ACCL...
THE LOST TEA...

"It was like finding ... have answers to que...
—J.W., chiroprac...

"Interesting, exciting, motivational. Real 'meat' for the soul."
—P.D., minister, Tampa, Fla.

"It has been extremely important to me in my spiritual journey. It has greatly clarified who I am and how my Christianity fit my new age spirituality."
—A.M., research scientist, St. Paul, Minn.

"Wonderful! I want more."
—C.T., host/entertainer, Madison, Tenn.

"Just what I needed to bring my ideas and personal experience into focus and balance. It's answering many important questions."
—D.S., field engineer, computers, Tyler, Tex.

"I'm a seeker of wisdom and truth. These books put me on the right path."
—V.L., retired fire fighter, Kensington, Conn.

"Wonderfully enlightening. It has changed my outlook on life, religion and spirituality completely."
—B.H., medical student, Webster, N.Y.

"Explains the big hole in the teachings of the traditional Christian church."
—S.B., registered nurse, Redmond, Wash.

"I have gained much knowledge and greater spiritual heights through this book."
—R.F., church organist, Peoria, Ill.

Treasure in the Mountain

THE LOST TEACHINGS OF JESUS

BOOK TWO

THE LOST TEACHINGS OF JESUS

Mark L. Prophet • Elizabeth Clare Prophet

❂

BOOK ONE
Missing Texts • Karma and Reincarnation

BOOK TWO
Mysteries of the Higher Self

BOOK THREE
Keys to Self-Transcendence

BOOK FOUR
Finding the God Within

THE LOST TEACHINGS OF JESUS

BOOK TWO

Mysteries of the Higher Self

MARK L. PROPHET
ELIZABETH CLARE PROPHET

SUMMIT UNIVERSITY 🛆 PRESS®

*To our beloved friends throughout the world
who have endured with us through
our trials and triumphs in Jesus Christ.
Without you his Lost Teachings
could not have been preached and
published in every nation.*

THE LOST TEACHINGS OF JESUS 2: *Mysteries of the Higher Self*
by Mark L. Prophet and Elizabeth Clare Prophet. Copyright © 1986,
1988, 1994 by Summit University Press. All rights reserved. No part
of this book may be used or reproduced in any manner whatsoever
without written permission, except by a reviewer who may quote brief
passages in a review. For information, write or call Summit University
Press, Box 5000, Livingston, MT 59047-5000. Telephone:
406-222-8300.

This is the second book in the four-volume pocketbook series
The Lost Teachings of Jesus, which contains the complete text
of the original two-volume hardcover edition of the same title.

Cover illustration: Adapted from Gustave Doré's *The Disciples
Plucking Corn on the Sabbath*. "And he said unto them, The
sabbath was made for man, and not man for the sabbath."
(Mark 2:27)

For information on the magnificent art of Nicholas Roerich
reproduced in this volume, write Nicholas Roerich Museum,
319 West 107th St., New York, NY 10025.

Library of Congress Catalog Card Number: 81-52784
ISBN: 0-916766-91-8

SUMMIT UNIVERSITY ❦ PRESS®
Summit University Press and ❦ are registered trademarks.

Printed in the United States of America
First Printing: 1988. Second Printing: 1989. Third Printing: 1991
Fourth Printing: 1992. Fifth Printing: 1994

THE LOST TEACHINGS OF JESUS
BOOK TWO *Contents*

1 CHAPTER FIVE

KAL-DESH:
THE INTERMINGLING OF
TIME AND SPACE

- 3 Every One of Us a Teacher
- 4 Thinking in Terms of the Head and the Heart
- 6 The Five Senses and Seven Chakras Reveal Reality
- 9 Living in the Mist and in the Crystal
- 12 Learning the Lessons of Our Past History
- 15 We Are the Sole Authors of Our Destiny
- 17 We Can Probe the Mystery of Self
- 18 The Problem of Desire
- 24 The Violet Fire and the Creative Fiat
- 26 The Human Animal Re-Creates Himself
- 30 The Second Coming of Christ
- 37 The Ancient Brotherhoods and the Fiat of Order

41 CHAPTER SIX

THE CHART OF THE I AM PRESENCE

- 43 Your Personal Relationship to God
- 45 Being a Manifestation of God
- 49 Diagram of God's Kingdom within You
- 50 The Violet Flame and the Law of Recompense
- 55 Where Is God?
- 58 Your Beloved I AM Presence
- 63 Draw Nigh unto Me and I Will Draw Nigh unto You
- 66 Your Finite Self and Your Four Lower Bodies
- 69 Etheric Octave—Threshold of the Second Coming
- 73 The Silver Cord
- 78 The Karmic Board Reduces the Silver Cord
- 82 The Threefold Flame of Life
- 86 The Only Begotten Son of the Father— Your Holy Christ Self
- 92 Balance the Threefold Flame
- 95 Your Causal Body
- 101 Accessing Your Cosmic Bank Account
- 104 Your Tube of Light

CHAPTER SEVEN

THE INTEGRATION OF THE CHAKRAS

- 121 The Missing Dimension in Physical Fitness
- 126 The Threefold Flame of the Heart
- 127 Light Mantras for the Heart
- 132 Vitality and Prana
- 135 The Powerful Throat Center
- 141 The Place of the Sun
- 142 The Inner Eye
- 147 The Chakra of Freedom
- 150 The Thousand-Petaled Lotus
- 152 The Base-of-the-Spine Chakra

CHAPTER EIGHT

THE ETERNAL VERITIES

- 159 The Sense of Selfhood
- 162 The Good Samaritan
- 164 Love Defined
- 168 Self-Worth and Self-Needs
- 170 The Wick of Self
- 173 Our Identity a Continuum in Christ
- 177 Why Do We Endow Ourselves with Mortality?

- 180 The Answer Lies in the Mystery Schools
- 184 You're Not Sinners. You Simply Are Not Awake!

187 CHAPTER NINE

A CONTINUATION OF OPPORTUNITY

- 189 What and Who Is Real?
- 200 Christ the Judge of the Quick and the Dead
- 204 Psychological Problems of the Ego in Rebellion
- 206 Call to Archangel Michael
- 211 The Belief in a Personal Devil
- 213 Our Victory over Life's Challenges
- 217 Free Will—the Necessary Fly in the Ointment
- 222 Serpents Take the Low Road, Lead Mankind Astray
- 224 The Conspiracy against the Children of the Light
- 229 The Lost Teachings of Jesus on Planetary History
- 233 Initiation at the Twelve Gates of the Holy City
- 237 We Have Lived Before

- 238 Mankind's Ignorance of the Law of Karma
- 247 Truth Vanquishes Doctrinal Delusions
- 250 Reembodiment: The Mercy and Justice of the Law
- 253 The Living Christ Is the Universal Saviour
- 255 The Romanization of Christ and Christianity
- 265 The Age of Apostasy and an Angry God Is Not Over
- 269 Christ, the Law, the I AM in Every Man
- 272 "Behold, What Manner of Love..."
- 275 The Church's Doctrine of Sin Begets More Sin

280 NOTES

308 INDEX OF SCRIPTURE

314 INDEX

Illustrations

PLATES — *Painting and Illustrations*

   ii *Treasure in the Mountain*

111 THE CHART OF YOUR DIVINE SELF AND THE CHAKRAS

   111 *Your Divine Self*

   112 *The Ascended Master Jesus Christ*

   113 *The Ascended Master Saint Germain*

   114 *Seven Chakras in the Body of Man*

   115 *Seat of the Soul Chakra*

   115 *Base of the Spine Chakra*

   116 *Throat Chakra*

   116 *Solar Plexus Chakra*

   117 *Heart Chakra*

   118 *Crown Chakra*

   118 *Third Eye Chakra*

Chapter Five

KAL-DESH: THE INTERMINGLING OF TIME AND SPACE

Kal-Desh:
The Intermingling of Time and Space

We would speak about time, *kala* in the Sanskrit, and space, *desha* in the Sanskrit,[1] and of the intermingling of time and space. And we would speak of it in terms of past history and the future, or that which is to be, and the fulfillment of the cycles of life.

Every One of Us a Teacher

For, not too long ago we were sitting in a high chair, drooling out our oatmeal upon our chin. And now we are here, quite a ways from that particular sorry state, and we are supposed to have a greater knowledge and a higher concept of what life is all about so that we can teach our children—as that old song goes, "Mother, teach thy children..."

Every one of us is a teacher. But we sometimes forget that we have this role to play. We sometimes think of ourselves as someone who is the victim of tyrants—as though life itself were a tyrant, as though our teachers were tyrants, as though everywhere we turned everything were in a tyrannical state and we ought to rebel against it.[2]

Then we suddenly stop, and we begin to realize what I began to realize long ago: that the meanest teacher I ever had in school—my Latin teacher—was, in reality, the one who taught me the most.

We ought to ask ourselves this question: Do we really want a sweet and beautiful personality that will pat us on the back and say, "Yes, you have learned all your lessons, Johnny. Mary, you know everything. You're just wonderful!" when in reality we're down in the D class? Is that what we want?

Shouldn't we look up to those who may seem to us to be tyrants by reason of their diligence and desire to chasten our souls, as God himself does? Shouldn't we look up to them as our most dedicated instructors, who teach us the very best of life that's free but whose precepts are meaningless to us unless we accept them?

And so we rebel no more, but we welcome the chastening rod that speaks in the Lord's name and says to us, "Whom I love, I chasten."[3]

Thinking in Terms of the Head and the Heart

Let us stop for a moment, and let us begin to think in terms of thought. Yes, think in terms of thought. What is thought? We have heard of the ancient Thoth, the Atlantean, the great master Thoth.[4] And we come to realize, if we pause to think upon the relationship of words, that *thought* and *Thoth* are perhaps one—that the word *thought* may even have sprung from his name. But whether or not it did is not so important as the fact that we are endowed with the capacity to think.

Yet, this great think tank that we have here [pointing to the brain] and this great think tank that we have here [pointing to the heart] are not always functioning together as they are supposed to. For, you see, man is supposed to think both with his head and his heart. And what happens is that he separates the heart and the head, and we find that the heart, expressing the feelings of man, leads the head.

And so, in almost every case where you are dealing with motivation—for example, in the field of salesmanship—and you want to sell someone something, you appeal to their head and you say, "Well, this particular product is going to do you a lot of good," but you don't get very enthusiastic about it. And you cite some facts and figures and graphs, and everyone looks unimpressed as though nothing has happened, and really nothing has.

And then, after a while you begin to get the idea. You get the message of the heart. You begin to wax enthusiastic. And in your enthusiasm you are creating an infectious feeling which is easily picked up at the emotional level by anyone.

And what is emotion? It is E—*energy*—in motion. You have created a feeling. And wherever there is a feeling created, good or bad, the feeling will lead the head—and, in most people, it will win every time.

So, if the husband is thinking with his head and the wife is feeling with her heart, the wife will have her way. But if the reverse is true, strange as it may seem, he will have his way. And this is always the case. It's the heart that leads.

But, in reality, it is not intended to be just that way. We are supposed to learn to think with our heart and govern our feelings so that we are not always carried away by the tides of emotion. But when we are able to feel with our head and think with our heart and do both in both places, then we have a great duality going for us and a masterful situation where we, if we will it so, can be in total command of ourselves.

We are our own man or our own woman. We are able to think the way God wants us to think—to think with our head, to think with our heart, to feel with our head and to feel with our heart. For we can learn to do this, as difficult as it may seem.

The Five Senses and Seven Chakras Reveal Reality

Now, in connection with thought, I am going to ask you to think with me as we begin to explore the great sphere of reality that is made known to us through the avenues of our five senses.

Our five senses telegraph to our inner self what is taking place. They reveal the world to us, but they reveal only a part of it. Therefore, unless we have the endowment of the quickened capacities of the higher senses, we cannot penetrate the totality of the world within.

And so we come to the place where we are going to climb the thirty-three steps of the spinal ladder to the place of the skull, Golgotha, where the Christ is crucified between the two malefactors[5] — the anterior and posterior lobes of the pituitary gland.

Now, you think about that for a moment. And if you *can't* solve the mystery of it, then decide that you're going to search further until you *can* solve the mystery of it, because it is filled with significance for each individual. And it correlates to the blossoming of the spiritual flowers on the spinal stalk. These are the great spiritual centers (chakras) culminating in the thousand-petaled lotus of light, right here at the crown of the head where the pulsation of the crystal cord can be observed in the newborn babe.

When the thousand-petaled lotus of light opens up, it reveals the whole universe to man. There is absolutely nothing hidden from one's eyes when the crown chakra is opened, but only the full penetration of the inward man reaching out and perceiving all things in the light of just what those things in actuality are.

Now, fortunately or unfortunately, many people like to be very pragmatic. They like to think in terms of results right now. And this, of course, can be very good. It has its value. But sometimes it does not give a clear picture of what has just happened to us or what is about to happen to us. We're interested not in a bubble that's floating in a level that is almost infinite in its horizontal plane, but we want to know the relationship of this bubble to the plane, to the surface whose incline we are measuring.[6]

Similarly, unless we have some arbitrary markings upon the scale of our judgments, our values will be warped because either we will see through the eyes of contemporary society or we will read—and read as other people read—but never read to think beyond what other people are thinking. We will be achieving what is known as mediocrity.

I cannot believe that it is God's will that man, endowed with his image, is intended to think in terms of mediocrity. We are intended to think big!—to think gigantic thoughts but to tether it all to reality. And this reality has already been established for us. We are not in a world where reality does not exist.

There are those who have come to this planet and who have had the oatmeal drooling down their chins just as we did, who today are spiritual Masters—masters of themselves and of their destiny. Once they walked amongst us and today they are still in contact with us.

If your spiritual centers are whirling with light—those little transformers (seven chakras) that God has all wrapped up inside of you—you may feel the cosmic energy flowing through you when in the presence of one of the Masters or while listening to their dictations on tape. It will pass through you and you'll know it.

If your centers are closed, you may not feel the Master Jesus' vibration, but you'll still hear his words and benefit from his instruction. And you'll

Living in the Mist and in the Crystal

So now we come to the point of time, which we will deal with first, this *kal*—this infinite calculation of the finite.

Because, you see, all we can ever do with a piece of string that represents all known history is break it up into segments. We call them years. We take this piece of string and we arbitrarily make our mark on it. We say this is such and such a year, and this is such and such a year. Two thousand years ago, Christ was born. We put that on the string and we call it A.D., the year of our Lord.

Well, when we come to the end of the string, we come to the end of history today; then we take another string. We don't tie them together. We just stretch this one out in a line continuing in the same direction because it's forward moving. Our history has met our present, and the future is unknown.

Now we realize that we really don't know just what is going to happen because, as Kahlil Gibran in his book *The Prophet* says, "Life, and all that lives, is conceived in the mist and not in the crystal. And who knows but a crystal is mist in decay?"[7]

So then, you see, there are some people who have this little idea in their brains. They say to themselves, "Well, what I *think* is not so important, it's what I *do* that counts." But I'm going to tell you that what you think *is* important, and what you do is also important. And I'm going to show it to you by Kahlil Gibran's statement.

Let us take the man who thinks the evil thought of adultery. According to the scriptures, a man who looks at a woman with lust in his heart has already committed adultery.[8] Remember this now. Jesus said it: if he thinks it in his heart, he has already committed the act—that is to say, in his heart.

So, a man said to me one day, "Well, it doesn't make any difference if I commit adultery, because I've already thought it and therefore I'm committed to it." I wish to prove to you that this is where the man is wrong in his thinking.

We live in the mist and we live in the crystal. The mist is the state of thought wherein we begin the thought processes that may or may not eventuate in the crystal. When Judas Iscariot was thinking that he was going to betray Christ, it was still in the mist. But the Master read his thought and said to him, "That which thou doest, do quickly."[9] And having received the sop, he went out immediately and betrayed him.

Now, when he betrayed him, that was crystallization. The mist of thought had crystallized and it could not be changed. It was the unalterable act. His fantasy had become fact. It was a fait accompli. The moment the deed was done, it was history. Thought had passed through the nexus and by the lever of the will became the action indelibly stamped on akasha. Karma.

No matter what deed you contemplate, as long as it is not crystallized into action, there is still hope that you will avoid the karma of deeds that will accrue to your life record *only* when the act is committed.

Wise is the man who does not allow himself to fall into the pit of wrong thought in the first place. But if he find himself in wrong thought, wise is he who will quickly correct himself before it becomes a recorded deed in the second place. As the Master said, "You can't help it if a bird lands on your head, but you don't have to let him build a nest in your hair!"

And that's the whole idea for all of us. To exercise control over ourselves is to realize that we live in the mist of thought, which we must tether to Truth and Righteousness before a momentum becomes "bigger than both of us" and topples the energies of both thought and feeling into words and deeds we later regret.

When we come to the realm of thought crystallization, it is far better to watch our thoughts before they manifest in the arena of action, because the karma (consequences) of thought is still not as great as the karma (consequences) of deeds. For the karma of deeds affects the lives of other people more physically and therefore often irrevocably; whereas with the karma of thought, though the effect may be more psychological, it can be healed and sealed and the damage undone "before it is too late," as they say—before the die is cast.

The fact is that transmutation is as a rule easier on the mental plane than on the physical—but not always, as in the case of mental cruelty and emotional abuse. But then, these are also the result of acts.

As long as we are dealing with just our own private thought—although it still may be error, often carrying a 'thought karma' proportionate to its duration—it can be pulled back, our desire purified, and the plot sequence taken out of consciousness by our own free will and the correct application of cosmic law.

Now, it's a wonderful thing that there is hope for people after they've erred. And it's a wonderful thing that there's hope for people before they've erred. But I still think that an ounce of prevention, as my mother told me, is worth a pound of cure. Don't you?

Learning the Lessons of Our Past History

Now then, enough with the ordinary human consciousness of just doing things. Let's look backwards and forwards in history and go to the very foundations of our own soul's evolution. We can go back to the hanging gardens of Babylon. We can see the great tower of Babel. We can still perceive, in thought, Sodom and Gomorrah.

We can experience the past, as Risë Stevens

did in the old amphitheater in Athens. While she was singing Orpheo's aria of lamentation at the foot of the Acropolis, the scene bathed in moonlight, she "lost all touch with reality" and felt herself in ancient Greece, "mentally and physically" living a former life in which she had acted on that very stage. Later she wrote about the incident, saying she finished the aria as in a trance and "fell prostrate on the body of Euridice." It took five minutes of thunderous applause to bring her back to the present.[10]

We *have* lived in the past and we *have* lived in the present. And we *have* also lived in the future that has become our past and our present. But our tomorrows cannot be any better for us than our todays and our yesterdays unless we transcend both and become the masters of our fate.

Since we have made our home in the past, the past has its effect upon our lives. In fact, unless we learn the alchemy of change, our past becomes our present *and* our future! And we may be its prisoner, and all we will have to look forward to in life are the replays which we ourselves project upon the screen of life—when we ought to cast ourselves in new and futuristic roles.

Thus, the present and the future can only be a clean white page if we clear our world of the causes we ourselves set in motion yesterday. If we don't, as sure as God made green apples, they will come home to roost as today's or tomorrow's "Surprise!"

Yes, yesterday's karmic involvements produce sideshows and side effects that have a magnetism all their own. Their force, or forcefield, can be felt; they have both weight and gravity. Call it astrology or fate or what you will, the fact remains that all too often we allow the effects of causes we and we alone created (and which we therefore are obliged to uncreate) to deter us from center stage and the spotlight of our own I AM Presence, who expects us to perform well—both in the mist and in the crystal.

Most of us like to think only in terms of this particular embodiment, this life. We like to think of our mother and our father and the old homestead and the good old days. Some people in this room go back to the horse-and-buggy days, and some remember the Model T and some the Model A. Some, of course, have a little different background—they only remember television! But we find in the record and the memory of the psyche that all of us go back somewhere into the distant past.

And some of us can go back farther than others. We can go back to the ruins and the records of the Sumerian civilization beyond the pale of current Mideast crises. We can go back to the building of the ancient pyramids and to the moment of the carving of the Sphinx.

We can go back through our soul memories to many countries and many climes; and the recordings stored in the unconscious, written in our "inward parts,"[11] as Jeremiah tells us, reveal to us many things.

And so, we can read and learn the lessons of our own past history and see to it, if we will it so, that our history does not repeat itself by our neglectfulness in studying the chemistry of our hearts and the elements that make up our actions, reactions, and the unfortunate distractions that impel us by the karma of desire from the highway of our God.

Some of us walked where Jesus walked. Some of us can literally remember Golgotha. Some of us can remember other times and other places. We have participated in various enterprises throughout history. Some people here were in the War of the Roses. Some remember King Henry VIII. Some sailed the seas with Christopher Columbus. Others, of course, have been paupers. Some have been princes. And some have really been kings and queens.

We Are the Sole Authors of Our Destiny

We have been many things. And we have not always been on top of the heap, nor have we always been at the bottom. Sometimes we've been in the middle. And sometimes we've been caught in between. We've been through lots of different situations in our past lives. And our future will be exactly what we make it. In fact, the script is already written. Only we can unwrite it, for we are the sole authors of our destiny.

This is why the Masters are so interested in our state of consciousness. They want us to be able to probe all of the past, to learn its lessons dispassionately, and then to look to the future with hope and joy born of the idea that God has placed the pen in our hands: We can rewrite the past upon the pages of the future!

I think it's a great tragedy that most of us just live from day to day. I mean, we get up each day and we say, "I wonder just what this day is going to bring forth, in time, for me. What is it going to bring forth?"

"Well," we say, "I don't know."

Isn't it a tragedy that we have so little governing power over our lives that we say we don't know? Especially when at subconscious levels we know the end from the beginning, because we've seen it all before—before we ever took embodiment in this life.

Don't you think that when God said to man, "Be fruitful and multiply and replenish the earth and subdue it, take dominion over the creatures of the sea, the air, and the earth!"—in other words, "Rule the earth!"—don't you think he intended him to exercise control over himself and his environment through careful planning and conscientious striving—even probing the mysteries of self and science?

It's a great travesty of the Law that we have not availed ourselves of the promises of self-mastery foreordained in the covenants and commandments of God. Why, we are not even masters enough of the fates to know, to be, and to determine what is going to happen to us in a single day, any day, of our lives! Instead of making things happen, we just sit back and let the future decide itself—instead of realizing that we *are* our past, our present, and our future.

Therefore, no matter what we do, we are deciding to be, to remain as we were, to appear, and to appear to change but to change not at all—to seem to be, but to be not—to feel, taste, smell, and still to see or not to see. Alas, the choices are infinite, but we are still finite and can only outpicture a few. Let them be wise in the mist so we will not have to undo the crystal—molecule by molecule.

We Can Probe the Mystery of Self

Must we forever think the future is a great mystery and that we can never pierce the veil and divest the mystery of its mystery? Dear hearts, the future will only be the mystery *we* make it or the mystery *we* unveil.

Well, we can probe the mystery of self, if we want to. Through the Masters' Teachings, through spiritual insight, we can look ahead. And not only can we look ahead, but we can plan ahead. We can make things happen.

There are two kinds of people: the kind who make things happen and the kind who watch them happen. Now, we're interested in being able to make things happen. Is this wrong? Does God blame us for making things happen? On the contrary, he blames us for just watching them happen. Because when we watch them happen, we are not participating at all in the constructivism that lies as a coiled spring within ourselves.

Oh, you say, you don't have any power within yourself. Well, I'm here to assure you that if you follow the true Teachings of Jesus taught by the Ascended Masters, and if you follow them long enough, the Teachings themselves will prove to you beyond question that you do have the power *and the ultimate power* to make things happen in your world. And when you prove to yourself that you can do it, why then you will see that you can govern your life from now on. And your future can be tailor-made just the way you want it!

But, of course, people will always come up with this question: "Well, how will I want it? And how will I know how I want it? I don't even know how I want my life to be today, let alone tomorrow and the next day and the next."

But, you see, dear heart, you have already created your yesterdays, your todays, and your tomorrows. And unless and until you get in the driver's seat and become the charioteer in your own race against karma, you are not going to be first at the finish line. Your own human creation may very well beat you to the punch!

The Problem of Desire

Well, let's talk about giving someone a million dollars. You give them a million dollars and they're overwhelmed with the gift, but they don't know what to do with it. Of course, everybody says, "Well, I know what I'd do if I had a million dollars." And they can think of all kinds of things they would do with that money. But, you see, it isn't quite that easy.

Now, I can't speak from the experience of having had someone give me a million dollars, but I have had people give me gifts in the course of my life. And I have had the experience of walking into stores and really not knowing just how to spend a certain amount of money that I had in my pocket that I thought I ought to spend.

But you know what the biggest problem was? It was the problem of so many wants, so many desires that it became a question of: "What shall I select that I can buy with this amount of money, because I don't have enough to buy everything I see? What will I pick out? What can I buy?"

And the ideas would come so thick and fast, it was like a blizzard. You know, you're in a snowstorm and you're batted from one side of the store to the other. And in the end you go home with the money in your pocket—yet it was burning a hole in your pocket when you came into the store—and you say, "Well, I guess I'd rather have the money than anything," because you can't settle on any one thing that you really want.

This shows that man has a real problem. His real problem is that he needs to learn to school his desire, to master this chaotic condition of the mind where he cannot settle upon one particular thing that he feels is most important in his life.

I think, then, that all of us should stop for a while this business of just thinking randomly in what we will call the stream of consciousness. Most people think in the stream-of-consciousness mode. And do you know that the planetary stream of consciousness is muddied from the refuse of human thought and feeling that has been dumped into it from all over the world?

Because of this pollution we have to learn to protect our aura and our astral body against the impinging negative thoughts of the world—those "arrows of outrageous fortune" that beset Hamlet. We have to learn to upraise the shield of the mind in order to shut them out of our consciousness so that we can build great positive passions for what God wants us to have for ourselves.

Otherwise, you see, we cannot even receive the gifts that God has to give to us. He's got all kinds of gifts to give to us and he's right ready to hand them to us now. But we can't receive them until we have purified our desires. Do you understand this?

The desire is important. But, you see, desire is a key which may be understood through the esoteric interpretation of the two syllables of the word: *desire*. *De* stands for your divinity—the *De*ity of your selfhood—in other words, your Mighty I AM Presence. And what is *sire*? It means lord, the term whereby we address the Son of God. Put them together and you get God and the Son of God:* *Desire*.

Another way of looking at this word and the co-creative power it conveys is to realize that *Deity*

---
*or the Mighty I AM Presence and the Holy Christ Self

sires—begets or brings into being—the Son of God out of the depths of his own desiring.

And if you want to understand the science of Being, you should know that your I AM Presence through the "Sire"—your own beloved Christ Self—bestows upon you through the power of the spoken Word the same power to re-create yourself in the image of Higher Consciousness by which you came forth from Elohim in the beginning!

"Let there be Light!"[12]
This is the original fiat
 of the LORD who made heaven and earth.
"Let there be Light!"
Say it now with determination.
With the deep desiring of your heart.
With the Peace-commanding presence
 of your Christ Self.

"Let there be Light!"
Say it into the teeth of every problem
 and temptation.
Say it in your mind and in the most secret secrets
 of your heart.
Say it in your desires and in the musings
 of your soul.

"Let there be Light!"
Say it for loved ones.
Use this divine decree to heal the sick—
 to challenge evildoers and to bring order
 out of the chaos of global crisis.

Speak it in the eye of God's whirlwind
   and in the center of his fury and
   when elemental forces rampage in fire and flood.
Speak it on the shores of life,
   to your beloved and your children
   when they are happy and carefree
   and when they are bowed down
   by the void of noncaring, noncreativity.
And when Darkness covers the land
   and the face of the earth is consumed
   with war and plague and famine and death,
   say to the whole earth and to the Sun:
   Let there be Light!

"Let there be Light!"
Speak it in the dark night of despair
   and in the morning's light of joy.
Speak it to thy God who loves thee
   and shall love thee evermore,
   who says to thee even in this moment of eternity:
   "Let there be Light!"

Give answer, O my soul.
Tell Him thou hast heard.
He longeth for thy confirmation...
   "And there was Light!"

Yes, it was desire and the spoken Word that struck the first note of cosmos, and it will be your desire as God's desire in you yoked with the command to Light that will strike the true chord of your identity.

So, what have we got to do? We have got to learn that we are acting creatively as God acts creatively, that we are co-creators with him of our destiny and that by purifying our thoughts—the offspring of our minds—we will be siring a true and noble lineage made in the image of our Christ. And then we will actually produce in our world what we want to produce.

Yes, the thought that you create is the offspring of your mind. And the way you create it is the same way that Leonardo da Vinci created. You have got to learn how to create. And this requires the purification of both the mind and the heart.

But first we must bring our desire and our desire body into alignment with the desire of God. We must study what Deity sires, what the Creator creates, and then pattern our designs after the heavenly patterns. We must study the lost Word and pattern our speech after his speech, as it is written: "The heavens declare the glory of God; and the firmament sheweth his handywork. Day unto day uttereth speech, and night unto night sheweth knowledge."*

De-signs are the Deity's signature on every component of his creation—every leaf, flower and star. And, do you know something? You also sign your name to your creations—just like a famous designer—because every thought and feeling, <u>motive and momentum</u> contains the microscopic signet

---

*"The heavens declare the glory of God, the vault of heaven proclaims his handiwork; day discourses of it to day, night to night hands on the knowledge." Ps. 19:1, 2, Jerusalem Bible translation.

of your molecular and electronic blueprint. You can never deny your creations, whether human or divine, just as you cannot stamp out your etchings in the crystal unless you learn the alchemy of change.

The Violet Fire and the Creative Fiat

It's the violet fire! You've got to get the violet fire—both to create what you want and to uncreate what you don't want. And that's what Jesus and Saint Germain and El Morya sent us here to do. To teach you how to use the violet fire. And that's exactly what we're going to do.

But don't skip over first principles: The body should be kept clean, because a clean body breeds clean thought. Whatever you feed the mind should be glorious, should be miraculous, should be beautiful, should be wise, should be comforting to humanity, should, as with scientific precision, produce something good in the world.

Do you see how important it is that you grasp this thought? Because through this thought you can purify your own concepts and then, you see, this world of time becomes a world where you can step from the present into the space of the past.

And soon you can learn to move through the realm of ideation where ideas are being born and then conveyed along the corridor of the mind, where they take on thought and feeling modes just before they thread the needle of the drive and the shuttle of action. You can learn the laws of spiritual alchemy to transmute by violet fire the base metals of your human consciousness into the refined gold of the divine.

Well, you may think that you can't change the past. Because it's the crystal. So, for the time being step over here into the mist and experiment with the laws of change that can change the future.

It doesn't matter what you have been in the past—how weak or worrisome you've been, how you've frittered and failed, or what you have or haven't discovered. I'm interested in awakening within you the realization that the power of God in yourself has every answer that you need for every human problem.

I don't care what that problem is! God has the answer. And the answer, of course, can best be conveyed if we go back to what Jesus actually taught and said to the inner circle of his disciples and what he's saying to us today. For example, we have illustrated here in symbolic form the violet transmuting flame [pointing to the violet flame surrounding the lower figure in the Chart; see Chapter 13] and soon we're going to be giving creative fiats called decrees with that violet flame.

If you can understand the Chart of Your Real Self, you can understand the Almighty One individualized and personified in your Beloved I AM Presence. You can understand its relationship to the Christ of your being, the one anointed with the Light of the Son of God. And you can understand the relationship of your soul (which, while in embodiment, occupies the relative position of the lower figure) to your Higher Self and the I AM THAT I AM.

So I'm just about ready to give you as complete and thorough an understanding of that whole kingdom of God within you as you'll get anywhere. And when I do you'll be as thrilled as the day you were born in God. Because it'll put you in that go position to be what you were and what you still are: a co-creator with God.

So hang on to your hats because the mysteries of God are so wonderful they'll just blow away all your old thinking caps—and not only you, but your mind and your thought/feeling modes will be truly born again in the encounter with the Universal Christ.

The Human Animal Re-Creates Himself

Robert Louis Stevenson said, "The world is so full of a number of things, I'm sure we should all be as happy as kings."[13] But we aren't, are we?

Look around you on the street as people walk up and down. Park your car sometime—or park your carcass in your car—and as you sit there, just look at the people's faces. And tell me if you don't think that's entertaining.

Why, I remember that in Sutton, Nebraska, one time during World War II, I went down to the main street of the town, and as I walked down the street in my military uniform, everybody in town who happened to be parked along the street was

The Human Animal Re-Creates Himself 27

looking at me. Now, I wasn't just embarrassed or self-conscious—they actually were looking.

So I decided to get into one of the cars and sit there, too. And so I sat there, and as I was sitting in one of these cars looking at the people, I took note of the faces of the people coming by. And I realized that this was really a very entertaining situation. It was a substitute for going to the movies. I could study the lines and expressions of their faces, read the records of their past lives—and of this life—and learn why people do the things they do.

Then after a while, the lookers-on went into the restaurant. They had a cup of coffee and some sandwiches, and they relaxed a little bit after they'd had their entertainment.

Well, it's really interesting when you stop and think of just how people function. The human animal has become just that—an animal in the zoo on exhibit. Because no higher image has been set before him as a goal or standard. So he unknowingly re-creates himself daily after the image of the earthly creature.

I cannot believe that Almighty God, who framed this universe and made this beautiful earth and all the stars and planets out in space, ever intended the creation that he put here to take dominion over this planet to function the way they are functioning today. In fact, I don't guess at it: I know that they're not supposed to be the kind of people they are today.

We're not supposed to have war. We're not supposed to have human greed. We're not supposed to have unkindness between people. We're not supposed to have bad motives, we're supposed to have good motives. And we're supposed to have good movies instead of bad ones coming out of Hollywood.

But in many cases we don't have either good motives or good movies! And as a result, we often don't have either good messages or good momentums in the media as a positive creative force in society. And this, too, is our responsibility. For the mist and the crystal are all right there on film passing to the frames of consciousness that then frame the actions of our lives.

Wherever man is, man creates. And the manifestation is the projection of someone's self upon the minds of other 'selfs'—or elfs, as the case may be. And failure is everywhere around us, but the trick is we must much more abound and surround our defeats with the good feats of our faith and the feets of Victory's legions marching!

Of course, many more people love the Beatles than love Christ—so the Beatles tell us. But somehow or other, I don't believe that. Because I know I don't love the Beatles. I may love their souls, but I certainly don't love the Beatles. Nor do I love their phonograph records.

And I don't love to stick a hypodermic needle in my arm in order to give me a kick! In fact, all I have to do is look up and I already have my kick for the day and for all the days to come. Because if you look up at your Presence—once you've learned to look up to your God Presence—and realize that that is the only part of yourself that is absolutely real, then you're going to look back and you're going to say, "Well, I guess when I was a baby I hadn't yet realized all that God wanted me to be"—that oatmeal again and the toodle that comes toddling along.

By gosh, we needed some support in those days or we fell flat on our faces! And then we had to learn to take our little hands and put them on the desk and take our little fingers and learn to hold a pencil and write. Then we had to take the beatings in the schoolyard that many of the children take. Then we had to go through the fear of a beating at home if the report card wasn't up to the standards that Father and Mother thought it should be! And all kinds of experiences.

We were exposed to theft, where people tried to induce us to steal in the dime stores. We were exposed to pornographic pictures and drug paraphernalia. We've had all kinds of struggles toward morality, toward decency, toward God. We live in a time when everybody's pulled this way and then they're pulled that way. And sometimes people don't know which way to go.

Some people have had no experience in the Church. Some people have had no experience with God. Other people have had a lot of interesting experiences with God—enough so that they're turned off by the Church or else they've been burned off. And they don't exactly like the idea of some of the pastors trying to tell them if they don't be good, they're going to go to Hades and burn forever on some kind of a spit—roasted like a turkey on Thanksgiving Day!

I can't accept this idea because I know that God doesn't intend to do this to anybody—simply because, as a father, I wouldn't do it to my own children.[14] And I'm sure that I'm not better than God, you see.

The Second Coming of Christ

We've talked a little about time and the stream of time and ourselves floating down the stream, like the bright colored leaves of autumn, coursing through our destiny. And we have said that we are moved by a power higher than our own that we can harness to chart our own compass in life and be the captains of our ships—instead of chips of wood floating as flotsam and jetsam eventually to be submerged by the stream of our own karmic crystals.

Now, I'd like to talk briefly about space. We always think of space in terms of the great vastness that rolls before the eye in the mountains or at the seashore or on the open plains of the West. If you take a trip across America by car, you'll have some idea of just how big this country is. And then, if you go across it in a jet—from New York to California—you'll seem to be annihilating space by speed.

And when you annihilate space by speed, you

also experience the annihilation of time. This is quite an experience in physics and mathematics. If we were to take off in a spaceship from planet earth and go to some star so many light-years away in such and such a period of time, transcending the speed of light and then come back—even though, let's say, only five years had elapsed for us, by the time we got back to earth, all the people we had ever known would be dead, because a hundred years would have passed.

This is a bit of a ridiculous picture, but nevertheless a true one, which gives us something to think about in terms of the Second Coming of Christ. People say, "Well, Christ is coming back to this earth again." Well, I hope so. But they think of it in this way: They say that a cloud is coming, and it's coming out of the East. But they don't even know what the cloud is or what the East is.

But they say it's coming out of the East and it's going to be somewhere up in the Eastern sky and Christ is coming in that cloud. And then all the people in the world that are now alive are going to be able to see him.[15] But if you know anything about logistics and the cramming of people into space, you know that if you were standing on top of the Washington Monument and you had all the people who live in the District of Columbia gathered around you on the ground, they couldn't see you from the periphery of that group nor could they see you from below. They wouldn't see you and you wouldn't see them.

So you have to begin to understand that many of the scriptural references are significant only in terms of the individual—you and I and our personal relationship with God and his Christ. It's a matter of our realization of what we read and what we run with—what we know and what we are.

Do you think for one minute that if you had ascended with Jesus from Bethany's hill (if you'd been standing right beside him and you'd both gone up together) that you'd be dead now? Of course not! And neither is he. And if you had been standing there and he had ascended and you didn't, he'd still be alive, the Ascended Master, and you'd still be alive, the unascended disciple—wondering why you didn't make it when he did. And so here you are two thousand years later determined to find out how he did it so you can do it, too. Well, I'm here to tell you tonight that you've come to the right place.

Jesus said, "I am alive forevermore, and have the keys of hell and of death."[16] The Master is here to give you the keys to time and space and to eternal Life.

We have to understand, then, that the Second Coming of Christ does not have to occur in the physical sense of him floating in on a big white cloud—and everybody down here looks up and they see him like they would the Hindenburg dirigible floating through space.

We have to understand that the Second Coming of Christ is the specific event that occurs because the hearts of men have prepared themselves to receive him in all generations—not only in this one but in all generations. Otherwise the Everlasting Gospel could not be preached. Because Christ must first come in your hearts. Because if Christ had not first come in your heart—and this is the real Second Coming—then you could not understand the Everlasting Gospel even if you heard it preached.[17]

How could he preach to you the Everlasting Gospel if he'd come a hundred years ago and we were living now? If Christ had come a hundred years ago in time and we're living now, where would we stand then—if he'd come and gone? Or if he was still here ruling everything, supposedly, as they sometimes think of it? Well then, of course people wouldn't have any free will, would they—if he ruled it all? If he made them do exactly what he wanted them to do, he would be taking their free will away from them.

The solution to all of this is the Truth that the First Coming of Christ is in the exemplar, the son of man Jesus, who fully expressed the Light and was the Word incarnate, and that the Second Coming is in you. This glorious event takes place when the Son of God comes to live and reign in your heart and mind and soul and temple—because you have prepared him room.

When this planet achieves its immortal perfection, it will be because man has accepted the fiat of Almighty God, because man has recognized the great creative potential that is inside of him and is beginning to exercise it. As he begins to exercise that spiritual prerogative, then, you see, he achieves greatness.

And in that state of mind or frame of reference, he sees Christ within him, Christ above him and Christ all around him. And he experiences the Second Coming of Christ into his temple—the First Coming, of course, being his original creation in the beginning when Christ was formed in him and he was formed in Christ.

But that doesn't mean the Bible prophecies won't come true. The prophecies are, in fact, just like Jesus himself—"the same yesterday and today and forever."[18] They are coming true in the Eternal Now—whenever you are ready. For you are also the creator of your own time and space.

And when you look at your beloved Christ Self depicted on the Chart, if you so desire you'll also see him in your mind's eye as he is—coming into your heart and mind in the clouds of heavenly consciousness. And when you experience this mystery in your being, your heart and mind will feel and know at once his power and great glory. (The Second Coming of Jesus Christ is likewise glorified in the coming of the Ascended Master Jesus Christ as he delivers his Everlasting Gospel in the full power of the spoken Word through his Messengers.)

Well, once you experience his Second Coming in this manner and you meet me somewhere on the highway of Life between time and space and eternity, and I ask you when is Christ's Second

Coming, do you know what your answer will be? Why, you'll say to me, "He never ever went away and he never came back—he's always been—the same Christ with me—yesterday, today, and forever. It is I who went away and I who have come back."

And then you'll realize what you just said and you'll know that even so, your own comings and goings in and out of God's kingdom and in and out of embodiment have also been relative—only real in time and space. And when the eternal Mind within you gets through devouring your karmic cycles in time and space, why then you'll know that the Real You never left Home!

But don't get ahead of yourself on this evolutionary string. Because before you realize all of this you're going to have to thread the eye of the needle with that Gemini mind of God which Morya speaks about to his chelas, and which the Master, bless his heart, has through many lifetimes truly become.

This is the mind that leads to that spiritual greatness which, because it is true mastery, is outpictured through and tethered to the physical form and consciousness. This type of greatness that is not of this world, but comes from above and blesses that which is beneath, is brought forth from previous lives and other spheres of soul experience.

Now, Rabindranath Tagore achieved a certain greatness in the field of poetry. We have had many great poets in the world. We've had many great sculptors. We've had great teachers. We've had great doctors. We've had great avatars. Mighty souls have brought Truth to humanity and awakened the people. But, my goodness, none of them have been able to save the world.

Tagore can't save the world. I can't save the world. You can't save the world. In the end, each individual—and I'm saying this to the little children who are here—has to take the gift that God has given us (the gift of Life, first of all) and reach out in time and space and realize that we're natives of eternity, that we're here in this universe, we're in this mighty soundless sound stream—for a reason.

We're in it, and we've got to listen to it and vibrate with the cosmic sound. We've got to vibrate with the Cosmic Logos, the lost Word. We've got to let the Word begin to move in our lives.

And when that Word moves, we will be moved by God's intent. And when we are, we will learn how to control our thoughts. Because *the* controlling *thought* of the Mind of God will be our example. But it will be neither the controller nor the comptroller, because we will be in command of our thought by free will and by our individual exercise of some facet of the Great Thought of God, where all the desiring and the siring of the creation began.

Because, in the final analysis it's the God-control *we* allow in *our* lives that is going to save the world—one times one times the One. In *kal/desh* it is the individual and his individualization of the God flame that provides the only key to unlock our eternality. The flame, the One, the God-control and *you*.

The Ancient Brotherhoods and the Fiat of Order

If you can't control your thoughts, if your thoughts are wandering around like will-o'-the-wisps on a swamp wherever they happen to go, nothing will really be happening at all except chaos. And chaos is the illusion that something is happening, when actually nothing is happening that's real in the Mind of God.

So when you think something's happening when it's not—like on a psychedelic trip into the astral plane—you are also a part of that illusion which is the definition of chaos. 'Tis then that Tiamat, the great dragon of chaos,[19] is eating us up, devouring us.

Unless we're devouring God—assimilating his Thought and his Mind as Jesus taught, "Except ye eat the flesh of the son of man [who is the Son of God incarnate] and drink his blood, ye have no life in you"[20]—we ourselves will be eaten up by forces of the anti-Self beyond our control, that is, our control of *kal* and *desh*.

And God is not glorified in the Tiamat scenario because he cannot be glorified in chaos. Because God is order. And man is order. And the twain are made one in the glory of the universal Order of Light's perfection.

This is why the ancient Brotherhoods established the fiat of order. They established the fiat of order because only by obedience to the Law of the One and by order and by a quickening in consciousness can man achieve the brilliance of the Mind of

God in his own mind. And when he does, there are changes that he will work in the world—both in and through and beyond time and space.

This is the sacred fire that has been forever and forever central to the th-r-r-one of God. And I said it purposely like the old Scotsman, th-r-r-one, because I wanted to illustrate the three-in-one of the threefold flame—of Power, Wisdom, and Love in man: the three-in-one consisting of the Father, the Son, and the Holy Spirit, you see, focusing through the body, the mind, and the soul.

When we understand these parallel triune aspects according to the law of the equilateral triangle and we put our understanding into practice by obedience to God's laws, we can see that by visualizing ourselves working with the great hierarchies of Light—angels, archangels, Elohim and elemental builders of form (whose offices of cosmic service were established long before we ever knew who we were)—we are going to have extraordinary experiences like the ancient Masters used to have.

We will not be just ordinary people. We will be the sort of people—believe this or not—that could stand here and disappear right in front of our eyes. We'll be people that, in the body or out of the body, could go to the ancient temples—in Egypt and in the fastnesses of the Himalayas, beneath the seas and under the polar caps or in the center of the earth, wherever there are retreats of the Great White Brotherhood—and hear the great mystic songs of the Masters and the music of the spheres. We will be able to absorb the Light of eternity right here in time.

And we will be able to enjoy ourselves a thousand times more, a million times more, infinitely more than we ever possibly could in this rat race we call human life, which has been made a rat race because everybody is trying to rush around in their horseless chariots. Running around with, hopefully, two lights and a taillight on—maybe two taillights—and a little aerial sticking up, listening to some radio station that's putting out acid rock or classical rock or punk rock or country Western rock or just plain old rock 'n' roll.

It's all the same because it all takes you to the same place—the place where you really don't want to go if you know what's good for you. But then, in time and space where everything's relative, or so they say, most people don't know what's good for them. And they don't know because their teachers haven't taught them.

The preachers haven't opened their understanding to the true meaning of the scriptures of Life written in our hearts and in our memories and in the akashic records that reveal Christ and his disciples conversing with the adepts in the Himalayas, both listening and demonstrating the Word, that reveal the ancient Masters and their circles of devotees sitting beneath the Tree of Life in the Garden of God. And thus the shepherds in every field have not fed their sheep with sufficient Christ-love to satiate their spirits and melt their self-images of worthlessness frozen in time and space.

And you go down the street and you see the boys and girls with long hair or shaved heads or astral cuts and colors, mohawks and spikes, and chains around their arms and legs and necks that look like they just stepped out of some Atlantean time warp. And they're bobbing along, bouncing up and down—probably injected with acid—LSD, STP, and God only knows what else. And they're going down the street, not knowing where they're going, and sometimes they bump into people. But then, that happens to the sane element of our society, too, doesn't it? They bump into people, too.

So, you see, I won't be able tonight to give you very much more than I've already given you because, for goodness' sake! it's ten after nine and I'm supposed to quit at nine o'clock. So, I've gone ten minutes over what I'm supposed to. I've bumped into the cudgel of time and my space is no longer.

You see, no matter what we know, as long as we're in the world we're still subject to *kal/desh*. So about all I can do is tell you that I hope you will have success in getting rid of this great dragon Tiamat—that right now is devouring my tale!—and learn to bring order out of your lives. And I can promise you that you can learn a great deal about how Jesus conquered *kal/desh* from the Ascended Masters of the Great White Brotherhood, if you want to.

So make the most of your opportunity in *kal/desh* to weave the fabric of eternity.

I'll see you in my next chapter!

Chapter Six

THE CHART OF THE I AM PRESENCE

The Chart of the I AM Presence

Your Personal Relationship to God

Let's talk about the Chart of the I AM Presence and you. It is a form-presentation of your electronic reality (see page 111). This Chart can be very beneficial to you personally if, through the understanding of it, you can learn to think of yourself as you really are and forget yourself as you are not.

Now, the self that is not was revealed to John by one of the seven angels as "the beast that was, and is not, and yet is."[1] This is the synthetic self made out of the synthetic image. Down deep in our hearts, we all know that this is the self we allow to get in our way a lot of the time. That is, the human gets in God's way, when, in fact, our souls are really created in the Divine Image.

You see, the Chart helps you to realize the Reality of yourself. And when you know the meaning of it, you will never again be alone—not if you practice the great truth embodied in it.

Now, if you didn't have an eye picture of yourself at all, if you had never seen yourself in a mirror or in a photograph, it would be somewhat difficult for you to actually know yourself—to understand who you really are. The same principle applies to the knowledge of the Presence.

Here we are dealing with something that is invisible to our physical senses but visible to our cosmic senses—the senses of the soul. This 'eye picture' of the Chart has brought that magnificent, invisible but all-powerful Electronic Presence of ourselves before our gaze for one purpose: to inform us as to the Reality of ourselves.

Consequently, our ability to respond to the ancient maxim inscribed on the temples of Atlantis and later in the temple of Apollo at Delphi—"Man, Know Thyself"—is aided magnificently by the Chart.

This Chart is valuable. It is perhaps the most valuable possession you can have outside of the Reality for which it is a symbol. And it has a purpose—and that is to quicken in our consciousness the advent of the Presence in our lives, of the Holy Christ Self, the violet fire, and the tube of light.

You may not see your Presence—but you do see this Chart. And that's the important thing, because the Chart is a scientific explanation of your Reality, *your Divine Reality*. It shows you your own relationship to God.

If, early in this century, this Chart could have been in the hands of the Christian churches, accepted by their pastors, taught to their parishioners, and understood and practiced by millions of people, we would have an entirely different world today.

You wouldn't have your global problems of

Communism, juvenile delinquency, crime, drugs, the manipulation of our money and energy by the international bankers and big oil, and many other serious conditions—because eye contact with the visual image awakens the soul's memory of pre-existence and independence from the time/space continuum.

Just seeing the Chart reconnects the soul to the inner knowledge of its tie to the Source of universal Light, Love, Energy, and Consciousness. And this awareness of one's individual relationship to God alone produces miracles of expanded potential and joy and soul satisfaction!

The Chart is self-knowledge—Self-knowledge! And this is power. Translated into action, it is your ultimate power to work the works of God on earth[2] and ascend to his throne at the conclusion of this life.

Being a Manifestation of God

Quite a few years ago I heard someone say to another person, "Who in the world do you think you are? Do you think you're God or something?" No doubt you have heard people say such things to one another. Is that bad? Is it bad to equate one's potential with God's?

Well, it must be terrible, because Jesus was thrown out of his hometown and practically pushed headlong over the brow of a hill because he presented himself in the synagogue of Nazareth as the Anointed One of Isaiah's prophecy.[3] And later, because he said, "I AM the Son of God," they would have stoned him and taken him but he escaped out of their hands.[4]

People are very touchy about their gods, whether they have just one or many; and they don't like anyone to claim that they are God, i.e., a manifestation of God—even though Jesus taught them by example that it was not robbery for the Son of God to make himself equal with God,[5] admonished them to be perfect as their heavenly Father was perfect,[6] and showed Paul how to embody the same mind (of God) that was in himself.[7]

Well, being a manifestation of God simply means that the stream is the issue of the Source. After all, if the stream of your consciousness comes from God—directly from your I AM Presence, as it is illustrated in this Chart—then isn't that stream *of* God? Isn't it actually God?

When we say you are a "lifestream," we mean you are a "stream of Life"—of the Life that is God; for the terms *Life* and *God* are synonymous. Often the Ascended Masters address us affectionately as "precious lifestreams," in the same way they would say "dear hearts" or "beloved ones." And this is because they know us as the Light-emanation, or *Light-stream*—a ray of Light from God's heart.

Jesus taught that the stream cannot be any different than the source—as his brother James said: Does a fountain send forth at the same place sweet water and bitter? Can a fig tree bear olive berries or a vine figs? So no fountain can give forth salt water and fresh.[8] Thus we are the fruit of God's

Tree of Life—the thought-emanation of his Mind bearing the seed of the Christ potential. We are God's, fully his—spirits of his very Spirit.

One of the tricks of the evil forces on this planet is what is known as intimidation. That's why you have to know who you are in relationship to God and your Beloved I AM Presence. Because they intimidate you through inferiority; they try to make you feel so small and so insignificant and so little that you figure, "Well, I haven't got a chance to run in this race anyway. I might as well quit before I start."

The Chart is the most immaculate proof of the fact that you *do* have a chance, because there isn't a man or a woman or a child that God created on this or any other planet who does not have this exact relationship to him. Because you are a lifestream of God, you can walk the earth as a jointheir with Christ Jesus. This means that you stand to inherit the same Christhood, the same Sonship which Jesus had and demonstrated.

And this is the true teaching of the apostle Paul. If you don't believe me, then read Romans 8:14–17 and tell me what it means. And I'll tell you that this Chart is an illustration of the teaching which the Ascended Master Jesus Christ gave directly to Paul:

> For as many as are led by the Spirit of God [*the 'Presence' of God, whose name is I AM*], they are the sons [*suns*] of God [*they are the Light-emanations of God*].

For ye have not received the spirit of bondage again to fear [*bondage to the law of karma, without grace*]; but ye have received the Spirit of adoption, whereby we cry, Abba, Father. [*As we have been adopted by the Cosmic Christ, who is personified in our Christ Self, we may now call in his name directly to the Mighty I AM Presence.*]

The Spirit [*of the I AM Presence*] itself beareth witness with our spirit [*through our divine spark, our threefold flame, and our souls*] that we are the children of God:

And if children, then heirs; heirs of God and joint-heirs with Christ [*every child of God stands to inherit the full potential of the Universal Christ, or Light (of the only begotten Son of God), individualized in his Beloved Christ Self*]; if so be that we suffer with him [*if we bear our own burden, or karma, as well as his burden of Light*] that we may be also glorified together.

This teaching does not deny the divinity of Jesus; it affirms him, and the Godhead dwelling in him, bodily.[9] It also affirms Jesus, as well as the Christ that he incarnated, as being within your range. It makes it possible for you to reach up and touch the hem of his garment. It shows you how and why you can have an intimate relationship with him—and, through him, with God.

Jesus himself taught us so simply the requirements that must be met in order for us to enjoy the

Presence of the Father and the Son indwelling with us—precisely as illustrated in this Chart: "If a man love me, he will keep my words; and my Father will love him, and we will come unto him and make our abode with him."[10]

This contact with your Lord and Saviour may be very different from what you realize at this point. In the case of beloved Paul, the Lord not only converted him in the divine encounter on the Damascus way, but he personally overshadowed his ministry and tutored his soul in the mysteries of God *every step of the way.*

And the Lord will do it for you through your own I AM Presence and Holy Christ Self, if you just make the call and lovingly obey the answer.

Now, let us examine that Chart very closely, because it is the key to your discipleship under the Lord Jesus Christ.

Diagram of God's Kingdom within You

Here is the threefold flame in your heart. Here is the silver cord connecting you to your Mighty I AM Presence. Here is your Holy Christ Self— your Real Self, who is sometimes called your Higher Consciousness or Higher Mental Body— standing between you and your God Presence. And, of course, this is the tube of light, sealing you in the white light, and the blue flame reinforcing its protection, called up all around you through that great defender of your faith, Archangel Michael.

This is your causal body surrounding the One

whose name is I AM THAT I AM. These bands contain the treasures of heaven; together they comprise your causal body and focus the Cosmic Christ Consciousness of your Higher Self.

Here we have illustrated the dove of the Holy Spirit descending from the Father upon the Christ Self that signifies the baptism of the Holy Spirit. It is the Paraclete, whose love passes through the silver cord to fill the heart and soul and mind of your lower self until that self becomes *wholly* the vessel of the Light, truly the temple of the *Holy* Ghost.

Then you have the love radiance of the Christ in this beautiful expanding heart of your Holy Christ Self, the golden flame of illumination identifying him as the Tutor of your soul and the Healer.

Here you have a lighthouse, its great beams sweeping out over the sea of humanity's consciousness symbolizing the All-Seeing Eye of God, the Watchman of the night illumining the Homeward path.

Here (all around you inside your tube of light) you have the violet flame, in one way the most important part of the revelation of the Chart because it's the key to transmutation—the washing of your being with the sacred fire.

The Violet Flame and the Law of Recompense

As I have told you before, there're two things that are sure: death and taxes. So goes the saying of Ben Franklin.[11] And you'll never get out of this world alive except through the ascension. And the only way you can really make your ascension is through the violet flame.

There is no person who has ever made his ascension who hasn't had the violet flame given to him some way or another. All may not have had the formula written down. All may not have addressed the LORD, "Beloved mighty victorious Presence of God, I AM in me...," etc., as we are taught to do when we invoke the violet flame from God's altar, but in some way, perhaps on the inner planes, they had to have reached the state of consciousness of the seventh ray where they could call forth the violet flame to consume their human creation.

Because if you don't consume your human creation, dear hearts, you are never going to be able to win the battle of life—because if you don't master your human creation, your human creation will master you, rest assured of it.

There's no two ways about a thing like this. We like to think that there's two ways; but this is only the human, and the human consciousness is constantly changing its mind. One minute he's running hot and the next minute he's running cold. The human is the most unpredictable despot of our natures.

Don't let it fool you; it will try. It will tell you that God isn't going to do anything about it anyway, that he's not concerned with you because you are so little. Well, Jesus said, "One jot or one tittle shall in no wise pass from the law [i.e., the law of

Moses and the law of Christ, both being reflective of the responsibilities of karma] till all be fulfilled."[12]

Now, a jot and a tittle are pretty small portions on the karmic scales. But if it gives you any consolation, your enemies will suffer to the uttermost for the things they do to you. And, consequently, you will suffer just as much, in fact more so—because you know better!—for anything you do to them.

So the safest thing to do is to forget vengeance and forget and forgive immediately, because it just doesn't pay to carry it out to the last farthing and seek your pound of flesh, "Shylock," because when you get your pound of flesh, it is an empty victory. And a vendetta is never a happy circumstance.

There is a moment of triumph when the enemy lies bleeding on the ground before you—he the vanquished, you the victor. But this is soon replaced by the remorse of the spirit when the pangs of guilt give you pause to wonder if, in depriving another of life, liberty, and happiness, you will ever sleep again the sleep of beatitude in God.

So forget and forsake the idea of vengeance in any matter. You have the promise of your Creator—"Vengeance is mine; I will repay, saith the LORD"[13]—and he will keep his promise if you don't interfere and try to take matters into your own hands.

Defend yourself if you have to. I don't think any one of you should give up your life to just anyone because they want to take it. I don't say you shouldn't protect yourself. But, by the grace of God, you should also protect yourself against yourself—because it's alright to protect yourself at any given moment.

But don't carry that too far and "let the sun go down upon your wrath"[14] and then find out that while you were sound asleep, the force of your human mind went out and created something that caused someone else to suffer or to die.

Remember, as we have said, there's a part of your psyche that—if you go to bed harboring anger against another in your heart or in your mind—could go out and actually cause that one to die. A lot of people don't know this. And the next day might come and you'd hear, "Oh, they passed away." And then you'd say, "Well, good enough, they deserved it! They hurt me and I'm pretty important. That's what they got. They got it. They deserved it."

Well, what happens when the Lords of Karma confront you with the record of your energy sent forth as a poisoned arrow and say, "You did this"? So it's best that people "put it into the flame," as we say—the all-consuming violet flame. Forget—forget every wrong as soon as it happens. If you will only do that, you will not be engaging in karma-making action.

And then the violet flame that you use with the plus factor of your Christ Self will be able to remove some of that crusty old karma that's down inside your four lower bodies somewhere lurking—and it needs to be scraped off just like you scrape the barnacles off the bottom of a ship. You need more than a spring housecleaning. Your hull needs a complete overhaul by violet flame!

But if you're so busy creating more human nonsense—and I know of some people (I'd rather not mention them by name) who used to have a violet-flame service, and then they'd have a good fight outside the sanctuary right afterward, the idea being that they'd invoke the violet flame to pay their anticipated debts, you see, and build up their credit in advance—well, this doesn't work because the record is clear:

The purpose of the violet flame is to shed mercy upon the earth. And if people are going to have mercy, they've got to be merciful. And if they're going to think that they can use the violet flame just to make themselves feel good and clean up their human creation—the worst of the scum off the surface so that their pores can breathe for a while—and then they are going to start in with their old hate and hate creations and their fighting and wrangling and human viciousness and discord and keep saying to the Law, "We won't pay! Let the violet flame pay for all our transgressions, for we are above the Law...," let them know that sooner or later the Great Law will make them pay.

And the first thing they know, the violet flame will not be working for them the way it should, because they'll get so clogged up that the Lords of

Karma will come down and say, "Wait a minute. You haven't paid your debt and we're turning off your light and power. We're not going to give you any more violet flame!"

Now, I am saying this in a jovial sort of way but, believe you me, there is an inner law that's involved in this, and this could happen. It could happen that you would lose your efficacy in the use of the violet flame by abusing it. So, let's hold on to the violet flame by using common sense and not go out wasting our energy and creating more karma just because we've now balanced a little and we "feel so good."

The last word on the subject of new-age truth is that no matter how much you think you know or how much of an adept you think you are, you are never above the Law. In fact, you are always under the rod of Christ and the commandments of Moses.

Those who invoke the violet flame, therefore, must know that they must operate under the laws governing its use, beginning with faith, hope, and charity toward all—faith in God, hope in his Christ for every man, and charity toward the evolving soul.

Where Is God?

Let us understand that man has been confused by the time-spatial relationship of himself to Himself. How many angels can dance on the head of a pin? The answer is an infinite number, because angels do not displace time and space.

When it comes to spatial relationships, we believe that two people can't occupy the same square foot at the same time. We say it's just not possible. If we get into a revolving door and there's someone else in there with us, somebody might get hurt! Somehow we can't get it through our heads that maybe, if we knew how, we could walk right through that revolving door—or one another!

So, because of our concrete conceptions, we have a little difficulty in fixing in our mind's eye just where God is. "Well, where is God?"

Where is he? Where indeed! He's everywhere.

Well, this doesn't quite satisfy a child. And somehow even child-man is not quite satisfied with it. We always have the idea that God should be somewhere and that maybe if we knew just where to look for him, we could go and find him.

That's why Jesus warned there would arise false Christs and false prophets proclaiming a flesh-and-blood messiah that could be located in time and space, saying: "Look, here is Christ!" or "Look, he is there!" But the Master said, "Believe not, go not, for the kingdom of God is *within you*."[15] Now, let us see what he meant.

Past, present, and future, the kingdom of God is within you. Well, what is God's kingdom? It is his realm—the realm of his habitation and the realm of his Mind. It would be the dwelling place of his Spirit—and the farthest reaching out of his consciousness. From the point of center where he declares, "I AM...," to the bounds of beingness where the Word "...THAT I AM" resounds, the name of God defines his infinite awareness of himself. Indeed HE IS WHERE HE IS!

Jesus the Christ, God's son who knew his Father well, told you and me that God's kingdom—not part of it, but the whole infinitude of his universal Mind—is inside of us. He meant that within every one of you God's kingdom already is: it always has been and it always will be so for every son and daughter of God.

This Chart is a diagram of God's kingdom within you. In his Teaching on the kingdom within, Jesus also taught by example that it is not blasphemy for you as a son of God to think of yourself as being made in the image and likeness of God, because God created all of his sons in his image and his likeness. So what's wrong with thinking that you *are* this image!

Paul even said we all are changed into the image of the glory of the LORD.[16] And the glory of the LORD, the Shekinah, is the Word, the Light, or Christ, of the I AM Presence. Indeed, we shall bear the "image of the heavenly"[17] Self—our Real Self, who is Christ.

Yes, Christ is the image of the invisible God. And this Christ is the firstborn of each of us. Christ is our original Self. This Self we now see as the Mediator between the soul (the lower figure in the Chart) and the immortal Spirit of the I AM (the upper figure). Your beloved Christ Self in whose image you were made is shown as the middle figure who stands between heaven and earth as your open door to the glory of the LORD above (some witnesses of the Light call the I AM Presence "Jehovah").

Physically speaking, your body may not look just like God, but you're not your body any more than you are your dress or your suit of clothes or your overcoat. Your body is something you wear. It may fit you like a glove, or you may think it does; but you may find out that it doesn't fit you so well, when you find out what you really look like. So let's take a look at who is God where you are, and who you look like at inner levels.

Your Beloved I AM Presence

The upper figure in the Chart is the individualized God Presence of each one of us. This which is called your Mighty I AM Presence, and the Light-manifestation thereof—who is called your Holy Christ Self—is representative of your true Being.

Your I AM Presence is your electronic body of Light. This electronic body of Light is the actual image of God; and every person has the image of God individualized for him. It is an exact replica of the Electronic Presence of God in what is called the Great Central Sun, or the Hub. This is the core of cosmos whence, through the Logos of Alpha and Omega, all of the star systems emanate and the physical creation sprang forth as the counterpart of the spiritual.

Everything in the material universe comes forth from this great center of Light—which itself is the nexus, or go-between, between Spirit and Matter. The Great Central Sun is the focus of the Cosmic Christ consciousness of all life. It contains the image, or divine pattern, for the whole of creation just as your Christ Self contains the image of your soul and your divine plan.

And so this ray of light above the Presence at the very top of the Chart symbolizes the continuation of the crystal cord that connects your heart, through your Christ Self, through your I AM Presence, to the Heart of the Cosmic Christ in the Great Central Sun—and to the Sun behind the sun, the spiritual First Cause behind the material center: the One Supreme God, the Almighty.

Thus, you are very well connected! And every soul who has come from God has an individual I AM Presence, which is an extension of the being of God individualized for him.

The knowledge of the image and likeness of God with you brings you closer to God than you have ever been before. This Presence is actually 'in the air' above your physical body right now and it always has been. Many people have seen this Presence when they were a child and they thought that it was an angel, a beautiful angel hovering over them. But it was the Divine Presence.

Remember John's description of the "mighty angel come down from heaven"? He saw him clothed with a cloud and a rainbow on his head, his face brilliant like the sun and his feet as pillars of fire.[18] Now, that's as apt a description of your own Mighty I AM Presence as you'll get anywhere.

Moses also described the 'Presence' of Yahweh as "the angel of the LORD" who appeared in a flame. Next thing you know, it's the LORD himself who calls Moses out of the midst of the burning bush.[19]

The fact is that that which the prophets and patriarchs interpreted as the LORD's angel was the LORD himself, who would *personify* himself before man, whether through the I AM Presence or one of the Archangels or through the Christic manifestation of the Mighty I AM Presence, whom the prophets addressed as the Ancient of Days[20] or the LORD of hosts.

You see, the I AM Presence is an individualized and very personalized expression of our God, who is Spirit, who is living Truth, who is Mind, who is Principle—as some of our Christian Science and Unity friends like to think of the Presence of Divine Love.

Therefore, for the purposes of intimate communion and verbal one-on-one communication with man (the manifestation of himself), God may assume the form of the man he made so that man will recognize God as his Creator. And this apparition is in the pure likeness of the Son of God, the middle figure in the Chart.

Doesn't that make sense? Don't your children recognize you because you are like them and they are like you?

We are dealing, then, with the One Supreme God—the Almighty, the Maker of heaven and earth—who is one Spirit everywhere present, who sends comfort to his offspring by sending to each one the greatest gift and the only gift that could totally comfort his sons and daughters when they are journeying in that far country—the Matter cosmos. He sends the gift of his Presence, his Electronic Presence individualized for each and every one of his children.

When your children are away from home, aren't they comforted to have a photograph of you as a remembrance? Well, our loving Father, who knows our hearts and how much we miss him and need to feel his nearness, took a photograph of himself and duplicated it for every one of us! And because he is the God of very gods, that photo contains the full momentum of himself—it's just like having the Godhead dwelling with us bodily.

In fact it is, because, you see, this "photograph" is not made of paper and chemicals; it's made of Light. Why, it's made of the very same substance he's made of—or it wouldn't be a duplicate, would it?

Jesus revealed the Almighty to John the Beloved in this wise: "I AM Alpha and Omega, the beginning and the ending which is and which was and which is to come...."[21] Therefore we know that the beginning and the ending of every man and of all creation is God.

Now, this God, who admittedly is everywhere

yet centers his 'Beingness' in the heart of the Great Central Sun, has the power to duplicate his image and make as many luminous presences (focuses) of himself as he wishes.

Just like a woman with a lump of dough. She rolls it out with a rolling pin and she gets out a cookie cutter that looks like a little gingerbread man. She can stamp out as many cookies as she wants to and they all look alike. So don't expect you're going to find anything different about your I AM Presence and mine.

Jesus' I AM Presence looks just like yours. This is the common denominator. This is the coequality of the sons and daughters of God. He created you equal in the sense that he gave you an I AM Presence—he gave you a Divine Self.

"Hear, O Israel: The LORD our God is one LORD!"[22]

When we pray "Our Father...," inherent in that address is the acknowledgment by each one of us that our Father belongs to each one of us somehow uniquely. He may be *your* Father, but he's also *my* Father. We share him but when we're alone with him, he's all ours. We feel complete in him and we feel his very personal caring for us alone.

It's like a family of five children. They share their parents, but each one senses a very private and personal relationship with Daddy and Mommy—or should, if the parents truly understand their role and their children's need to feel very special in those moments of being supremely loved for their intrinsic worth, rather than as part of the group.

So when you realize that your Beloved I AM Presence is in fact the omnipresence of the Father made very tangible right where you are, when you realize that it is both the privilege and the power of the Father to so identify himself to each of his children, when you realize that he is one God, he is the Almighty, and he can do anything—including give you an exclusive Mighty I AM Presence that is yours alone—then you will really know just how much God loves you!

And then you will know that this love is available to you—ever flowing like a mountain stream that never runs dry because it is fed from snowy heights—and that it is yours to give to everybody you know or don't know.

Your Father has given to you, because you are his very own, a limitless Source of light, love, wisdom, joy, peace, and healing power—vested in the Mighty I AM Presence. And all you have to do is call it forth in his name, and it will pour through you to his other children until they, too, learn to depend on their own God Source.

Draw Nigh unto Me and I Will Draw Nigh unto You

This Divine Presence abides in the atmosphere from seven to seventy feet or more above your head, and it varies in its locale. One minute it may be up seventy or eighty feet, and then again it's down to twenty feet. And what governs it is this covenant of your Maker: "Draw nigh unto me and I will draw nigh unto you," saith the LORD.[23]

When you draw nigh to God and your thoughts are high and kind, the Presence will drop down around you. When you're engaged in vicious human activities of criticism and gossip or doing the things that consume your energy in the wrong way, the Presence pulls away from you because your discord and dishonesty with your True Self actually repels the LORD.

Think of it—your vibration can be a repellent to the Godhead. Maybe now you understand why God doesn't always seem to be there when you need him. (Discord of any kind puts a wedge of darkness between your soul and your Highest and most Perfect Love. Then you hear the unbearable words spoken to Eli, "Be ye far from me."[24])

When we lose touch with our Presence, we also lose the protection of the 'angel of the LORD'. And that's why we need the tube of light and why we need to learn how to call it forth by Christ command from the heart of the I AM Presence.

You understand that when you gaze at a blinding light, no matter how bright it gets, as long as it's blinding, you can't see it anyway. So there has to be a contrast. And that's the beauty of heaven, because I think God puts us down here on earth so that by becoming acquainted with all the vibratory actions that occur down here, we can really learn to appreciate heaven.

It's like someone knocking their head against a cement wall. They say it feels so good when they quit! And that's the truth of it—because after you get socked by your own karma and a few other people's karma, you get to the point where you don't know which way is up and which way is down. Why, then you're ready for heaven—we hope!

It reminds me of the story of the young enlisted man who was very nervous about going overseas. And he was so nervous and shaking all over that he was actually breaking out in a cold sweat. And so his friend came up to him to comfort him and he said, "Well, I tell you, my buddy, I wouldn't worry too much about that—there's always a possibility that you won't pass your physical."

"Well," the soldier said, "that's true."

"And there're two chances for you right there," he said. "You either pass your physical or you don't, and then," he said, "if you should pass your physical, you may go overseas and you may not. They may decide to use you in the States."

He replied, "That's true. I do have two chances."

So he said, "Well, another thing, too, when you get overseas, you may be sent into battle and you may not be sent into battle. So, you see, you'll have two chances." Then he said, "And if you get sent into battle, you may get killed and you may not get killed, and," he said, "even if you get killed, you still have two chances!"

So that's a very down-to-earth way of looking

at the calculated risk each of us takes every day of our lives. When John Kennedy was asked not long before his death if he feared an assassination attempt, he said, "To get out of bed each day is a calculated risk." Each day as we get back into the four lower bodies that comprise the lower figure in the Chart—the outer man—we are taking our chances with the risky business of earthly living.

I don't want two chances, do you? I'd rather take the one chance. This is the greatest chance that you can take—the chance of a lifetime to identify with God through your own Beloved I AM Presence. So, identify with God. It's your guarantee of 100-percent success—not necessarily down here through the lower figure, but up here through your Christ Self.

But you have to bring your Higher Self down here to your lower self and superimpose the 'Big Me' over the 'little me'. Then you take charge and, as a wise parent, you control that little "so and so," and you don't let him get in the way of your Great God Reality.

Your Finite Self and Your Four Lower Bodies

Now, natural science, divine science, is magnificent to behold and nowhere more so than in our own body—and ultimately in the seven bodies of man—a cosmos 'all inside' patterned after the seven creative forces of Elohim.

The lower figure in the Chart is symbolical of your finite self, your soul lodged in a human form. I don't like to compare you to a piece of bologna, but it's useful to do so for a moment's digression. Bologna actually has a skin around it and you cram the meat down in there, and it's in its skin, you see. Well, that's the way we are. We're crammed down into this body and we're in our skin, aren't we? Whether we like it or not, or are comfortable or not, we are there.

This human figure down here in the Chart is symbolical of the little man that's down here in his skin—having all told, uppers and lowers, seven bodies, of course. (The I AM Presence, Causal Body, and Holy Christ Self are considered to be the three upper bodies.)

The four lower bodies of man, vehicles of vibration and consciousness in the Matter universe, are his "coats of skins,"[25] as the Bible calls them. It is said that the material body is made of the earth element "from dust to dust."[26] Though an earthen vessel, it is composed of more of Light's energy than most people realize; and therefore, the physical envelope is the focus of integration in the physical octave of the other three bodies.

The mental, or air, body—the vessel of cognition, thought processes, reason, logic, and concentration for decisive and discriminatory action—is just beneath the etheric in vibratory rate. When it is purified holy, it becomes the pure vessel of the Christ Mind, and the etheric and mental bodies are fused as one.

The desire, or water, body—the vessel where the feelings and emotions undulate with the currents of desire stimulated by memory, mind, will, or external causation—is larger and more dominant than the more concentrated mental body. Whereas the Christ Mind ought to dominate both mind and emotions, if the desire body is not disciplined and under the control of the Holy Spirit through the Higher Self, it can cause shipwreck to the soul's evolution lifetime after lifetime.

The physical body is the focus of integration for the evolving soul, which must gain its freedom and self-mastery in the physical octave. The etheric chakras, the seven major with the eighth, are anchored in the three lower bodies; these—including the threefold flame in the secret chamber of the heart and the seed atom as well as the Kundalini (the Life-force) at the base-of-the-spine chakra[27]—are the centers for the spiritual fire and the interchange of the higher and lower energies for the purpose of spiritualization, transmutation and the emission of Light, or the Christ consciousness, to the planetary body.

While each of the four lower bodies has many levels of awareness (conscious, subconscious, and superconscious), "the form of the fourth is like the Son of God,"[28] as the astonished Nebuchadnezzar observed. The etheric body, most like the Christ Self, is mirrored in the physical. But the image is not always clear, as it is troubled and murky with the record and karma of the mental and feeling (astral) bodies. These intercept the pure polarity of the fire and earth elements held naturally between the etheric blueprint and the physical form.

Thus, you can see why the highest vibrating of the four lower bodies is the etheric (the memory, or fire) body. It contains the records both of your soul's preexistence in heaven above (stored in your causal body and Christ Mind) and of your soul's experiences in physical embodiment here below (stored in your subconscious, the astral sheath and lower electronic belt[29]).

Whatever the plane of your activities, the memory body contains the Tablets of *Mem*—the electronic, computerized recordings of all vibrations and energy impulses you have ever sent forth through your soul and its higher and lower vehicles. This life record is written on innumerable discs of light which comprise the changing, evolving identity pattern of the soul merging with the Spirit. It is this life record (the L-field) which determines the patterns which will be outpictured in the three lower vehicles—the mental body, the desire body, and the physical body. (Only the violet flame can permanently alter the effect by thoroughly transmuting the cause.)

Etheric Octave—Threshold of the Second Coming

The etheric body of man the microcosm—as well as the etheric body of planet earth, the macrocosm—is perceived as the heaven-world. It is recorded that Enoch was taken up to the ten heavens.[30] These are distinct planes of consciousness through which the soul evolves in its ascent to God. What we call the etheric octave is the plane to which the Lord Jesus Christ descends (from the highest heaven where he is seated "on the right hand of God"[31]) in his 'Second Coming'.

Paul described his coming as "with a shout, with the voice of the archangel, and with the trump of God."[32] He said that those who are one in Christ's consciousness (those in physical embodiment as well as those who have passed on and are in the etheric plane) shall be caught up together in the clouds (the etheric octave) to meet the Lord in the air (in the plane of the Christ Mind).

By the Lord's descending grace and our willing ascent on the path of attainment, we will meet in the etheric octave of the heaven-world and from there we will follow in the footsteps of Enoch, who by faith "was translated that he should not see death, and was not found because God had translated him: for before his translation he had this testimony, that he pleased God."

And we will mount with Enoch the planes of heaven above, viewing their respective hierarchical orders. These include the plane of Jesus Christ's habitation ("In my Father's house are many mansions.... I go to prepare a place for you...that where 'I AM', there ye may be also"[33]), the Ascended Master octaves of light, the realms of archangels, Elohim, and so on, all leading, spiral upon spiral of infinity, to the throne of the Most High God.

Thus, the etheric body and plane is the meeting ground of heaven and earth where, one by one, souls advancing up the mountain experience the Second Advent of Christ, the rapture, and the resurrection.

The Ascended Masters teach that the Second Coming of Jesus (descending in clouds of glory, as depicted in the Chart) is the descent of the Lord to quicken our soul's consciousness of "his" Christ as "our" Christ—the Universal One, the Only Begotten of the Father. This is the common loaf, or Light, we share and identify as our own Real Self.

Their message is that those who are caught up in the Spirit of Christ through their fiery hearts and the purified etheric vessel (waiting in this earthly life or in the next world) will see Jesus Christ descending, and through him know the image of the Son of God as the God Reality to which they, too, shall indeed ascend.

The author of Hebrews saw that "it was therefore necessary that the patterns of things in the heavens should be purified" in order that Christ Jesus, our High Priest, who comes to us through the person of our Christ Self, might enter our etheric abode, thence to appear for us in the I AM Presence of God.[34]

Because we have altered the heavenly, or etheric, patterns of our lifestream (reflected in the DNA chain as our precise genetic code), we must purify these by the violet flame (the blood, or essence, of Christ) so that the lower mind, the desire body, and physical body might also be remade after Christ's image and the fourfold vessel become the temple of the God who would take up his abode with us.

All of us have an inner awareness of our Christ image, both by self-knowledge and through the auric emanations of our own Christ Self-awareness. By the many layers of consciousness both higher and lower which play upon the 'plastic' substance of these four sheaths, the human personality is formed. The first sheath (the etheric) is incorporeal, for it is impressed with sacred fire; the mental and emotional bodies are subject to certain disintegration factors, but not entirely—the physical, of course, being subject to total dissolution.

The identity patterns of the mental and emotional bodies together with their 'nucleus' are retained from one embodiment to the next as an electronic matrix in the etheric sheath. These records are reproduced lifetime after lifetime on vessels fashioned of earth's frequencies for another round of the soul's self-discovery and self-mastery in the physical plane.

Thus, the reincarnation of the soul in new coats of skins that are most compatible and well suited to her evolution is by a mathematical formula made to order by one's own self-creating actions and thought/feeling impulses which continually mold and shape the outer man.

Though we do not always see "in the flesh" of one another the reflected image of the Anointed One, we may commune with heart and soul and mind of dearest friend and see beyond the veils of skins the Son of man in all his splendor. It is this man we love so dearly—in the plane of reality where our friendships are sealed, our true loves revealed.

It was his hope in the Universal Christ image that led Job to exclaim, "Yet in my flesh [in my genetic code outpictured in my flesh and blood] shall I *see* God!"[35]

The path of the foursquare gospel made plain in the Teachings of the Ascended Masters is the means whereby the soul wed to Christ takes dominion over the four lower bodies and the four planes of Matter simultaneously.

Through the joyous process of soul-purification—transmutation—the earthly patterns are transformed by the heavenly, and the goal of the ascension is attained when the seven bodies of man, as Above so below, are become as one: the soul united with the I AM Presence through the Christ Self now occupying the totality of Being. This, then, is the likeness of the Son of God who dwells forevermore as the One. In all seven planes of Being he is the Ascended Master.

Even so, Ascended Master Jesus Christ, come into my temple—Come into the seven planes of my being!—and dwell with me, my Lord, forevermore.

The Silver Cord

Now, the flow of light between the Spirit of the living God and your soul is over the silver cord. It is the thread of light and the thread of contact, not only with God but also with all souls ascended in the white light who comprise the Great White Brotherhood. (The terms *silver cord* and *crystal cord* are synonymous, being descriptive of men's perceptions of the 'umbilical cord' of the soul, tied to and fed by the Spirit.)

The silver cord originates in the Godhead in the Great Central Sun. You can visualize it as a ribbon of light descending down infinity to your Mighty I AM Presence, passing through your Christ Self to nourish your soul and your four lower bodies. Everyone who is of God has the magnificent 'crystal' cord connecting all planes of his being—heart to heart—to the Sun.

The forgiveness that pours through this crystal cord is absolutely unbelievable! You are dealing with what Saint John saw as the River of Life.[36] The River of Life is crystal. It is radiant. It is bubbling. It is effervescent. And it is individualized for you and for me. All children of the Light have it. It will make you truly, divinely happy.

You don't need any champagne if you can put yourself in God's campaign! Because you have everything you need in the heart of the Presence and it's delivered to your doorstep over this iridescent crystal flowing Life-stream.

The silver cord enters the four lower bodies through the crown; its pulsations can be seen physically by observing the soft spot on a baby's head. Once the silver cord stabilizes the breath and the heartbeat at birth, and the threefold flame is rekindled in the "secret chamber of the heart"[37] and the child begins to "wax strong in spirit,"[38] the soft spot begins to close over. By the time the child is about two years old, it is no longer visible.

While in the womb, the baby lives by the heart flame and crystal cord of the mother. The moment of the cutting of the umbilical cord—when the Holy Spirit has breathed the breath of Life into the form—is the symbolical moment (and sometimes the actual moment, depending on the correct timing of the cutting of the cord) of the descent of the baby's own silver cord from the Beloved I AM Presence. The baby's first cry or sound is often indicative of its sudden recognition of the burst of flame in the heart, of the sacred breath infilling the lungs, and of the bodily sensations now keenly felt.

A long time ago, back in the old Methodist church way out in the country, to the music of a little old organ they used to sing, "When breaks Life's Golden Bowl, / Or the Pitcher at the Fount, / Or the silver cord be loosed, / Then upward shall I mount / Fling wide the pearly gates..."[39] You see, they talked about it as it was spoken of by the preacher Ecclesiastes.

Clairvoyants way back in the 1800s reported standing over dying people and watching the loosening of the silver cord. Spiritualist mediums observed when attending departing souls at their deathbed that something silvery seemed to disconnect from their body and float up into the air.

They described it as a beautiful silver ribbon they could see with their inner sight.[40]

In his autobiography, Charles Lindbergh tells of an experience he had during the twenty-second hour of his transatlantic flight in the *Spirit of St. Louis* when he sensed a "tenuous strand" connected to his body:

"I had been without sleep for nearly two days and two nights. My conscious mind had lost control of its body. My movements were made by instinct, not by will." Then he became aware of what he called "phantoms" grouped in the fuselage behind him.

"Gradually, the apparent difference between self and phantoms faded and I, too, existed independently of time and matter. I felt myself departing from my body as I imagine a spirit would depart—emanating into the cockpit, extending through the fuselage as though no frame or fabric walls were there, angling upward, outward, until I re-formed in an awareness far distant from the human form I left in a fast-flying transatlantic plane. But I remained connected to my body through a long-extended strand, a strand related to the form of man, a strand so tenuous that it could have been severed by a breath, an ethereal breath unrelated to the propeller's wash.

"Then I re-formed slowly as a man again, returning from spatial distances to my plane and body, condensing and collapsing into earthly qualities."[41]

Thus, a man of our time, an aviator, one not in the religious field, saw the silver cord as the lifeline connecting his spirit to his body and experienced his soul's independence from the human form. This is exactly what the Chart depicts.

We learn that the actual cause of death is the cutting of this silver cord (an act of God), which causes the threefold flame to "go out" in the physical body. And this is the accurate and true meaning of Ecclesiastes 12:6–7, which reads: "... or ever the silver cord be loosed, or the golden bowl be broken, or the pitcher be broken at the fountain, or the wheel broken at the cistern [metaphor for the withdrawal of the silver cord and the simultaneous withdrawal of the threefold flame—i.e., the 'breaking' of the heart, the going out of the breath of Life and with it the soul, and the taking up of the light from the chakras—'wheels']. Then shall the dust return to the earth as it was, and the spirit shall return unto God who gave it."

When the silver cord and threefold flame (the 'spirit' or 'spirit spark') are withdrawn from the lower vehicles, the physical heart stops beating and the life-force and breath which animated the form return to the heart of the Christ Self and the etheric plane. The soul of Light also rises—with the accumulated light of the chakras which has been woven into the wedding garment—to the etheric plane where it abides 'dressed' in the etheric sheath until its next incarnation, when the three lower vehicles are remagnetized by the inner blueprint during gestation in the womb.

If the soul is dark, destructive, and given to the passions and possessiveness of this world, it gravitates to the astral planes of the lower vehicles to the hellish existence of its own making and liking. Reincarnating in the lower order of things, the soul experiences the replay of the cycles of death and mortality in and out of the body until the awakening to Christ and the desire to be free sets the soul on the path of self-liberation under the disciplines of so-called spirit guides, some of whom are really the angels and Ascended Masters.

The Karmic Board Reduces the Silver Cord

Going back into past ages, we see, as the Ascended Master who is called the Great Divine Director* points out in his series of Pearls of Wisdom entitled "The Mechanization Concept," that this silver cord was as large in diameter as the tube of light, and the stream of energy from your Presence was just magnificent. It came down all around you. You didn't have to invoke the tube of light because that was flowing naturally from the fount of the Godhead day and night.

Men lived to be eight and nine hundred years old[42] because, you see, this vital shower, like a Niagara Falls, was pouring Life and Life's essence into their physical forms. It kept out imperfection.

---

*also known as the Master R, who founded the House of Rakoczy and the retreat of the Great White Brotherhood in Transylvania and is the teacher and sponsor of Saint Germain

The Karmic Board Reduces the Silver Cord 79

It kept out disease. It maintained their souls' contact with God.

Then mankind began to abuse the Law. And so, by divine decree reflected in an edict of the Karmic Board, set forth in order to prevent mankind from misusing greater and greater quantities of God's energy (because we are all accountable for how much energy we use or misuse), God took away this tremendous shower of energy and reduced the silver cord to its present size.

That you may profit from the Great Divine Director's own words, I shall read them to you at this time:

> Some of the students are aware that when it became necessary to restrict mankind because of his viciousness and bestiality, the Lords of Karma did cut the allotment of cosmic energy for many lifestreams upon the planet until the stream of Life flowing into the body of man at the top of the head (which had once been the size of the tube of light) became a very narrow cord of silvery light-substance through which a relatively minute portion of energy could flow.
>
> Because there is a relationship between the apportioned size of the lifestream, or silver cord, and the spectrum of consciousness upon which man's awareness vibrates, the reduction in the actual size of the cord caused a corresponding decrease in the

number of years of the allotted life span of mankind as well as a gradual shrinking of the spectrum of consciousness.

You will recall that in the days of Methuselah men did live to be many hundreds of years old. Then the shrinking of the rate of descending energy was reflected in a shrinking of the life span, together with the aforementioned spectrum of consciousness.

In a practical manner, this meant that the vibratory peaks of happiness which could be experienced by man and those of consciousness and of awareness were also diminished. And while, through the power of various spiritual exercises, mankind have been able to expand their consciousness, the physical vessel of man and his brain structure have continually impeded the flow of the vital essences because of the shrinking of the cup of consciousness.[43]

We see that the function of the silver cord is of ultimate importance, because the silver cord is the lifeline to our Presence. And, as the Great Divine Director teaches, for those willing to make the calls the lifeline can be expanded.

But bear in mind, dear hearts, that all of us are responsible for the energy we draw down from our Presence. Therefore, we must ask that we may receive the Light of the Christ consciousness and use that energy constructively always.[44] And this is the prerogative of every soul, whether you're in a male or female body—to magnetize the Christ and thereby become one with the Eternal Bridegroom.[45]

I've seen nervous people—like you see sometimes at some of these jazz places, where boys and girls are chewing gum and diddling with one foot and they just don't know what to do with themselves. They're just bouncing with energy.

Just think of all that nervous energy, all sent out in undisciplined thought and feeling. Is it any wonder they're nervous? Now, bring that energy under control and use it to heal the cells of the body. Bring that energy under control and use it to make the mind still. And the mind, then, becomes a clear pool, and in that clear pool the reflection of your Real Self can shine.

You see, as long as you have a choppy surface, you don't know whether you look like Fatty Arbuckle or Slim Jim. You don't know who you look like! If you look in the water, one minute you look fat and the next you look thin, and the image is shaking like a leaf. But still that pool, and you see a true reflection of yourself.

And if you can avoid the sin of Narcissus, you beautiful ladies and good-looking men, I mean—if you can resist falling in love with your own image (in the egocentrism of the human consciousness) and then falling in and drowning in the pool of self, you will behold instead your beloved Christ Self, whose loving face will rekindle in you the desire to be wed spiritually to the Divine Spouse.

The Threefold Flame of Life

In this little circle down here, shown in the center of the chest of the lower figure of yourself, is what is known as the threefold flame of Life. That flame of Life is one-sixteenth of an inch high inside of your physical heart.

You may say, "Well, if it's there, why hasn't medical science discovered it?" Well, the minute they get into it, you are no longer living and the flame is gone out. But that flame is there. And that flame is the flame of your life.

The threefold flame has three plumes—a blue plume, a yellow plume, and a pink plume. This may sound very strange to you, but it is true, and these three plumes form the pattern of the fleur-de-lis. Most of you are familiar with this French lily which is a very beautiful motif—the emblem of the House of Bourbon.

Truly, the threefold flame is the divine right of every son of God. It is the seat of his conscious divinity. Through this tiny spark the identity of God can be known and contemplated. It is the sacred fire of creation, the preserver of Life, and the all-consuming Presence of Love.

Also called the holy Christ-flame and the threefold flame of liberty, this flame flower of the heart increases the divinity of the soul while blessing its humanity. It traces the inner blueprint on the parchment of Life. It shapes the soul's destiny in earth and fire, endows it with air and water, aerating the mind, washing the desire. It generates life and warmth, friendship and peace, kindling the noblest aspirations toward heaven, enlivening the earth with happiness and love of Home.

Consider, then, the three plumes that make up this tripartite light. The blue plume is the anchor point in your world for the will of God the Father; it sparks your willpower, your faith, and your God-determination to outpicture your divine plan through the four lower bodies. The golden yellow plume anchors the discriminating intelligence, the wisdom, the illumination, and the mind of God in Christ. The pink plume anchors the love, compassion, mercy, tenderness, and the grace of God, the Holy Spirit, together with the practical know-how to put the divine plan into action.

Saint Germain taught us about the threefold flame in a heart-to-heart Valentine message. His teaching is yours to contemplate:

> Your heart is indeed one of the choicest gifts of God. Within it there is a central chamber surrounded by a forcefield of such light and protection that we call it a "cosmic interval."
>
> It is a chamber separated from Matter and no probing could ever discover it. It occupies simultaneously not only the third and fourth dimensions but also other dimensions unknown to man.
>
> This central chamber, called the altar

of the heart, is thus the connecting point of the mighty silver cord of light that descends from your God Presence to sustain the beating of your physical heart, giving you life, purpose, and cosmic integration.

I urge all men to treasure this point of contact that they have with Life by giving conscious recognition to it. You do not need to understand by sophisticated language or scientific postulation the how, why, and wherefore of this activity.

Be content to know that God is there and that within you there is a point of contact with the Divine, a spark of fire from the Creator's own heart called the threefold flame of Life. There it burns as the triune essence of Love, Wisdom, and Power.

Each acknowledgment paid daily to the flame within your heart will amplify the power and illumination of Love within your being. Each such attention will produce a new sense of dimension for you, if not outwardly apparent then subconsciously manifest within the folds of your inner thoughts.

Neglect not, then, your heart as the altar of God. Neglect it not as the sun of your manifest being. Draw from God the power of Love and amplify it within your heart. Then send it out into the world at large as the bulwark of that which shall overcome the darkness of the planet, saying:

I AM the Light of the Heart
Shining in the darkness of being
And changing all into the golden treasury
Of the Mind of Christ.

I AM projecting my Love
Out into the world
To erase all errors
And to break down all barriers.

I AM the power of infinite Love,
Amplifying itself
Until it is victorious,
World without end![46]

This precious prayer of Saint Germain is more powerful than you realize. It draws the holy angels—Faith, Hope and Charity, who bear the Light of the Trinity to your heart, fanning the fires of this little sixteenth-inch-high flame, which is your signet of eternal Life.

As the flame of your Holy Christ Self, it is truly "the ornament of a meek and quiet spirit,"[47] as Peter said. Burning on the heart's altar as the votive light of the Father—tended by the hidden, or inner, man of the heart,[48] whose image of the Only Begotten of the Father is clearly outlined within its self-enveloping flames—this threefold light is the replica in sacred fire of the Holy Trinity.

Without this holiness unto the LORD,[49] beloved, this spark of the Divine, you would be as beasts of the field. Not particularly evil, but not particularly good either, you would lack the free will to choose to transcend the genetic patterns of the species and the potential to become divine. Without this endowment, you would exercise no choice of right or wrong, feel no conscience, desire no betterment of self, share no co-creative powers with Elohim through the spoken Word, and know not the all-encompassing Love of the Master-disciple (Guru-chela) relationship.

All the evildoers in whom the divine spark has grown cold (by their own willful neglect and blasphemy against the Godhead) have lost forever their original capacity to seek and find the Source of the creative fires. They have sunk below the level of the beasts; for they have sinned against the Holy Ghost, would not repent, and are hollow even of the hope of spiritual evolution through the sons of God—which even the blessed elementals yet retain.

Truly, with all thy getting, get the dominion over thy human self, by this flame of thy Divine Self.

Ask Saint Germain to help you. He will.

Use his mantra affirming the "I AM" as the Light of your heart. It contains his momentum of devotion to the sacred fire whereby he has demonstrated the spirit's mastery over the elements by the alchemy of the threefold flame.[50]

The Only Begotten Son of the Father— Your Holy Christ Self

The Holy Christ Self is the Mediator between God and man. God in the absolute sense of Spirit is wholly perfect. He is not even aware of what we call sin or iniquity or any evil vibration. Of him the prophet declared, "Thou art of purer eyes than to behold evil and canst not look on iniquity..."[51] Therefore, he created the "Christ Mind"—which descended to the midpoint (the etheric octave) between our highest and lowest self-expression.

This replica of the only begotten Son of the Father, full of grace and truth, serves as the Mediator of each lifestream before the throne of God. He is the Advocate before the Father, The LORD Our Righteousness whose coming was foretold by the prophet Jeremiah.[52]

This Son (or Light) of the Presence came forth to do the will of God as the Father's own representative at your side. His is the still small voice of 'conscience' you hear whenever you are willing to listen.

Jesus was both the actual and symbolical representative of this Christ Self. Jesus was the example, the one who self-realized the Christ Mind and was at one with it at all times. Jesus himself was not the only begotten Son of the Father. The Christ of him was and is the only begotten Son of the Father; and Jesus was the pure vessel of that Universal One. He was the One Sent, chosen from among the Sons of heaven to embody the Christ on earth as the avatar, the exemplar for all to follow for the two-thousand-year Piscean cycle.

When the soul of Jesus became one with the Christ, the son of man was called and he called himself the Son of God. This is the selfsame office to which you can aspire through the path of your personal Christhood on behalf of your family, community, nation, and even world.

Jesus was the embodiment of the Sun, or Light, of God on behalf of the *man*ifestation of earth's evolution. He was the Keeper of the Flame—of the threefold flame of Life—on our behalf until by our own devotion to the Source, we, too, might magnetize a sufficiency of the Sun Presence to intensify our own divinity and hold the balance for others until they, too, are able. Thus, teaching us how to be "my brother's keeper" is one of the fundamental purposes of the Great White Brotherhood.

Beloved Jesus' Christhood was both an office that he filled and a mantle that he bore. And before our very eyes the son of man became both the office and the mantle—which in turn shaped the very nature of his individual Sonship and mission. Jesus was uniquely the Christ and the Christ was uniquely Jesus. And this is the way it is intended to be for all of us—each one showing forth a very precious profile of the Universal One. And the ray of his divinity shone upon him and merged with his humanity. And this consummation of Love's Presence both with and in you will happen to you.

Jesus came to teach us by his example that every child of God has a Holy Christ Self and that the Holy Christ Self is the means to our individualization of the God flame according to the divine plan and free will of our lifestream. The Christ Self is the expression of the absolute love of God for each of his children, the very same love bestowed upon Jesus. Otherwise, God would have had a favorite son, Jesus, and all the rest of us would have been defrauded of our sovereign right to his kingdom.

I don't believe God did this, and I know you don't either.

We wouldn't have stood a ghost of a chance of getting anywhere with God except perhaps in the outer court. As it is now, we have the chance to sit, as it were, on the throne of our own divinity. We can be rulers over many things in the four planes of Matter by being faithful in a few things of the Spirit.[53] All things are possible with God, and this includes the raising of every lifestream that he ever created into his divine inheritance.

I used to wonder, as a child, how it could be that God only created Jesus, who I was taught was the only son that was really 'begotten' of God. Then Jesus revealed to me the truth. Your Holy Christ Self is begotten of your own I AM Presence in order to mediate between the human and the divine—for the express purpose of showing the soul how to correct its human faults. Your beloved Christ Self is your Teacher who inspires you through the intelligence of God's Mind and shows you how your lifestream down here can ascend back to your God Source up there, as Jesus did.

The Chart, then, illustrates to you that day by day you may put on the identity of the Son of God. As you live in a Christlike way, your Christ Self descends closer and closer to you until, by kind words and thoughts and pure feelings and actions motivated by goodwill, you and your blessed Christ Self become one.

It's like some Christians say they're being "partners with God." God will act through you through the Son of his heart. Through the threefold flame—that spark divine—you know Christ and in him you know your Father. Your soul and body temple, your mind and heart become illumined and radiant by the presence with you of this Emmanuel. And your light shines because you are anointed with the Light of your Christ Self. So you become like your elder brother Jesus, who was the "Anointed One"—Jesus, "the Christ."

This is the original meaning of the word *Christ*. One who is Christ is anointed with the Son-Light of God, one who becomes the very embodiment of that Light. Jesus is described as one in whom the Godhead dwelt bodily.

If you are to ascend to the heart of God, you must do so by first ascending to the level of your Christ Self. For only the Son of God who came down from heaven can ascend to the plane of the I AM Presence.[54] All in whom the Spirit of the LORD dwells can claim their present sonship as heirs of the promise. But only by becoming fully integrated with your Christ Self, body and soul,

The Only Begotten Son—Your Holy Christ Self   91

can you affirm in the physical plane, "I AM *the* Son of God"—i.e., the Christ of God incarnate.

Nonetheless, you can affirm right now that your Real Self is the Son of God and that, by right, you are a disciple of Jesus Christ on the path of becoming one with the Son of God. This is the goal of your life which God has ordained for you, as for Jesus. And when you attain it, you will know it and no one will need to tell you, and no one will be able to deny it.

You may walk the earth for many a decade or for centuries bearing the burden of the LORD's Light dwelling in you bodily, until one day the Father calls you Home and your soul, hid with Christ in God,[55] ascends to the I AM THAT I AM to go out no more. "For in him dwelleth all the fullness of the Godhead bodily. And ye are complete in him, which is the head of all principality and power."[56]

When Jesus was taken up "in a cloud" of infinite energy from Bethany's hill, two angels who looked like "men in white apparel" said to the disciples: "Ye men of Galilee, why stand ye gazing up into heaven? This same Jesus, which is taken up from you into heaven, shall so come in like manner as ye have seen him go into heaven."[57]

Even so, from the day of your ascension, my beloved, or even from states of attainment of God-mastery before the ascension, you may also come in like manner, stepping through the veil as the saints do at times to appear to those loved ones on earth, bearing witness to them of their God-potential in all the glory and radiance of the great Light you shall have become in Jesus' name and power.

The descent of the Ascended Master Jesus Christ into your world is most likely to occur through the consciousness of your own Christ Self. Those who saw him ascend were in the Christ consciousness, else they would not have witnessed the angels as well; and those who see him descending day by day are also witnesses of Christ in their own temples, by the same Spirit of the LORD.

Balance the Threefold Flame

Now, I want to explain that most of you do not have a balanced threefold flame. Some of you—we can see it—do have a lot of power and a lot of faith and your blue plume is big.

But some of you have very, very little love. Some of you have a lot of love. You're just so loving, you could just love the whole world! So you're a third-ray type. You've got a great big pink plume but a very tiny plume of illumination—you don't have a lot of real understanding yet.

Some of you have a great big plume of gold. You have all kinds of understanding, like the second-ray people, but you don't have much faith; and therefore, you don't put it to work. Or you don't have much love for people—just for yourself.

Now, what the Christ wants us to do is to *balance the threefold flame*. If we're a person with great faith and great power, we're a first-ray person. He wants us to learn to love one another. He wants us to obtain wisdom. With all thy getting get understanding.[58]

If we have a lot of worldly wisdom but very little love for the world, very little faith in the purposes of Life, he wants us to gain these other two legs of the tripod of being.

This is what all of you have to understand: our duty on earth is to first balance our threefold flame, and then expand the three plumes together—not just one aspect of being but all three of them. It is only by balancing all of the elements of the Trinity in our lives that we can actually attain the fullness of our Christ-perfection.

This is a decree you can give for this purpose. It's called "Balance the Threefold Flame in Me!"

> In the name of the beloved mighty victorious Presence of God, I AM in me, and my very own beloved Holy Christ Self, I call to beloved Helios and Vesta and the threefold flame of Love, Wisdom, and Power in the heart of the Great Central Sun, to beloved Morya El, beloved Lanto, beloved Paul the Venetian, beloved Mighty Victory, beloved Goddess of Liberty, the seven mighty Elohim, beloved Lanello, the entire Spirit of the Great White Brotherhood and the World Mother, elemental life—fire, air, water, and earth!

To balance, blaze, and expand the threefold flame within my heart until I AM manifesting all of thee and naught of the human remains.

Take complete dominion and control over my four lower bodies and raise me and all life by the power of the three-times-three into the glorious resurrection and ascension in the Light!

In the name of the Father, the Mother, the Son, and the Holy Spirit, I decree:

Balance the threefold flame in me! (3x)
  Beloved I AM!
Balance the threefold flame in me! (3x)
  Take thy command!
Balance the threefold flame in me! (3x)
  Magnify it each hour!
Balance the threefold flame in me! (3x)
  Love, Wisdom, and Power!

And in full Faith I consciously accept this manifest, manifest, manifest! (3x) right here and now with full Power, eternally sustained, all-powerfully active, ever expanding, and world enfolding until all are wholly ascended in the Light and free!

Beloved I AM! Beloved I AM! Beloved I AM!

Note: Use the word "Blaze" and then "Expand" in place of "Balance" for two alternate decrees once you have developed a momentum on "Balance."

Your Causal Body

Now we will discuss the point at which people begin to differ in the Divine Self. You have an I AM Presence and it looks just like everybody else's. It looks just like God's.

I always learned that if you put one and one together, you got two—that's all there is to it. You can't change mathematics. And therefore, you can't say that God is more God than himself, or that man is more or less God than God. Because if God created man in his own image, then he made him in his own image, period! There is no difference between the image of God and its manifestation in man! Man is not more or less the image of God; in his natural spiritual state he is simply the image—pure and undefiled.

We have to understand this in order to understand the Chart, because we've got to change our thinking. We can't keep thinking that we're just nothing, because nothing could not possibly come forth from nothing, and nothing could not possibly come forth from something, could it? Therefore, something comes forth from something; and what came forth, of course, is the Divine Man, *the divine manifestation*.

Oh, he doesn't look very divine now, does he?—when you see him lying drunk in the gutter, when you see him out here misbehaving and doing all kinds of unruly things. He doesn't look very divine, but upstairs he is. Up here, everybody who came forth from God is divine. There is absolutely no difference between your I AM Presence and my I AM Presence—because, as we have said, the Presence is the replica of God. And there is only one God.

But here's where the difference comes in. This is important. In the Bible it says, "For one star differeth from another star in glory. So also is the resurrection of the dead."[59] This means that people have causal bodies of varying size and magnitude. These circles of color bands are spherical bodies. They're not flat as they're painted on the Chart with pigment; these are spheres of energy, pulsating energy, permanent energy, eternal energy. They're spiritual Light energy radiating the color of their frequency and vibration.

Your causal body is shaped like a globe; the white fire core is in the very center enfolding the I AM Presence in its central sun of purity's Power and Light. This is the first, or primordial, sphere. The yellow sphere which surrounds it is the primal radiation of the Mind of God; and it contains the record and the momentum of all the intelligence, divinely illumined action, self-knowledge and wisdom that you have ever externalized from God. It is the second sphere.

And here is the pink, the core of love—the third sphere—and then mercy and the violet transmuting flame, the fourth. And then the purple-and-gold band of justice and the ritual of the Law outpictured as your service to life is the fifth sphere. And then the green, the healing and supply in your life, the abundance of Life, the sixth. And all of these are sealed in a magnificent blue-flame sphere, the seventh, of protection, perfection, fiery faith, and God's own goodwill.

You see, every time that you do a good deed on earth, the angels of record build up the size of your electronic body. The good deed is, in effect, a cause you set in motion, which multiplies its vibration around the world, begetting more of its kind as it ripples out to bless many more than the one who was first the recipient of your graciousness.

The light of virtuous acts automatically ascends to the corresponding ring of your causal body. Multiplied by your Christ Self, it returns again and again to increase the good of your divine potential. Therefore, when you need more light to accomplish more good works, you can draw forth from your causal body the 'treasures of heaven' you have stored there as your reserves.

For example, the white has all the colors of the rainbow in it; it's a symbol of purity. Every time that you permit purity to function in your world, every time you perform any soul-purifying ablution—you better believe that that is adding to the size of that band of white.

And every single thing that you do for yourself to keep yourself pure—beginning with your pure perception of all life, the immaculate concept of what is really real—is yours forever. You can never lose what you spiritually gain. And as you gain spiritually, you gain physically, mentally, emotionally, and etherically.

Everything you do out of *pure* love, *pure* truth, *pure* devotion, service for the sake of service and not self-gain adds to the size of the central white sphere—and the bigger it gets, the more purity-power you have in your world. And that's why one star differs from another star in glory.

"*In glory*"—this means in its glorying in God or in its glorification or magnification of the Word of God. So, the one catch about building your causal body rings is that whatever you do in your use (or glorification) of the seven rays, it must be "to the glory of God"[60] and in the service of some part or every part of his Life expressed in his children.

So if you do what you do to the glory of your ego and its self-serving ends, it doesn't count. *It doesn't count for grace.* You may get what you want—a glorified ego, fat with the riches and successes of this world, and a developed and even powerful personality down here—but you won't be storing up treasure in heaven.

None of that goes to build your causal body; instead it accumulates as the momentum of the lower electronic belt. This is the memorabilia of your human karma, which one day, piece by piece, you will want to put into the violet flame—because you won't need it anymore. Once transmuted, this energy, after having been reconsecrated by you in the building of the patterns of perfection on earth, will ascend to your causal body.

Now, let's take a look at that yellow sphere again. Every time you pick up the scriptures, the holy books of East and West, and you read and you run with the Word, or every time you study and demonstrate your mastery of the learning process of anything constructive—if it's to the joy of God's flame in you, you add to your storehouse of knowledge, and that adds to the size of the golden sphere of illumination. This is how you lay up for yourselves treasures in heaven where, Jesus said, "neither moth nor rust doth corrupt, and where thieves do not break through nor steal."[61]

Everything that you do where God works through you—of purity, of learning, or of expressing love, as in this pink band—every time you're loving and kind to any human being, immutably, it registers up there by God's I AM THAT I AM. The Law demands it!

So whatever you do of good down here in the human end (the lower figure in the Chart) is registered up there. That's why you never lose it. You can lose your body, you can even lose your mind, but you will never, never, never lose your causal body. It's there forever. Your soul came forth from it, and it will return to it. It is the place prepared in heaven by God and by your good works on earth.

What's this violet band here? Well, that's the quality of mercy that is not strained—"It droppeth as the gentle rain from heaven upon the place beneath. It is twice blest; it blesseth him that gives and him that takes."⁶² That's mercy and forgiveness and the alchemy of transmutation, ritual and diplomacy—take note of that.

And here, in the fiery blue-purple adorned with pure gold, is the path of Christ's ministration and service which you outpicture daily as you minister to all life, serving to set God's life free on earth.

And here is the green folding stuff you carry in your wallet; it's also chlorophyll—symbol of health and the abundant life, your physical/spiritual wholeness and supply. It's the ray you use for precipitation in conjunction with the alchemy of the seventh ray. It's the green of nature, the healing power of the universe. It's a combination of the yellow and the blue, isn't it?

It's the wisdom and the power to produce good health and honest wealth. That's in the green sphere. That's why many of your physicians today are using green in their operating rooms. Because that color is health, chlorophyll—the imprisoned Life-splendor of the sun.

It's also the light of Truth as science that sets you free from drudgery. It's spiritual Truth as the *true* Teachings of Christ and not the false. And it's the all-seeing, all-knowing eye of God that will act through you, through your Christ Self.

And what's that blue sphere? That's power. That's the first ray. That's the will of God. That's faith. Every time you have faith in divine things, you add to the size of that. It is the envelope of protection and power vouchsafed to you through your obedience to the will of God. Without love of the Father and submission to his goodwill for you and your loved ones, you cannot retain the power to act. Isn't that a beautiful sphere of radiant blue light!

Do you see how the Law works? You draw forth protection through your calls to God and Archangel Michael, and you seal yourself below as you are sealed above in this wonderful emanation of your causal body that protects you always.

Accessing Your Cosmic Bank Account

This is why the woman followed Jesus everywhere and came trembling to get ahold of his garment. Because she had so much blue ray, so much faith up in her causal body, that she knew if she could just touch the hem of his garment, she'd be healed—and she did and she was healed.

But did you take note of what happened? What did he say? He said, "Who touched me?"

Peter said, "Master, how can you say, Who touched me, when the whole multitude are pressing around you on every side?"

He said, "Nay, somebody has touched me, for I perceive that virtue is gone out of me."[63]

Take note of that. Out of his causal body, the virtue of God descended down the silver cord and came through his chakras, through his flesh form and went out through the hem of his garment. This is the energy of God, and it's also yours to conserve and to command. And when you are one with your Christ Self, you will also feel it pass through you and out of you.

So this is your causal body, or your heavenly storehouse; it's your cosmic bank. And every single one of you in this room has a different size causal body with different size spheres within it.

Now, if you're real wise, if you're really smart, you have a lot of intelligence vibrating in the yellow band of your causal body. If you're really full of power and you've got a lot of faith, you know—you've got a lot of blue energy up there. If you're in the healing arts or you're a banker—you've probably got a lot of green. And here, of course, you may be a very merciful person—you've got a lot of pink in your aura (Mary Magdalene had a lot of that)—you're a person of great love.

And that's why some of you people who are so little down here in the human—some of the little women we have here—you have an aura that is so big that it really belies your size. You are not limited by your physical envelope in these matters. You can be a spiritual giant and have a small physical form. Or you can be as big as I am and have a puny little aura, you know. So don't be fooled.

Now, how does the energy of the causal body, which is your cosmic bank, get down here into the physical plane so it's available to you to use at will for more good works in the name of the LORD?

The answer is very simple. It comes down through this silver cord; and it will intensify and accelerate in answer to your call. By your dynamic decrees and "good credit"—showing your wise investment of the light/energy/consciousness entrusted to your use from this cosmic bank account—you can access more and more of God's infinite resources day by day.

I have told the story about the little girl who had a balloon filled with helium so that the balloon always stayed up, and she held it on a string. And like Mary who had a little lamb that followed her wherever she went, the balloon followed the little girl wherever she went.

As long as you live, wherever you walk, just like the little girl running through the park with a big balloon and a string going up, you are right below your own causal body and your own I AM Presence, dangling on the end of the string. Except the string is a silver cord running down through your head, right down to your heart, and that's what beats your heart. And it goes with you everywhere you go, just like Mary's little lamb.

If you walk three steps to the right or to the left, your God Presence moves with you. How could it be otherwise? "Have not I commanded thee? Be strong and of a good courage. Be not afraid, neither be thou dismayed, for the LORD thy God is with thee whithersoever thou goest."[64]

So the Presence is never very far from any of you wherever you are. That's why the psalmist said, "If I ascend up into heaven, thou art there. If I make my bed in hell, behold, thou art there. If

I take the wings of the morning and dwell in the uttermost parts of the sea, even there shall thy hand lead me and thy right hand shall hold me."[65] It's because God goes with you—specifically, God individualized in your I AM Presence.

Now, can't you better imagine your Presence (the angel of his Presence) with you in hell than the Almighty God himself stepping down from his throne to follow you into hell? It makes perfect sense, you see, for God to create this blessed expression of himself to interact with you from day to day. For while his eye beholds you as "the apple of his eye,"[66] at the same time he is beholding the All-in-all of Cosmos so that it too, like your eternal Spirit, will be eternally sustained.

Your Tube of Light

The power of the Divine Presence was with Moses and the children of Israel as the LORD, the beloved Mighty I AM Presence, "went before them by day in a pillar of a cloud to lead them the way, and by night in a pillar of fire to give them light to go by day and night. He took not away the pillar of the cloud by day nor the pillar of fire by night from before the people."[67]

Your Mighty I AM Presence has existed from the moment God thought of it and it will exist forever as the thoughtform of his Mind for your perfection and protection. The rays of light from your Presence signify that your God Presence can reach any corner of the universe instantly with the speed of light. Therefore, you really have something omnipotent here, don't you? Omniscient—yes! Omnipresent because it's the Presence—that's right.

Remember the angel of God which went before the camp of Israel?[68] Well this 'angel' is the messenger of your I AM Presence. Why does your I AM Presence need a messenger? Because, as we have just said, your Presence is ever beholding God Good—creating, preserving, and sustaining worlds of perfection for your soul to inhabit.

Because the Divine Presence does not behold iniquity, the LORD's angel in the person of Archangel Michael as well as your own Christ Self does go before and behind your camp; and wherever the Christ Self is, there is the pillar of the cloud: before, behind, and in the midst of his chosen people is the Spirit of the Great White Brotherhood.

Now, here you are down here in a physical form. You make a call up through "the angel of the LORD," one of the archangels or angelic messengers, by your Holy Christ Self, to your Presence. And the immaculate, all-pure, all-powerful eye of your Presence answers you through the discriminating, all-seeing, all-knowing eye of your Christ Self and sends down the energy as the Light, Life, and Love of the Godhead. And the tube of light—the pillar of cloud by day and the pillar of fire by night—is created in answer to your call.

The call compels the answer and down comes the tube of light from the Presence. It drops like a curtain all around you and protects you against the harmful effects of the mass consciousness because it stops human creation from coming through.

Did you know that the vision of your Holy Christ Self, your seven chakras, the transmutation of karma, and the Chart of your Mighty I AM Presence was given to Joshua the high priest about five hundred years before Jesus Christ was born? Well, listen to this reading.

After the LORD chose to forgive and transmute Joshua's iniquity (sin, karma) and to change his garments—from filthy to the raiment and mitre of the high priest before the altar of God, standing in the office and the stead of the Holy Christ Self on behalf of the people—the LORD said to him:

> Hear now, O Joshua the high priest, thou and thy fellows that sit before thee, for they are men wondered at: for, behold, I will bring forth my servant the BRANCH.
>
> For behold the stone that I have laid before Joshua; upon one stone shall be seven eyes. Behold, I will engrave the graving thereof, saith the LORD of hosts, and I will remove the iniquity of that land in one day.
>
> In that day, saith the LORD of hosts, shall ye call every man his neighbour under the vine and under the fig tree.[69]

And this is the interpretation: My servant the BRANCH is the Person who embodies the Righteousness of God, who comes to replace the self-righteousness of the human. This Person, whom Jeremiah called The LORD Our Righteousness, as we have said, is your own beloved Holy Christ Self.

The BRANCH endows the individual soul with the capacity to be conscious of himself within Christ and to be conscious of Christ within himself. The stone is the unquickened, unredeemed, unanointed who shall receive through the BRANCH the consciousness of God focused in the seven chakras.

Micah says, "Every man shall sit under his own vine and fig tree."[70] The Vine is the beloved Christ Self, the fig tree is the I AM Presence and the causal body bearing the fruits of God consciousness in good works. The LORD is the Mighty I AM Presence, who is represented in the Christ Self.

In the coming kingdom, the reign of God's consciousness on earth, the people will no longer preach the LORD, every man to his neighbor, for they shall all know their Mighty I AM Presence and Christ Self.[71] And "my servant the BRANCH," the Righteousness of God with and in each soul, will serve as high priest at the altar of the living God.

Through Zechariah, the LORD prophesied to Joshua: your office foreshadows the coming of Christ incarnate in Jesus, the Lord; and then, in the fullness of the time ordained, it shall reveal that Christ as the Person, *Pure Son*, of each one's own divinity. This is the path of the return to Eden and the lost estate of God-dominion for every son of God.

Let's seal this revelation of your God Reality through and through with our "Violet Fire and Tube of Light Decree," dictated to me for you by the beloved Ascended Master Saint Germain.

Wherever you are in this glorious universe God made, in whatever plane of heaven or earth, won't you pause with me in the oneness of our communion in the Holy Spirit and send forth this call spoken aloud to God through your Beloved I AM Presence.

O my constant, loving I AM Presence, thou Light of God above me whose radiance forms a circle of fire before me to light my way:

I AM faithfully calling to thee to place a great pillar of Light from my own Mighty I AM God Presence all around me right now today! Keep it intact through every passing moment, manifesting as a shimmering shower of God's beautiful Light through which nothing human can ever pass. Into this beautiful electric circle of divinely charged energy direct a swift upsurge of the violet fire of Freedom's forgiving, transmuting flame!

Cause the ever expanding energy of this flame projected downward into the forcefield of my human energies to completely change every negative condition into the positive polarity of my own Great God

Self! Let the magic of its mercy so purify my world with Light that all whom I contact shall always be blessed with the fragrance of violets from God's own heart in memory of the blessed dawning day when all discord—cause, effect, record, and memory—is forever changed into the Victory of Light and the peace of the ascended Jesus Christ.

I AM now constantly accepting the full power and manifestation of this fiat of Light and calling it into instantaneous action by my own God-given free will and the power to accelerate without limit this sacred release of assistance from God's own heart until all men are ascended and God-free in the Light that never, never, never fails!

Thus it is written, and thus the LORD, the Mighty I AM Presence (YAHWEH), has sealed his promise by his 'angel'—by the "man with a measuring line in his hand," who now stands before you as the eternal Messiah, the same yesterday and today and forever, even your own beloved Christ Self. He has promised unto you, the living soul, the daughter of Zion, who has gone forth from his Spirit:

> I, saith the LORD, will be unto her a wall of fire round about, and will be the glory in the midst of her....
> Sing and rejoice, O daughter of Zion; for, lo, I come, and I will dwell in the midst of thee, saith the LORD.

And many nations shall be joined to the LORD in that day, and shall be my people. And I will dwell in the midst of thee, and thou shalt know that the LORD of hosts hath sent me unto thee.[72]

Peace be unto you, beloved, in the name I AM THAT I AM.

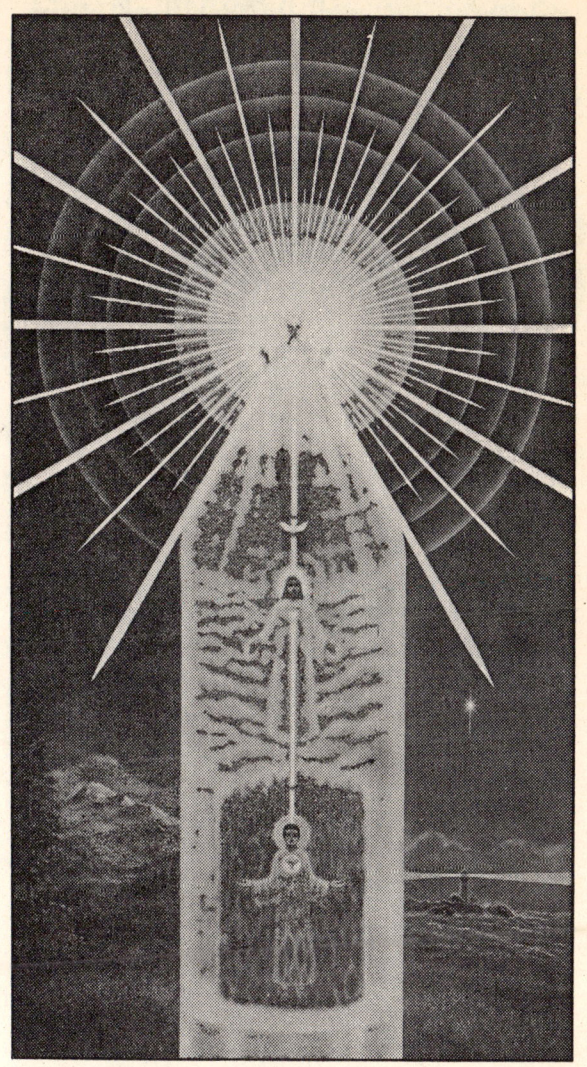

YOUR DIVINE SELF

THE ASCENDED MASTER JESUS CHRIST

THE ASCENDED MASTER SAINT GERMAIN

SEVEN CHAKRAS IN THE BODY OF MAN

Seat of the Soul Chakra
violet

Base of the Spine Chakra
white

THROAT CHAKRA
blue

SOLAR PLEXUS CHAKRA
purple and gold

HEART CHAKRA
pink

Crown Chakra
yellow

Third Eye Chakra
green

Chapter Seven

THE INTEGRATION OF THE CHAKRAS

The Integration of the Chakras

"The Fitness Craze," "Body Beautiful," "America in Training." How many headlines have you read about the benefits of physical exercise?

The current trends would have you believe that almost any problem you can think of can be cured through some sort of workout program. Books, magazines, and television shows abound, touting everything from aerobics to racquetball as the ultimate remedy for a wide range of maladies from simple stress to heart disease.

Health, as we all know, is a product of proper diet, positive mental attitude, enough sleep, and physical exercise—right? Well, maybe...

The Missing Dimension in Physical Fitness

While such activities are definitely valid, there has been a consistent omission of a very important element. The missing dimension in physical fitness has nothing to do with what we normally think of as health-promoting factors.

What we are talking about are centers of energy flow within your body that you cannot see or touch but that are as important to isolate and condition as your triceps. These centers are called *chakras*—the Sanskrit word meaning "wheel" or "disc." There are seven major chakras within your body.

You're probably wondering how in the world something you can't even see, let alone exercise, can be so important to fitness! Well, you *can* exercise your chakras. And even if you can't see them, you can feel them. More on this later.

To begin with, the physical body of an athlete is only one-quarter of the whole person. You also have your mental body (your thoughts and cognitive mind), your emotional body (feelings and desires), and your etheric body (your memory, containing layers of the subconscious and the superconscious mind as well as the blueprint of life) to train for the optimum performance in any situation—be it track, court, or gridiron.

These three other 'bodies' fulfill a very important role in any athletic training program. It is these which support the physical body and give it that extra determination to push through, to work those muscles, even when—and especially when—you feel that "burn" that lets you know you are making progress.

As anyone familiar with the world of physical fitness can testify, workouts are grueling and painful and exact a heavy toll on the body. Except for a possible endorphin-induced high, there is little immediate physical gratification. (Endorphins are chemicals produced by the body during periods of intense exertion that mimic the effects of opium on the brain. They contribute largely, along with pain-blocking enkephalins, to the phenomenon known as "runner's high.")

Another phenomenon known to many runners is the "wall." This is the point at which the body has used up all of its available glycogen and has no more energy to give to the muscles. Usually this is after twenty miles or so, when the body is physically exhausted. Sometimes drinking sugar water during the run will combat this problem. Most people, however, will get "exhausted" long before the wall is reached. For those who do not run regularly, to actually go twenty miles would be impossible without risking serious injury.

The point I am making here is that there are many who could run the twenty miles but stop at six or ten because they *think* or *feel* that they can't do it. If those people would get their mental and emotional bodies working with their physical, they would excel. This is only common sense.

Any gratification achieved through a fitness program is delayed. Be it drinking a glass of apple juice and taking a cool shower after the evening's program or long-term muscular gain, the joy of a workout is not the workout itself.

Consequently, unless you are someone who enjoys pain, there must be other factors driving you to put your body through its paces. These could be your *memories* of how good you felt last time you 'pumped iron', your *mental* determination to excel, or the desire to attain the *emotional* control that comes with the true mastery of any sport or martial art.

Take, for example, the case of John McEnroe, the tennis pro who plays a very good game but has been known to throw his racquet and berate the judges. His actions reveal a temporary absence of emotional control for which he receives no small amount of bad publicity.

In the Davis Cup tournament held in Buenos Aires, McEnroe was badly beaten. This was due in large part to the clay courts on which the games were played. Sullen and dejected, McEnroe broke his routine by remaining unusually quiet for the duration of the competition.

But even this despondency is a lack of emotional control. If McEnroe had really wanted to win that tournament, he would have had to maintain a positive attitude while at the same time keeping his lid on. This is the middle path of the Buddha—just enough of the right qualities at the right time, without ever losing control. In any event, he could probably play a much better game, as well as increase his popularity immensely, if he would integrate his "emotional body" with his physical.

Tennis, or even racquetball, requires a great deal of memory in addition to emotional control. Just think of the countless hours of practice McEnroe has spent. Not only must he have developed his forearm and trained his eye, but also he must remember with intimate detail which type of shot to use on what occasion and the exact angle of incidence and reflection of every ball that screams over the net and into his court. Once memorized in every cell, these responses must then become automated—like a bio-electric formula invoked and executed faster than the 'mind' can think.

As far as mental attitude is concerned, this is mainly being "psyched up" for the game. No matter how skilled your opponent, or what the playing surface is composed of, you must know you have the ability and determination to win.

Alright, you say, what does all of this have to do with your chakras? Thought you'd never ask!

Each body is separate and distinct—sharing, or intersecting through, the common coordinates of the seven chakras. In the physical, they are specifically attached through the central nervous and endocrine systems. The chakras are the central vehicles for the flow of light from your soul to your four bodies.

In order to maximize your potential, you must have a clear passage for the light and energy you receive from the Life Source each day to move freely through all of your bodies. If any chakra is clogged, it can throw one or more of your four bodies out of alignment. If one of the four lower bodies is out of alignment, you can't make the most of any of them.

All the push-ups in the world won't mean a thing if you are still fighting your own sense of limitation. Therefore, it behooves anyone who is really serious about fitness and well-being to study and know the chakras and their effects on training as well as all aspects of everyday life.

The Threefold Flame of the Heart

The central and most important organ of your body is your heart. Likewise, the central and most important chakra is the heart chakra, which contains the threefold flame. The threefold flame is the blossoming of light within your heart, anchored there through the descent of the crystal cord. It is not really a flame like a candle, but we can think of it more in terms of the bush that burned with fire and was not consumed.[1] The crystal cord is the thread of light which descends from your "I AM Presence," another name for your God Self.

Why is the flame in your heart called "threefold"? Because it embodies the three God-qualities of Power, Wisdom, and Love, also personified in the Trinity. Ideally, these are kept in balance. But few have the mastery to do this. Instead, people fill their hearts with hatred, fear, and malice, which on the spiritual level resemble lead or asphalt. (Heart disease, though on the decline, remains the biggest killer in the country. Small wonder.)

One of the most important parts of keeping fit is cleaning up and balancing the heart chakra. Just as the brain and organs depend on blood flow, so all other chakras depend on energy flow from the heart. Thus, when the heart is clogged through selfishness and possessiveness, which block this flow, all of the chakras suffer.

Secondly, after the threefold flame is balanced, it must then be expanded. Before the proverbial Fall of man, the threefold flame surrounded the body completely and reached a height of five to seven feet. At that time, the crystal cord was over nine feet in diameter, channeling tremendous amounts of divine energy into the heart chakra of man. This increased his longevity—hence the extraordinarily long life spans, earlier noted, of such antediluvian figures as Methuselah and Noah—and enabled him to perform what would now be considered as superhuman feats.

Finally, the heart chakra must be protected. It is extremely sensitive to all types of vibrations, both good and bad. This sensitivity must be guarded. Negative frequencies impinging upon the heart can cause heart attacks. Most dangerous are hatred, mental criticism, hardness of heart, envy, and even the death wish, which amounts to witchcraft. By failing to groom their thoughts and feelings with love, people actually engage in mental and emotional malpractice against one another on a day-to-day basis.

Light Mantras for the Heart

Saint Germain, the Master who is the keystone in the arch of the Aquarian age, has given us a mantra for the cleansing of our chakras. This mantra can be used in conjunction with all of the other mantras contained in this chapter. It is very simple and easy to remember and can be given aloud or under your breath any time things aren't going well or you feel a heaviness in your body or a burden on your heart.

I AM a being of violet fire,
I AM the purity God desires!

Similar in quality to the threefold flame in the heart, the violet fire, or violet flame, is specifically for the transmutation of negative karma, records of nonfulfillment in this or past lives, or negativity in any form. It is the flame of freedom and of the Holy Spirit which forgives sin by dissolving its cause, effect, record, and memory. It is the God-energy that frees the atoms, cells, and electrons in your four lower bodies to sing the song of their fiery destiny. And it will liberate all who use it—mentally, psychologically, and spiritually.

Saint Germain's mantra for the Aquarian age can be adapted for use with all chakras as follows:

My heart is a chakra of violet fire,
My heart is the purity God desires!

My throat chakra is a wheel of violet fire,
My throat chakra is the purity God desires!

My solar plexus is a sun of violet fire,
My solar plexus is the purity God desires!

My third eye is a center of violet fire,
My third eye is the purity God desires!

My soul chakra is a sphere of violet fire,
My soul is the purity God desires!

My crown chakra is a lotus of violet fire,
My crown chakra is the purity God desires!

My base chakra is a fount of violet fire,
My base chakra is the purity God desires!

Simply give the mantra corresponding to the specific chakra you feel needs cleansing, and give it until you feel a release from your tension, anxiety, or whatever problem you may have. Try it! It works.

For the purposes of visualization, the heart chakra, when at its optimum, emits a white fire clothed with shades of pink, rose, and ruby—depending on the intensity and purity of the love expressed. This rose of the heart has twelve petals. It is visualized over the place of the physical heart, although in the perfected state, it and its physical counterpart would be in the center of the chest.

See the threefold flame within it, with its three plumes of Power, Wisdom, and Love as flames of blue, gold, and pink respectively. As an added protection against world weight, you can see in your mind's eye a spinning disc of white light in front of the heart. For a real clearing action, give the "I AM Light" mantra.

When you say the mantra aloud, you are setting up a forcefield of light around your heart. This forcefield will keep away the 'bad vibes' and other assorted negative energies that tend at times to make things go wrong.

This is one of many practical applications of the science of the spoken Word. Through the correct use of the throat chakra in decrees such as this one, we become effectively co-creators with our Higher Consciousness. As spoken of in the Book of Job, "The Almighty shall be thy defence.... Thou shalt make thy prayer unto him, and he shall hear thee.... Thou shalt also decree a thing, and it shall be established unto thee: and the light shall shine upon thy ways."[2]

"I AM" is the name of God as spoken to Moses: Tell them, 'I AM' hath sent me unto you. This is my name for ever.[3] Therefore, when we affirm "I AM," we are affirming "*God in me is*" or "*God in me is the action of...*" Whatever follows—whether it be speech, prayer, mantra, or decree—it is self-realized because it is the power of God's name and his Be-ness that works creative change in our lives.

I AM Light

I AM Light, glowing Light,
Radiating Light, intensified Light.
God consumes my darkness,
Transmuting it into Light.

This day I AM a focus of the Central Sun.
Flowing through me is a crystal river,
A living fountain of Light
That can never be qualified
By human thought and feeling.

I AM an outpost of the Divine.
Such darkness as has used me is swallowed up
By the mighty river of Light which I AM.

I AM, I AM, I AM Light;
I live, I live, I live in Light.
I AM Light's fullest dimension;
I AM Light's purest intention.
I AM Light, Light, Light
Flooding the world everywhere I move,
Blessing, strengthening, and conveying
The purpose of the kingdom of heaven.

By meditating on the white fire surrounding the threefold flame in the secret chamber of your heart and giving the "I AM Light" mantra by Saint Francis (known today as the Ascended Master Kuthumi) for the protection of the heart chakra, you are really benefiting all of your chakras. As you know, oxygenated blood from the lungs must first pass through the heart before it can nourish the rest of the body. Similarly, the light from your I AM Presence must also pass through the heart. Whatever the heart contains is then carried to all the other chakras.

Indeed, the energy of the Life Source is the only real 'fountain of youth' in existence. (Ironically, Ponce de Leon and countless others have spent a major portion of their lives chasing that flaming youth which was really in their heart.)

As a result of the misuse of this energy, the crystal cord is today a mere thread, and the threefold flame measures an average height of one-sixteenth of an inch. If we are ever to regain our former power and vitality, we must prove ourselves the master over what we now have.

Vitality and Prana

As for vitality, it is the endless pursuit of this elusive quality which drives many fitness devotees to their efforts.

Why is running a natural high? Why do you feel so invigorated after a brisk walk or a good hard workout? What is it that makes you think more clearly and feel like you're really alive?

Prana. The Sanskrit word for "breath" or "breath of life." But it is much more than what we think of as breath. Prana is the life energy that vitalizes all living things and controls all activities in the body—physical and spiritual, mental and sensory. Without it, blood won't circulate, organs won't function, and the brain won't do its job.

The concept of a universal energy force has been taught for many centuries and in many cultures. The Sanskrit term *prana* has been compared to the *mana* of the Polynesians, to the Chinese *ch'i*, energy which circulates through the meridians detailed in the ancient science of acupuncture, to the Hebrew *ruach* ("spirit of life"), and to what scientists have in recent times called "bioplasma."

Prana is most easily absorbed into the body through the air, where it is found in its freest state. As you exercise—especially in fresh air and sunshine—you are inhaling, with each breath, air charged with this dynamic force. Like an electric current, it courses through an intricate system of nerve passages in the etheric body and is carried to every organ and part of the system, giving renewed strength and vigor.

Prana has its greatest concentration in the seven chakras, which serve as generating centers and focal points for this energy. The chakras regulate specific bodily functions, and at each of these energy centers the prana is collected and distributed to its destination.

Every activity—from muscle movement, to digestion, to thought itself—utilizes prana, and the supply needs to be constantly replenished to sustain good health. Unless enough fresh air reaches the lungs, for example, the venous blood (which accumulates waste from all parts of the body) cannot be purified or renewed with life. This poisonous waste matter, instead of being expelled, is then circulated through the body and poor health or disease ensues.

In fact, it is said that disease is due to an imbalance of prana. And some proponents of yoga believe that all sickness can be controlled when the proper flow of prana is restored. Along the same lines, in the West jogging has been used successfully as preventive medicine and even as therapeutic treatment for patients with heart problems. However, some practitioners believe jogging is harmful to the organs, the spine and sacrum.

Because all of the four lower bodies are interrelated, causes set into motion by prana are not limited to physical effects. A lack of prana can influence the mind and the emotions as well. Clinical tests have shown that there is a relationship between poor breathing and low IQ in children. And it's not hard to see how being confined to a stuffy room for too long can produce moodiness, depression, or apathy—instead of the buoyancy that an energy boost of fresh air and prana will provide.

Prana comes from God through many channels. The most reliable source of prana is clean air near moving water, charged with sunlight.

It can be postulated that the amount of prana in the air is a direct function of the concentration of negatively charged ions. (A negatively charged ion is an air molecule that is carrying one or more extra electrons. Similarly, a positively charged ion has been stripped of one or more electrons.)

I would not go so far as to say that prana *is* negatively charged ions, but let's just say that when the concentration of negative ions is naturally high, you can be reasonably sure there is some prana around.

Many studies have proven that the ion concentration in the air has a profound effect on the body. In working environments in the cities, positive ions which are detrimental to health are generated in quantity by central air-conditioning systems, pollution, and automobiles. On the other hand, rain and lightning storms generate negative ions which benefit the body. The ocean, rivers, streams, and all types of vegetation also contribute to the negative ionization of the air.

When you run along the beach on a clear day, you are doing far more to revitalize your physical temple than if you were to jog for twice the time through the back streets of Los Angeles. Once you take into consideration environmental factors, the where and when becomes as important as the how and for how long.

Since most of us do live in the city, it's important to find the time to go elsewhere—into nature to clear out our physical bodies of pollution and processed food, cleanse our chakras through fasting, meditation, and mantras, and bring the other three bodies into alignment.

The Powerful Throat Center

The next center we should be concerned with is the throat chakra. It is located over the physical throat, has sixteen petals, and is blue in color. It is the power chakra, and through the gift of speech unique to man, it can release large quantities of energy, both good and bad.

Through the disciplined use of the spoken word, we can make great progress in the toning of all of our chakras. With misuse—such as cursing in the name of God or Jesus Christ, gossip, criticism, sarcasm, angry words, or "unseemly conversation"—we do ourselves great harm as well as increase the planetary level of human effluvia.

Even irritation toward others and the voicing of that irritation causes imbalance within all of the chakras, because the throat is the command center through which our creative forces flow to all life, establishing the tenor of our aura and our person.

This concept is not new. Jesus admonished us, "Let your communication be, Yea, yea; Nay, nay: for whatsoever is more than these cometh of evil."[4] This was not meant to exclude necessary communication between persons but was a reminder to us of the seriousness of the misuse of the word; it also revealed his awareness of the power of the spoken word to affirm Truth.

Through the affirmation of Truth—"Yea, yea"—we channel it into action in our lives, and by denying error—"Nay, nay"—we cast out error's effects in our lives.

He also warned that "every idle word that men shall speak, they shall give account thereof in the day of judgment. For by thy words thou shalt be justified, and by thy words thou shalt be condemned."[5]

This shows that Jesus believed words were as important as actions, and that both would be weighed in the ultimate evaluation of the soul. It's also important to realize that idle chatter (like idle sex) drains you of the energy you need to focus for maximum performance. Too much talk and not enough action, like any other indulgence, squanders the life-force and reveals an absence of control and personal integration.

Despite its enormous significance in human relations, our society has deemphasized the word to such a degree that cynicism and incisiveness have become more important than true communication.

Now, as we all know, music is the barometer of society, and as the Scottish patriot Andrew Fletcher of Saltoun so aptly commented, "If a man were permitted to make all the ballads, he need not care who should make the laws of a nation."

Just tune in your radio to any popular station. Tell me if you can find four songs in a row where some aspect of life isn't being degraded. Everything is made common. Every action has a hidden motive. People are painted as having no sincerity in word or in deed. Even words themselves cease to have meaning in the minds of many. People can lie, curse, gossip, and it's all justified matter-of-factly with "It's just words."

Take, for example, the hit by the group Missing Persons. It speaks for itself. The lyricist is obviously following the current trends of musical cynicism, but he ends up making quite an accurate social comment. This is not to say that the words of the song really meant any more to him than to his imaginary listener.

"Words"
by Terry Bozzio & Warren Cuccurullo

> Do you hear me
> Do you care
> Do you hear me
> Do you care

My lips are moving and the
   sound's coming out
The words are audible but
   I have my doubts
That you realize what has been said

You look at me as if you're in a daze
It's like the feeling at the
   end of the page
When you realize you don't
   know what you just read

What are words for
When no one listens any more
What are words for
When no one listens
   what are words for
When no one listens there's
   no use talking at all

I might as well go up and
   talk to a wall
'Cause all the words are
   having no effect at all
It's a funny thing am I all alone

Something has to happen to
   change the direction
What little filters through is
   giving you the wrong impression
   it's a sorry state...[6]

Sorry, indeed. The sad part is that, to many, words have become empty—something to use to manipulate others or to express anger. Even though the song is not taken seriously by the majority of those who hear it, it is a most apt description for the way many people communicate.

Much of social interaction today is governed by the 'cocktail party' mentality of one-upmanship—along with the couching of every aggressive statement in terms of some sort of joke or good humor so as to be able to hurt another deeply without "ruffling anyone's feathers." And heaven forbid that the poor guy should take anyone seriously, lest he be greeted with more hoots of laughter and shouts of "Paranoid?" and "Can't take a joke?"

Generally, the way this is dealt with is that these 'sophisticates' develop a razor-sharp tongue, ready to counter each rapier thrust of caustic wit with an even more incisive jab. Then everyone laughs and supposedly none are the worse for the wear.

But are they? What about the deep-seated scars that this inflicts on the unsuspecting and sensitive individual? What about the sincere seeker whose nature will not allow him to participate in this type of game? Is he to be cast out of society, branded a simpleton?

Certainly all of this is not what the throat chakra is meant for. When an individual is accustomed to hearing mostly innuendo and sarcasm from everyone around him, who should be surprised that he "doesn't listen any more"?

In our society, more than anything else we need to realize the importance of the word. Now that communication has become all but automated, and computers 'talk' to each other faster and more accurately than people, we think of technology as the cure for all of our ills. Just look at the word *technology*. It comes from the Greek *techne*, meaning "art" or "craft," and *logos*, meaning "word." So here we are, in the *age of the art of the word*, and communication between individuals is one of our biggest problems!

David's prayer ought to become our own: "Let the words of my mouth and the meditation of my heart be acceptable in thy sight, O LORD, my strength and my redeemer."[7]

If we all thought about what we said each time we said it as if we were speaking to or in front of God, our conversations would be quite different. This, then, is the first step to the clearing of the throat chakra: to purify our speech.

The very strength of God's will we misuse in this center can become the power to engage the cosmic law in our life. Try this mantra of Christ's victory in you:

> Not my will,
> Not my will,
> Not my will,
> But Thine be done!

Mentally or verbally affirmed, it can even be used to maintain the rhythm of your exercise. Visualize the blue flame of Life's blueprint working through your throat chakra and spoken word to charge your body with the integrating will of the universe.

The Place of the Sun

Complementing the throat, below the heart, is the solar-plexus chakra. It is located at the navel and corresponds to the nerve center there. It has ten petals and its colors are a combination of rich purple and metallic gold. When you become agitated and feel that familiar discomfort "in the pit of your stomach," you know that it is your solar plexus that has been affected.

This energy is usually released through the throat in the form of disruptive verbiage. The solar plexus and the throat are corresponding chakras, and when in harmony, the energies of both converge in the heart for peaceful and loving communication. When one or the other is in disharmony, both chakras are involved.

Many of our emotions are expressed through these two chakras. You will notice that under normal circumstances, when people are expressing feelings of love, kindness, or any other positive emotion, they usually speak in a quiet and resonant tone of voice. As soon as the solar plexus is agitated, however, the pitch and the volume go up. This is most noticeable when the person is in a state of anger or anxiety.

Mastering the solar plexus requires the mastery of our emotions by harnessing ourselves to the divine will—by the sacred fire of the heart. When they are controlled, we can begin the purification of this chakra through meditation and dynamic decrees.

While visualizing the chakra as shown, give "The Balm of Gilead." This prayer will help calm your emotions (your *energies in motion*) whenever you feel agitated or ill at ease.

> O Love of God, immortal Love,
> Enfold all in thy ray:
> Send compassion from above
> To raise them all today!
> In the fullness of thy power,
> Shed thy glorious beams
> Upon the earth and all thereon
> Where life in shadow seems!
> Let the Light of God blaze forth
> To cut men free from pain:
> Raise them up and clothe them, God,
> With thy mighty I AM name!

The solar plexus is very much linked to the soul. Therefore, if this chakra is kept pure, you will be more in touch with your true feelings and self. Our emotions, magnifying the pure desire of the Higher Self, are intended to amplify the soul and the potential of the soul.

The Inner Eye

Ascending once again above the heart, we find the third-eye chakra. This center is just as important to keep free of human debris as any of the other six—even more so, because it is the orifice of spiritual vision.

Jesus, our beloved World Teacher, was speaking of this 'eye' when he said, "The light of the body is the eye. If therefore thine eye be single, thy whole body shall be full of light."[8]

Located at the center of the brow, it is emerald green when purified and has ninety-six petals (sometimes represented as two, as in the winged caduceus). Ideally, through the third eye, we should be able to anchor the vision of God, the vision of perfection.

Today, we live in a world of relativity and do not see or outpicture the absolute perfection of the God Self. When man was first created, before the descent of the soul into the planes of illusion (the Fall), he had the single-eyed vision of his original perfection in the third eye.

At the time of the Fall, when he partook of the fruit of the tree of the knowledge of relative good and evil, he fell into a state of duality. This is the propensity to see good and evil as relative qualities.

At the lowest point of the planetary evolution, some had lost the divine spark and walked the earth as animals. (It seems that Darwin was really a latecomer!) In actuality, mankind did not start as cavemen but descended to that state through neglect of devotion to the sacred fire of the heart and the misuse of the throat chakra and the third eye.

Since then, man has not been able to regain the fullness of his former faculties, although he may make great strides through the *exercise* of the heart chakra in devotion and meditation, the *exercise* of the throat chakra in the scientific use of the mantra or the dynamic decree of the Word, and the *exercise* of his spiritual vision by seeing the good (God) in friend and foe alike.

The very fact that America has enjoyed such prosperity over the last two centuries has to do with the fact that its people have had the third-eye vision of a higher standard of excellence to make things happen. Not only have we built a mighty nation of our own, but we have exported money and technology to almost every other nation on earth.

"Yes," you say, "but what about our economy? What about all of the unemployment?" Well, some of the nation's poor are those who have misused their chakras in the past, causing great harm to others, and are now experiencing the effects of causes they set in motion. And some of the rich have taken unfair advantage of the rest of us (through no fault of our own)—and that's their karma, too, which they will surely reap. And some of them already are—having returned in this life as the nation's debtors who cry the loudest for welfare payments and food stamps, now that the shoe is on the other foot. But even this can be undone by the violet flame.

Karma, after all, until submitted to Mercy's grace, is the iron law of cause and effect, more binding and all-encompassing than any earthly statute. That's why Jesus said, "The poor you have with you always."⁹ You see, there's always someone at the bottom of the socio-economic ladder. This is not to disallow the negative and even diabolical influence that our past and present leaders have had on the economy and employment picture.

Small comfort to the little people, the working people and the low-income brackets. But then, too, there is the karma of neglect where you fail to champion your economic rights or to challenge the power elite's international cartel who exercise control of the money, the banks, trade, and the economies of the nations. If the people don't stop complaining and start stumping for the Coming Revolution in Higher Consciousness, they may be lost before they are found centered in Saint Germain's fires of freedom.

It's a fact. The high and the mighty, the captains and kingmakers have interfered with the free market by monopoly capitalism, federal regulation and bureaucratic red tape for the small businessman, which has hurt a lot of good people who are the backbone of America. And, as we have said, they shall not escape their recompense. However, technically, there is no injustice in the universe. Everyone must face the reaper in the form of his own personal karma. Everyone must ultimately pay the price for the misuse of the light of God—the oppressors as well as the oppressed. There are no exceptions.

Now, getting back to the clearing of the third eye, this can be accomplished through meditation on perfect geometric forms, as well as through the raising of the energies of the lower chakras to the level of the third eye. "Behold the Good!" is truly the motto to espouse for strength of vision through this instrument of God's all-seeing eye.

To begin, visualize a disc of light superimposed over your forehead, like a miner's light, only brighter. See it spinning and filling your vision center with light, flushing out the misqualified substance of the ages from your chakra, cleansing it until it is a brilliant emerald green.

As you are holding this picture in your mind's eye, give the following mantra of the science of the Word:

> O disc of Light from heaven's height,
> Descend with all your perfection!
> Make our auras bright with freedom's Light
> And the Master's love and protection!

Then call to your Christ Self and affirm:

> I AM, I AM beholding All,
> Mine eye is single as I call;
> Raise me now and set me free,
> Thy holy image now to be.

Clearing the third eye is a very important step in soul evolution, as it is directly correlated to the soul chakra. Whatever is seen through the third eye is also mirrored in the soul.

As a practical measure, third-eye vision can be improved through the cleansing of the blood, the colon and the physical body in general. Toxins accumulated in the blood and fatty tissue as well as in the colon are a direct hindrance to that vision. A balanced program of fasting on fresh vegetable or fruit juices, as well as distilled water and herb teas, is a good place to start.

The Chakra of Freedom

All the images seen with the third eye are reflected in the soul. The soul is anchored to the physical body through the seat-of-the-soul chakra, halfway between the navel and the base of the spine. This chakra governs the genetic code, heredity, and the manufacture of the seed and the egg. The seat of the soul has six petals and is violet in color.

Because of the very close relation between the soul and the third eye, the soul is easily damaged by impure and imperfect thoughtforms and images. This is especially true with some of today's art.

Color is especially important. Pastel light-emitting hues are better than loud or muddier shades, which are detrimental—as are amorphous shapes. The pattern of Christ in the individual contains the geometry of the cosmos. Any dissonant or jagged art form is destructive to this geometry—disturbing to its reflection, from the eye image to every cell.

Long ago, advanced civilizations on the continent of Africa were brought down by perverted art and music, which eventually led to all forms of black magic and witchcraft being practiced there.

This has continued up to the present with voodoo, ritual murder, and sacrifice. These are extreme examples of the destruction of the soul chakra. Misuse of this and other chakras has caused vast devastation and, more than once, brought down a civilization or a continent.

The seat of the soul is the chakra of freedom. The movement toward 'artistic freedom' in many cases actually accomplished the reverse. Because some modern art forms pervert the inner symmetrical blueprint of the soul chakra, they take away from the freedom of the soul. For what the eye sees is instantly mirrored in the four lower bodies. Dissonance in art and music is without doubt self-disintegrating to those who give their attention and allegiance to it. Fohat follows the imaged key.

Parents with young children should be especially careful of what they allow their children to look upon and listen to. Some children today have never seen thoughtforms of perfection nor heard a chord of classical music. For them harmony has no definition.

It is vital that children have established within them certain archetypes, such as the Madonna and Child, the father figure in saints and heroes, flowers, and internally harmonious objects taken from nature in her unpolluted state. Through the very mathematics of the molecular structure of things, there is instilled in them the aspiration toward a path of self-discipline that can be won by striving for excellence in all of the four lower bodies.

The Chakra of Freedom   149

Man is not unique in the possession of chakras. States and nations also have spiritual centers—highly concentrated energy focuses which govern the interaction of their people, their destiny and their vibrations, personal characteristics, language, accents, customs, and mannerisms. People who have a certain karma to work out through the lessons and self-mastery imposed by the disciplines of a certain chakra will gravitate toward the corresponding city or state within their nation.

Los Angeles, the soul chakra of California as well as America, is the place of the greatest perversion of the freedom flame through the entertainment industry. (Does anyone really consider the *Texas Chainsaw Massacre* or *Scanners* to be worthwhile art?) This perversion causes a distortion of the soul chakra of all the youth who view these and other similar motion pictures.

Since the soul chakra is the creative center, whatever is created by those affected may then also be distorted. As these youth grow up to be tomorrow's parents, educators, civic leaders, and film producers, it becomes a self-fulfilling prophecy. They look upon a distorted creation and then create more distortion in every field (even in the fertile field of consciousness of their own children). This, in turn, is looked upon by others and distorted further.

Indeed, you can see how each year the movies are more violent, delve deeper into the collective unconscious, and portray more hopelessness to an ever younger age group. The only cure for this is for people who really care to begin purifying their soul chakras through meditation on images of beauty, symmetry, and Higher Consciousness. This is the first step.

Next, we must hold the visualization of the whirling sun disc, as with all of the other chakras, to flush out the substance that has built up with years of misuse of this vital center. Use of the violet flame is essential, especially in this mechanistic society which is in large measure devoid of the pure thoughtforms and images necessary to maintain soul (solar) consciousness.

The mantra for use with this chakra is very short, but when repeated—and accompanied by visualization and the violet flame—it will have an extremely beneficial effect. Remember, "I AM" means "God in me is."

> Light expand, Light expand,
> Light expand, expand, expand!
> Light I AM, Light I AM,
> Light I AM, I AM, I AM!

The Thousand-Petaled Lotus

The crown chakra is the chakra of illumination which regulates the mental faculties and memory. It is located at the top of the head and has 972 petals, which has gained it the name of the "thousand-petaled lotus." Yellow in color, the crown is the center through which we must attain

God consciousness (the awareness of yourself as a part of God). A clogged crown chakra can ruin your memory just as surely as drug abuse. In fact, the taking of drugs is one of the primary factors that leads to the polluting of this chakra.

Mental density, the lack of a "clear head" when you need it most, "spacing out"—these are the effects of misqualified energy in the crown chakra.

On the opposite end of the scale are those who pervert the crown chakra by overuse of their mental faculties. There is nothing wrong, and in fact everything right, with having brain power. What we are concerned with here are the 'eggheads'—people who believe that the only pursuits that matter are intellectual ones and who believe that those who are ignorant of the 'higher' knowledge which they possess are naïve and should have no say in the affairs of the world.

There are many in our universities and in our government and political arena today, as well as in top positions in major corporations, who fit into this category. It is they who feel that we need to be controlled for our own good—that the little people of this world lack the ability to govern themselves. It is they who try to calm us with facts and figures, while they slip their chains of control around our economy, our government, our educational system and our entire lives.

These individuals, the mentalists, instead of developing an attunement with the higher mind through the crown chakra, are constantly releasing the poison of their lies and half-truths which stem from a corresponding relative perspective of good and evil in the misused third eye.

This comes out of the aura in the form of a violent orange/black/silver astral discharge which is wont to intimidate anyone of "lesser sophistication." It seems that they are able, through the sheer force of their highly developed and highly manipulative mental bodies, to dupe the vast majority of the public.

If you are like most people in America, you have the earnest desire to see this country make it out of its current slump—to regain the lost glory and fervor of patriotism that has carried it through revolution, civil war, and global conflict. Most of us sincerely want to improve ourselves as well as our surroundings. In this case, a little violet flame coupled with the following mantra will go a long way.

> O Flame of Light bright and gold,
> O Flame most wondrous to behold,
> I AM in every brain cell shining,
> I AM Light's wisdom all divining.
> Ceaseless, flowing fount
> Of Illumination flaming,
> I AM, I AM, I AM Illumination.

The Base-of-the-Spine Chakra

The final chakra we are concerned with is the Mother chakra. This is the base-of-the-spine chakra, referred to simply as the "base chakra." It derives its name from its location at the base of the spine. But it is also the base of our physical (and spiritual) temple. The God-quality of this chakra is purity. Its color is white and it has four petals, forming the foundation of the pyramid of being.

The life-force of the base chakra is intended to be raised to the crown and the third eye by meditation on the I AM Presence. This will magnetize the energy upward. As the life-force, or Kundalini as it is called in the East, passes up through the channel connecting the chakras, it nourishes each one with the purity of the Mother light.

When the life-force is perverted or abused, it contaminates all other chakras. Or, if it is spent entirely, there is nothing left to rise to activate the polarity of light in the other chakras. Disease, disintegration, decay, old age, and death are the price mankind pay for the misuse of the energies of the base-of-the-spine chakra. In our society, this is the chakra which has been most flagrantly abused through impurity in all forms. Those who conserve the Mother light are the best performers and the most creative individuals in every field. The mantra that will help rid your four lower bodies of impurity is called "I AM Pure":

> By God's desire from on high,
> Accepted now as I draw nigh,
> Like falling snow with star-fire glow,
> Thy blessed Purity does bestow
> Its gift of Love to me.

> I AM pure, pure, pure
> By God's own word.
> I AM pure, pure, pure,
> O fiery sword.
> I AM pure, pure, pure,
> Truth is adored.
>
> Descend and make me Whole,
> Blessed Eucharist, fill my soul.
> I AM thy Law, I AM thy Light,
> O mold me in thy form so bright!
>
> Beloved I AM, Beloved I AM,
> Beloved I AM.

Now that you have cleared all of your chakras, go out and run! Go out and work that body until it won't work any more! You will feel an exhilaration you have never felt before, because now you have a complete program. Many professional athletes have discovered that they cannot survive in their training without the benefit of spiritual assistance.

Take, for example, the case of Toshihiko Seko, the winner of the Fukoka Marathon for three consecutive years. His entire life consists of training, both physically and spiritually. He is a devotee of Zen and, thanks to his trainer Kiyoshi Nakamura, he has developed "Zensoho"—running with Zen.

According to Nakamura, "The idea is to clear your mind of everything and to let your body function naturally, undisturbed by thoughts." Nakamura has studied all of the world's religions for over forty years. "You can learn from them all, just like everything in life," he explains. "We must study the Bible, scriptures, and all famous works. We must study nature—mountains, rivers, the stars, the sun and moon. All of them are our teachers."

Nakamura also subscribes to the belief that "physical training is only ten percent of the total preparation, the other ninety percent is mental."

In conclusion, many have come up with philosophies of training two or more of the four lower bodies while incorporating spiritual teachings from the world's religions. Seko is obviously utilizing a brand of this philosophy, with great results.

Why not take it a step further, then, and train all four of your bodies? Integrate them, clear out your chakras, breathe the prana of life, and gain maximum mastery over your total being.

I only hope that all who are aware of this teaching use it to its fullest. It is only through dedicated application of the law that change can be effected. Just as the weekend or occasional runner will never make it to the marathon, so the dabbler in this science of the chakras will never make it to the spiritual Olympics.

Chapter Eight
THE ETERNAL VERITIES

The Eternal Verities

Let us be aware of the eternal verities.

The world, the individual, and everything around us are cloaked with obscurity whenever the eternal verities do not manifest in our consciousness.

Whenever we are lost in a world of darkness and suspicion—of mistrust of the plans of the Infinite—whenever we are confused by the chaos at the crossroads of life, whenever we are uncertain of the way in which we ought to go—it is a matter of obscurity being cast across our pathway.

This obscurity does not come from God, nor does it derive from his goodness. It comes from the human realm, from the cocoon of mortal ignorance. It comes from a lack of knowledge of what life really is.

What, then, is the reality of life?

The Sense of Selfhood

Life is not darkness. Life is not chaos or confusion. Life is not an uncertain probing. Life is magnificent—even biologically.

The construction of the body is beautiful: our flesh and bones are intricately and wonderfully formed! And the brain—itself a recipient of the impulses of the eternal Mind—is a magnificent switchboard and a storehouse of infinite Truth.

Just pause and think, then, not only of the flesh and blood but of the consciousness which rests in the chalice of identity and gives identity to the chalice!

We are aware of a power outside of ourselves that at the same time is identifiable as the power within. This power defines right and wrong when all moral codes fall short of the mark. This power derives from the Real Self. And this is the beginning of the sense of self.

There is an innate sense of justice that is inside of us, superior in all of its rights and ramifications to all codes of justice that man through the years has manufactured—sometimes out of great wisdom and then again out of the complexity of word knowledge, a mere assimilation of facts and figures thrown together without rhyme or reason. Because these codifications of law have been accepted by humankind, precedence is established whether or not justice is served by it.

And these are not necessarily the eternal verities.

Today the whole human race needs to lean not upon the arm of flesh,[1] not upon the classification of mere human knowledge, but upon spiritual treasures of that wisdom which is to be found within the heart.

Such treasures of the gnosis of God are indeed within the heart, and they can be drawn forth to illumine the mind, even as they cast the light of Truth upon the screen of the mind and, in so doing, change our whole viewpoint.

And these are of necessity the eternal verities.

The majority of humankind are governed by their emotional energies, moving as they do according to acquired sensibilities and ideas that all of us have held, not always wise but ofttimes central to our ego. And this ebb and tide of the emotions is for the most part unreal, a chimera of the not-self—persistent yet persistently unreal.

What, then, is the reality of the Self?

In and through and out of all of this, we ourselves have an identity—an *id-entity*—a central focus of awareness. We call it "my self." Within this self we have an awareness of the I—of me, myself, and mine (id-entity extending to the periphery of the sense of the possessive self and beyond).

This self is in a state of becoming and it always will be—for such is the nature of an active Be-ness. The unwinding of the inner coils of this potential is an infinite process because the nucleus of Life is the infinite Light.

Because it has already been demonstrated to us that change is being wrought from day to day, we know that the 'I' of today is not the 'I' of yesterday; nor will it be the 'I' of tomorrow.

By a like token, the consciousness of today is not the consciousness of yesterday, and hopefully it will be better tomorrow. It will either move forward or backward. And if it moves forward on the crest of the forward movement of cosmic cycles, then certainly the self will take on new meaning, new relevance, and a new momentum.

This new phase of our *id-entity* can be cast in the light of the personal ego—where the struggle for recognition is ongoing—or it can be cast in the illuminating Presence of our God-identity.

And, if we permit it, the God-identity will engulf the human. And when it does, we shall no longer be compelled by the same transient desires. Little by little, they will fade away. They will lose their meaning as we take on in our consciousness new desires of the Spirit.

The Good Samaritan

We read the story of the Good Samaritan who came upon the wayfarer lying by the side of the road, bruised and beaten by thieves and left half dead, a man he knew not, a man for whom he had formed no attachments, a man who could not reward him—just a man lying there, on whom the priests had cast a disdainful eye and passed by.

What did he do? In his richness of spirit, his strength, and his solid sense of knowing who he was, he could step out from himself to serve the ends of someone he did not know. He bound up his wounds, took him upon his horse, carried him to an inn and paid the fee for his lodging so he could have a comfortable bed in which to rest.[2]

This was an act outside of the self—yet at the same time it was supremely within the security of a healthy self-completeness. It was a concern other than the immediate concern of his own needs. It was reflective of his recognition of the soul's need to serve others—and not for the glorification of the ego, not to be identified with some great movement. It was a surge of the flame of charity, not necessarily Christlike, but an urge simply to act on behalf of a fellow human being who was in need.

And by his act, he identified more closely with the goodness of God than those who, even then, made religion their business but not their life. This God whom he served, deliberately or not, had already stated through Christ that it is sometimes wise to leave the ninety and nine who are securely within the sheepfold and go in search of that which is lost[3]—the little wandering lamb caught in the brambles who is not only without comfort but also without apparent worth to the total picture.

Truly, the ability to save that which is lost, that which has strayed from the centrality of Life— to save to the uttermost—reveals the levels of one's own wholeness, a wholeness that is nourished by the Greater Whole and therefore always has something to give to another's sense of incompleteness. Whenever you behold the Good Samaritan, say to yourself, "There goes one destined to become the Good Shepherd."[4]

We are aware of the fact that when we deal with the Spirit and when we deal with God, we are dealing with an infinite power that has awareness of us whether or not we have awareness of him. He is aware of us not as insignificant, not as dispensable to his design (as one of the herd or the so-called mindless Atlantean masses that can be mechanically replaced and never missed).

No, he seeks to convey to us a higher, a holier, a purer sense, a more beautiful consciousness, emphatically *because* we have an identity *in him* that is not only supremely significant to his own, but one which is indispensable and would be sorely missed—simply because he loves us as his own and as his own individed Self. We are his, fully, freely, forever.

Love Defined

Let us then ask ourselves what motivates the action of the Good Samaritan.

Love.

But love has been defined so many times, and so many times selfishly. Here is love without expectation. We do not even find record that the Good Samaritan thought that he was going to receive some reward for his deed in the hereafter. He simply acted out of the compulsion of the needs of another soul with whom he identified, perhaps saying to himself, "There but for the grace of God lay I, the hapless victim of robbers, naked and wounded. I will do what I can for him."

Love to be truly Love must begin with the love of self in the sense of self-appreciation. One must have the sense that one is of some worth and therefore worthy to be loved. If one judges oneself unworthy, of no value to God or man, then the self-love that ought to be will turn to self-hatred.

Only if a man can love himself, can he love his neighbor. Only if he can love his neighbor, can he love his God. And if a man hate himself, he will hate both his neighbor and his God. Therefore Jesus said, "Love thy neighbor as thyself"[5]—i.e., as though he were *thy self* and as though he were *thy Real Self*.

The Master also revealed the great truth that we already treat our neighbors with the same contemptuous or possessive love with which we treat ourselves (*our souls*)—and, for that matter, our Real Self, the inner Christ. If you would have immediate and keen insight into your personal psychology, just analyze for a moment how you treat your neighbor and you will know how you feel about yourself and your God.

Let us realize, then, that we must always search our hearts for the motives of our actions. And ever strive for the purer reason. But if we find there a selfish motive, if we see clearly that we are attempting to underwrite ourselves in our charities and kindnesses, we should first understand that, in any case, it is neither healthy nor proper to condemn ourselves. Because, if I act selfishly to serve the needs of another, it is still a higher purpose than if I act selfishly to serve only the needs of myself.

It should also be remembered that to take to

oneself today in order to give of oneself tomorrow is always better than to act from the amoral premise of: "Never mind what happens to anybody else—what will *I* get out of it? I want to know what's in it for *me!*"

If we act entirely selfishly, you see, just serving what we think will produce something for ourselves, both in the immediate and the long-term goals of our lives, then we are not very high at all on the spiritual ladder. And all of this striving of the self *for* the self may well smack of a pseudo-righteousness, a self-assertiveness that is formulated by what *we* do or what *we* think, as if we of ourselves could make ourselves to be 'good gods'. (Ye gods!)

So, we understand that there are times when one has to think in terms of a 'selfishness' that must be exercised so that later one may be generous.

Now, this may not always be the highest form of devotion or the highest form of self-sacrificing love. But it may very well be a legitimate step on the path leading to the highest Love—when the Christ in us declares, "Take, eat, this is my Body which is broken for you..."[6]—and the soul, fully integrated with the Light, no longer feels its sense of self threatened by such a statement of self-givingness.

For the soul has attained sufficient identity in God to give away part or all of its 'corpus' and yet remain centered in the flaming vortex of self-declared Being: "I AM WHO I AM."[7]

And so, as we live our lives, we may observe that we are motivated by this selfishness that may subsequently become generous, even magnanimous; and this of itself may include the desire to love because we desire to be loved. When one loves, one is often loved—although there are many cases of unrequited love.

We see that when that love-exchange emanates from the Real Self, it is true and blessed because it does not come forth from beneath, but it is magnetized from on high. And thus it fulfills one's reason for being in the ultimate self-givingness—the reciprocal love of God in man and man in God.

When love does not emanate from the God Source, by and by it becomes apparent that something is missing, and the soul waits for the real thing—*someone who is Real!*—while the heart languishes for the ever more perfect union through the highest and truest Love.

These steps and stages of love are not self-contradictory. On the contrary, each step is taken through an unfolding awareness of individuality, an individuality that must first exist in order to love—and then must love in order to exist.

Individuality may become selfish when, self-satisfied, it sits on a rung of the ladder to bask in the light of its own achievement, failing to recognize that as the seasons pass, the tree of self must share its fruit with those who must needs taste of another's selflessness in order to attain their own.

Such a self-satisfaction robs us of the joy of

self-givingness and deprives us of the need to feel self-emptied so that we may strive again to be filled—so that we may live again another day to give again.

Self-Worth and Self-Needs

Man climbs the stairway to Reality—not in one giant leap, but up he goes, step by step. He may skip a step here or there but he will continue to climb if he maintains his interest in doing so.

Thus, motivation from within is essential if one is to consciously climb. And that motivation can only derive from the mantra of the true disciple's heart: "Lord, I AM worthy. Make me worthier still." Try whispering it in your heart—to him. It affirms a healthy sense of well-being—I am worthy *because* God, the "I AM" in me, is worthy. But it also acknowledges the *need* to strive and the *need* for help.

If you think you have no needs, if you are highly self-satisfied, you, then, have no need to climb. Only the dead have no self-worth and no needs. The quick have both self-worth and self-needs. Therefore, in true Love they speak to their Christ—"Lord, I AM worthy. And because you made me worthy, Lord, make me worthier still."

Did you know that some people have so little self-worth that they don't even think they're good enough to talk to Christ? If that's so, then you can't even say the Lord's Prayer or make this simple declaration: "Lord, I AM worthy. Make me worthier still."

By God, if you are going anywhere in life, you have got to know that God in you is worthy! And, if you don't, stop right now and ask him to show you that *he* is, and that because he is, *you* are!

No greater insult to the Godhead could be muttered than the cowardly confession "I have no worth." For in this the coward declares, "My God has no worth."

"O thou ungrateful wretch, knowest thou not that he that made thee is worthy, and that thou art in his image worthy, if thou wilt rise up and be all that he made thee to be?"

Indeed, there is no greater wretchedness that can come to the human soul than the denial of self-worth. Such a state of mind is suicidal—killing both soul and Spirit in man. For the denial of the Creator cancels out the creature (as effect cannot be sustained without Cause), while the denial of the creature obliterates the omnipotence of the Creator.

Life is a polarity, "as Above so below"—as in heaven so on earth, as in Spirit so in Matter. Each side confirms the other and so the worlds are sustained. Self-denial in either sphere cuts the spinal cord, and God is dead in man and man is dead in God.

The greatest need of real people is to find their self-worth in God.

Most people today, because they don't like themselves, seek to climb socially. They seek to climb financially. They seek to climb the ladder of fame and fortune that will lead them to a position where they can receive the adulation of others. Their sense of self wants to be honored.

Actually, they do it because they don't like their Real Self and they like their unreal self too much—but even this 'self-like' is the other side of self-dislike and a self-destruct drive that turns to self-hatred.

Beware the man who hates himself, for he is the most dangerous man on the face of the earth. Beware the man who has no capacity for self-love, for in him the divine spark has gone out.

But there is a self-love that, in the extreme, is self-hatred. Beware of it also, for all the works of that man are evil—verily the self-canceling energy veil of hatred—and "his days are as grass," as it is written of the flesh that is without the spirit, "for the wind passeth over it and it is gone, and the place thereof shall know it no more."[8]

O God, how shall I escape to the eternal verities!

The Wick of Self

Only *perfect* Love will cast out that fear[9] which leads to the death of the soul through the blind pursuits of a blind self-hatred. Let us renew our sense of self and be renewed thereby...

But this self is only the wick. And the wick stands there in the tallow of matter, yet it is meaningless until kindled by the flame of God's grace. A thousand wicks standing side by side in a sameness that reveals no separate identity—until one wick says, "I desire the quickening, I elect to glow, I desire to light a world that it might see—and that I might see 'face to face' the reflected light of a million souls."

When the grace of God as his holy purpose enfolds the soul, when there is a pulsation of infinite reality that descends and fills the consciousness with the beautiful Spirit of God—when all of that surrounds one and one feels it (if the spiritual senses and the chakras are activated), then you know that the flame of God's grace has kindled the wick of identity.

The wick is only a structure. It is that *somethingness*, rather than that *nothingness*, which alone is ours to offer—in order that Life might burst forth in all its vibrant reality where we are. The wick is the means whereby these noble aspirations we feel of wanting to be a good person— "good and kind"—may be quickened by the flame of higher purpose.

You see, the goodness and kindness must start with the human wick, consuming and being consumed (i.e., self-purifying) by human virtue and meritorious deeds. But, by and by, in the self-burning (i.e., the self-refinement), the divine alchemy is activated by the heat of spiritual desire, and the striving spirit becomes one with the sacred fire itself—of our own *Christ* goodness and *Christ* kindness.[10]

Without the enkindling flame, human goodness dies and is not reborn. But with the flame and a wick to ignite—a wick whose self-determination is that freewill creativity which burns with a self-consuming compassion for life—by and by the Spirit comes to dwell with us and illumines the whole house. One candle sets the soul of a universe aglow.

The wick of self is not a God Self-awareness until it exercises its *potential* to be. In so doing, it must muster the courage to be (by the very process) self-consumed. And here our case must rest in the faith that the all-consuming flame will deliver to us a permanent Selfhood—one that we cannot now see or hear or taste or touch.

We must believe that that Self exists as Cause behind effect of lesser self we now know. We must believe in the flame as we believe in God. We must believe that God loves us. And that his purpose for us is that we may live forever with him as individed flames of his kindling Reality.

If we have not personally experienced God's quickening Love—the kindling of the sacred fire on the altar of being—then it is a unique and glorious experience that awaits us. For his Love is truly all-consuming. It consumes all within our human loves that remains unlike the divine and transforms our paltry motives of self-gain into our highest expression of Selfhood, one to which we ourselves could not attain...without his flame.

The Spirit of the Most High God comes into our temple for the kindling of the wick. And we are made aware that this flame now burning within is not something that we created, nor indeed could, but a Thing-In-Itself (the *Ding an sich*).

It is the Self-created. Formulated not from the dust—as "dust thou art, to dust shalt thou return"[11]—but of and from the Beyond. (We cannot control It; but It controls us. We cannot subdue It; but It subdues us.) Nor did It spring forth from the tallow at the moment of the kindling.

Yet the flame was there, inherently within us. It preexisted us, etched the crystal, fired the clay and kept the midnight watch of our gestation, self-creation in the womb of time...It was always there—anywhere and everywhere our love should suddenly spring forth to greet the fiery purpose of his own—there, there the flame that always was!

Our Identity a Continuum in Christ

Our minds possess the capacity to be stirred. And our emotions as well. Our beings can be shaken to the roots by unreality as well as by Reality. Too many times have we responded to the vibrations of the spoilers who have told us: "You don't have a chance. Only *the* Son of God has a chance. And you're not *a* son of God, 'cause *there's only one Son of God!*"

Falser words were never spoken. Our Father has told us that he created us in his own image.[12] Is there a higher image than the image of God? No. And the image of God is Christ—the Light-emanation of the Logos.

So then, we perceive that long ago where the

mists of time and space disappear in the eternality of the Great God Self—back, back on the belt of our soul's eternal evolution, the self-evident Truth is known: "Before Abraham was, I AM."[13]

These were the words of the World Teacher Jesus Christ, the Anointed One, cupbearer of the LORD's Light—the Son of God who knew his identity to be a continuum in Christ.

Now *we* see, now *we* say: Before Abraham was, I AM—I EXIST in God's consciousness in the image of Christ. 'My' Christ is the same as 'his' Christ—the One (sun/sphere of radiant Being) whose many reflective fragments establish Be-ness not only in Jesus, 'my Lord', but in every soul that has ever received the gift of Life as self-awareness through the Son, back to the first fiery breath of creation.

And it was a creation of and by and in that same Logos that, in order to create 'me', placed a portion of himself within me. For without his essence inbreathing in me the sacred fire breath, without *himself*, was not anything made that was made—including me! For, as our Lord revealed it unto his beloved disciple, "That was the true Light which lighteth every man that cometh into the world."[14]

We were all there—if we have a soul, if we have a spark of God inside of us. We were there at the supreme moment when the first monadic expression was created, when the first manifestation sprang forth. We were there then. And we are there now.

Oh yes, we were—*and are*—spiritual! We didn't have these 'coats of skins'[15]—these four lower bodies we now need to navigate the denser spheres. The memory of that moment may not be thoroughly enlivened within us. Some of us may say with Saint Paul:

> For we know in part and we prophesy in part, but when that which is perfect is come, then that which is in part shall be done away....
>
> For now we see through a glass, darkly; but then face to face. Now I know in part, but then shall I know even as also I AM known [as the 'I AM' in me is known and confirmed by the voice of the Spirit above and my soul's reflection below].[16]

We can dispense with all our disorderliness, our untidiness of consciousness—and the soot that has marred the expression of the divine image. We can dispense with it all. We can cast aside purse and scrip.[17] We can cast aside our hungers and our desires. We can part with them all—once we are engulfed with the divine intent.

We can do this because he speaks to us and says, "I AM come that you might have Life and that you might have it more abundantly. I AM the Christ of you speaking from the innermost recesses of your creative Being. I AM the Good Shepherd. I give my Life, the essence of my Light, so that you, my soul, may live."[18]

When the abundant Life begins to express itself within us, the moment that pulsation engulfs us we are changed from glory to Glory—from the glory of this world to the Glory of the next.

With our faces unveiled, we behold in the mirror of God our true image in Christ, and by the flame—*The Flame* of Holy Spirit—the appearance of a man or a woman is changed into the selfsame image of Christ into which beloved Jesus was changed, from the lesser glory of the son of man to the greater Glory of the Son of God, even as by the Spirit of the LORD.[19]

No sudden inspiration carries us from the first to the thirty-third step, but without the first step none other can be taken. The taking of the first step of initiation is an act which may not even be preceded by any spiritual awareness at all, but may come suddenly, as with the rushing of a mighty wind[20] we are "face to face" in the encounter with our Lord.

For the first time, our eyes are opened and we know him. We see that he *is there*. We see that the Spirit *is there*—a living symbol and more!—the magnificence of the Person of Reality in whose face *we see* ourselves as the creation of the first begotten.

We are also the issue of the Only Begotten of the Father, full of grace and truth.[21] We are the offspring of the Eternal Mind and joint-heirs[22] with all who have issued forth from the same Fount!

Descending from the Cosmic Christ image,

the great glyph of the I AM Presence which is above us all, the symbol of our 'Personhood' becomes clothed upon with the reality of the personal Christ. And the Anointed One steps forth in our consciousness. The Son has returned.

Suddenly the Lord has returned to his temple,[23] and just as suddenly *we know* that through the long dark night of our sense of mortality he has never really been away. With Martha we say:

"Yea, Lord: I believe that thou art the Christ, the Son of God, which should come into the world."[24]

And we are truly born again.

With him we are alive forevermore.

With him we shout unto the stars: "Behold! I AM everywhere in the consciousness of God."

We have taken the first step on the path of Christic initiation unto Personhood in God.

But where did it all start—this fantastic, fabricated, celebrated sense of selfhood outside of God which we now starkly see face to face—mask to mask—and desire to discard? Where indeed.

Why Do We Endow Ourselves with Mortality?

You see, only we ourselves could have endowed ourselves with mortal consciousness. In the mists of an antiquity older than old, we captured the historical stream of monadic man, mortal man, whose prehistoric image resembled not at all the original. Yet we entered that primitive form. How could we forget!

While all of these wounded ones, golemlike,[25] haunt the dark centuries of mankind's infancy when the creation had not yet identified itself with the living Word, child-man sleeps in embryonic twilight, and the long night of the womb is the void of a spiritual creation yet to be—becoming...waiting to appear.

At one point there was a turning into the Dark, and the ones darkened by their dark decision to turn away from the Light and live in their own self-created shames and shadows, in their turn manufactured other dark ones—and the counterfeit race of mechanization man was spawned in a coil of self-doubt and dubious nondecision.

These bodies, vacant and vacated, yet roam the planet infested with howling demons who clamor for more and more noise, dreading the echo of their own godlessness in the empty chambers of a house neither occupied nor enlightened by the Word.

In ages past, before the dawn of recorded history, the real manifestation of God stood forth in the ancient temples and the Masters walked the earth and discoursed with the Children of the One on the mysteries of creation.

And they spoke not of Darkness but of Light—not of Antichrist but of Christ. They spoke of the radiating power of Light, the energy of Light, the freedom of Light, and the capacity of man, as the manifestation of Elohim, to express the goodness of God, the desires of God, and even the

Why Do We Endow Ourselves with Mortality? 179

magical principles of dominion over the elements of his world.

"Take dominion over the earth!" This was the command of the Divine Us.[26] And this we once knew and obeyed.

But today, every man sits under his own separate vine and his own separate fig tree.[27] But what does this independence profit the soul if he knows not the universal schemata of the interdependence of souls through each one's I AM Presence, as the Tree of Life,[28] and each one's beloved Christ Self, as the Vine[29] with whose righteous Branch[30] he must, in all his *in-dependent self*, equate?

Instead of kinship with the Life that is God, man today drifts further and further from being a part of the reality of God. He is estranged, as one floating at sea upon a raft is separated from the mainstream of life.

He may feel a physical, sympathetic kinship with the frequenters of the barrooms of the world. He may have a sort of psychic empathy with their pseudo, surface self through their raucous revelry and noisy sounds and rhythms, vainly music.

He may feel for their untidy desires of human creation that are never satisfied because they come from "beneath," from a bottomless pit which demands more and more satisfaction but can never get it: Because the Light that would satisfy the soul is devoured by the 'black hole' of the not-self, which, as a consequence thereof, always feels empty and never has anything to give except its own emptiness. And the vacuous ones congregate because they alone understand each other's existential existence.

The Answer Lies in the Mystery Schools

What, then, is the answer? The answer lies in the Teachings of the Ascended Masters restored in the mystery schools—not in the soul-damning indictments of the churches of today whose impotent messages, mind you, are broadcast to the world as preachments that distort and contort the original comfort of the Word to His own.

Ever since their expulsion from the heavenly courts and councils, the fallen angels, embodied among men (mortal yet influential beyond the run-of-the-mill Homo sapiens), have substituted social reform for the everlasting gospel of Truth[31] alive and vibrant within you, an endowment from your Father.

Why, all man's needs, artificially met by socialistic schemes, would come to him automatically—and scientifically!—once he had received the kindling Light and the immersion of his soul in the grace of God, and the Lord had entered his temple because he himself had kept the flame of Love.

Like the Good Samaritan, he couldn't help but go out and do good and create just laws to serve his fellowmen—*if* he were filled with the Spirit, *if* he were remade in the image of God. Because he would simply *be* true to his own nature.

Many of the restraining laws of today are of no more benefit than the leash that restrains the dog from escaping his master! Today many are breaking the leash. They refuse to be bound. And this is not necessarily a positive sign.

In the case of the Ascended Masters, they have not demonstrated that they themselves are anything else but men on a leash—willingly tied and obedient to the laws of God.

But in the case of the laws of control, the leash is the headlong desire of the fallen ones for domination over humanity.[32] They, the reprobate angels who were cast out of the higher octaves of light, want to control the people—their human procreation and their divinely co-creative Real Self, both coexisting within the individual. Furthermore, they want to be thought wise. Oh, how they want to be thought wise!

And they create movements and they create unrest to control the restless masses—without ever *truly* understanding or *truly* giving allegiance to the *intent* of God and the *reality* of God or the mystery schools hidden in the everlasting hills. They don't admit to understanding the mystic brotherhoods and they don't admit to understanding their power.

Yet the Great White Brotherhood and the power of the Ascended Masters is active and felt today throughout the whole fabric of civilization. And through their Messengers they gather their own in the Mystery School as in the last days of

CHAPTER 8 • THE ETERNAL VERITIES

Atlantis and Lemuria[33] to teach them the power of the Word by which their souls and the worlds were framed.

The fallen angels in embodiment seem not to take note of the historical fact that they will lose their temporal life. Most certainly they will. And if, during the course of that temporal life, they do not achieve some Reality, some sense of the power of God that is within them, and begin to exercise it, they will indeed be cast into the 'outer darkness'[34] of their own creation.

And if they have not made contact with the Brotherhood or sustained in honor the thread of contact they once had with the Ascended Masters, they will have no one to fetch them out of that darkness. Furthermore, if, having heard the Word of Truth, these rebellious angels do not repent of their evildoings and bow before the Universal Christ, "there remaineth," according to the doctrine of Christ recorded in Hebrews, "no more sacrifice for sins, but a certain fearful looking for of judgment and fiery indignation, which shall devour the adversaries."[35]

Thus suspended in limbo during the period awaiting rebirth, they will in all likelihood glean very little or nothing at all from the universe. Waiting for the next opportunity either to "make things right" and "set the record straight" or to squander what little they have left in the cup, they will be in a spiritually embryonic state in the incubator of life. This semi-awareness is in no way conducive to the kindling within them of the realities of the Spirit, which must be enlivened and quickened by a conscious acceptance (whether in the body or out) of the Christic Initiator.

This is the meaning of "the quick and the dead."[36] Both are here amongst us. There are very few who are quick, and there are many who are dead: some who were once alive and have chosen to be dead, and others who have never lived and cannot die except they first be quickened, then exercise the conscious choice to be or not to be. And the Christ, whose flame burns brightly in each of us, is ordained of God to be their judge and ours.

We have, then, a responsibility toward our Creator and toward the Lord of all to seek out the Mystery School sponsored by the Great White Brotherhood. Only by attunement with the World Teachers and with the cosmic reality of the message of Jesus Christ can man today derive the satisfactions and the instructions that will show him in due course of time (if he patiently wait for it[37]) the true path of his own resurrection unto his highest Self.

It does take time—and space. You can't turn the tide of centuries of the karma of self-delusion in one moment, but you can start. And that's why God gave us the good earth and another day to seek and find him. It does take the turning of cycles. And your allotted span remaining in this life is the most precious gift you have. For out of it you can forge and win true Selfhood.

So, you see, you need all of that instruction that is vouchsafed to you by the Holy Spirit through your own beloved Christ Self as you sit at the feet of the Master Jesus and the saints with him who teach and initiate your soul at the Place Prepared.

For in the failure to heed the Master's voice, many who have rejected his Path have found that when the sands in the hourglass have run out they have gone the way of the wandering stars to whom was reserved the mists of darkness forever.[38]

You're Not Sinners. You Simply Are Not Awake!

Without the enlightenment of the Holy Spirit taught to us by the Ascended Masters, who are our elder brothers and sisters on the path of Life, our consciousness may be nothing more than a tramp consciousness that goes from haven to haven or place to place without ever gleaning any sense of its purpose or any understanding of what actually is the intrinsic worth of the soul that cannot be weighed by human scales.

You can have the ageless Teaching of the Truth of your being—the eternal verities. It's here for the asking. I will not beg you—nor will any Ascended Master anywhere in the universe beg you. We are not going to beg you to accept our offering, like a beggar with a begging bowl in reverse.

This is not a matter of a sawdust trail where you come to the altar and get down on your knees and beat your breast and say, "O Lord, be merciful unto me, a sinner."

You're not sinners. You simply are not awake!

I don't say it to all. I say it to many in the world, because it is so. And I, too, was a part of that impoverished sense of selfhood passed on to me by the false pastors. And by His grace I was healed of it. And I walked, step by step, up those stairs.

I have not reached the top of the ladder. Nor have any that I know reached the top of the ladder, but all are struggling toward the top—moving toward it. The word perhaps should not be "struggle" in one sense, but still there is always the struggle between the flesh and the Spirit. And anyone who denies it has not walked the way of the real overcomers, the revolutionaries of the Spirit who have won against the odds of their personal and planetary karma.

And so our friends the Ascended Masters, as graduates cum laude of the Mystery School, definitely have something to offer us. In traveling all over the world to the farthest reaches of the globe, I have not found anything quite like the Teachings of the Great White Brotherhood.

I have never found such instruction as we have been given from the Masters of Wisdom—so pure in its form, so magnificent in its outreach, so unselfish, so completely beautiful, and so demonstrable. You can demonstrate it in your life. And it *will* change your world—and not for the worse but for the better.

That great exponent of freedom, Saint Germain—whose bobtail biography appears in *Encyclopaedia Britannica*[39] in some stance of error—is himself a great Western adept, known also as a prince of the House of Rakoczy (descended from the royal house of Hungary, his retreat having once been in Transylvania, now remapped as Romania).

Today Saint Germain is the greatest defender of real freedom to humanity that you will ever find on this planet. Jesus Christ and Saint Germain working together are architects of this age. And they are lovingly, willingly, joyously extending their help to humanity. But the Law says: Call unto me and I will answer you.[40]

We don't ask you to make a public display of yourself. You can call in your own heart to God, and no one need know it. And in answer to your call, God will send his servant-Sons, the Ascended Masters, to teach you. They have promised to do his will by helping those of us who are here on earth earnestly involved in the process of winning our ascension.

We have seen the results of their service in a fiery demonstration of joy and happiness and wisdom and an influx of beauty into the lives of our students.

And all that we have we offer to the world without money and without price.[41]

Chapter Nine

A CONTINUATION OF OPPORTUNITY

A Continuation of Opportunity

Isn't it a marvelous thing that the heart can sing? We sing with our lips, and our poor dumb voices we raise, but the real singing is within the heart, within the soul.

Of course, the angels never have to strain or exert themselves, possessing that dynamic flexibility of vocal cords made of electronic light-essence as real and tangible as our own bodies, yet having the buoyancy that we ourselves once knew before we took form here in this world.

What and Who Is Real?

We read of how the morning stars once sang together for joy,[1] and this is far more than poetic expression. It is a version of Reality—the Reality we hear within the corridors of self, dim and feetlike...voices heard at a distance.

Yet somehow we know it is Real.

Now, here is the interesting thing about life. Life is not the way most men have apprehended it to be. Life, real life, is different. Real life is a surge of dynamism.

Take the story of the great prophet Elijah[2] and of the word of the LORD which came to him in a cave on Mount Horeb after he had fasted forty days and forty nights. God spoke to him and said, "Go forth and stand upon the mount before the LORD."

And it is written that when the LORD passed by, "a great and strong wind rent the mountains and brake in pieces the rocks before the LORD; but the LORD was not in the wind. And after the wind an earthquake, but the LORD was not in the earthquake. And after the earthquake a fire, but the LORD was not in the fire. And after the fire a still small voice."

And God was in the still small voice.

This is the dynamic interchange between God and man that awaits us in the mountain of our Higher Consciousness.

This is Reality. This is the real God and the real man that great artists such as Leonardo, Michelangelo, Rembrandt, Titian, and Veronese have sought to capture on canvas and in frescoes and that great musicians like Palestrina, Schubert, Beethoven, Chopin, and Wagner have sought to capture harmonically.

And they did such an excellent job, the old masters, that today the trend toward modernism is away from the very techniques they taught, a departure from the classical beauty they sought to convey. They were too good!

They were too real. So is God. And so was Elijah!

What and Who Is Real?   191

It is not necessary for us to speak on modern art and music (they speak for themselves, and loudly, stridently), but it is necessary that we speak concerning the old masters and the thoughtforms they drew down from the inner planes—the "heavenly patterns"[3] reflective of their perception of the Divine Image. And this is what is the enduring Reality behind the mask of our human personality momentums.

Many of these thoughtforms are with us still. They are keys for our meditation on the Sublime Self—the unconscious symbolism needed by mothers with child whose attunement with the inner blueprint of the unborn soul will assist that returning one to realize his inner potential in coming into physical embodiment once again.

For although we have passed a Victorian age and an age of innocence in America, we stand on the threshold of great discovery and a true renaissance of the Spirit when the divine art shall appear as the Word made flesh. And the religion of the new age will be founded upon the Rock of a universal Christ Self-awareness.

Not six thousand years but a million years of culture and more are with us. And yet, in the midst of all of this—all of our technological progress, from space conquests to genetic engineering—man is still crying: Whence? How? Whither?

Where did I come from? Where am I going? and How am I going to get there?

What is the meaning of life? Why is there so

much political and religious strife? Why such unrest within the psyche of man? Why must man suffer?

Why can't I find the answers *now* and discover my true identity *today*? Why can't I probe beyond the conscious mind, and the memory that chooses to forget, to the near and distant past recorded in the subconscious—and beyond to the superconscious realm of causation?

Everywhere the search for who and what is Real!

These questions are being asked. The answer is simple, but it takes a child mind to accept it. The intellect refuses to accept a simple answer and it chooses to complicate it. Yet the highest intelligence is the intelligence of the Christ Mind that is the childlike mind. This is higher than all.

It is the universal intelligence which in Jakob Boehme (1575–1624) raised this humble German cobbler to a position of philosophical eminence. He was exalted—just as any man can be exalted by God, by the Great Spirit—by the simple truth he knew that "Christ was perpetuated in all men as a glowing spark of divine light..."[4]

In the Indian saint Sri Anandamayi Ma (1896–1982), the same divine light appears. Although she had but two years of schooling, she astounded scholars and statesmen, the simple and great from around the world by responding to their questions with profound truths and wisdom that God revealed to her, always what each one needed.

What and Who Is Real? 193

One intellectual said, "Though She is almost illiterate, all our learning is put to shame by Her great wisdom."[5]

Hers was not the wisdom of the intellect, but of the Mind of God. Once Paramahansa Yogananda (1893–1952) asked Ma, as she was called, to tell him something of her life.

> Father, there is little to tell. My consciousness has never associated itself with this temporary body. Before I came on this earth, Father, "I was the same." I grew into womanhood, but still "I was the same." When the family in which I had been born made arrangements to have this body married, "I was the same." And, Father, in front of you now, "I am the same." Even afterwards, though the dance of creation changes around me in the hall of eternity, "I shall be the same."[6]

As one devotee wrote, "Mataji's words evidently are not just ordinary words, but vehicles of power and light that open up one's understanding, that bring about definite changes in the person to whom they are addressed."[7] Her schooling was left to the Universal Christ, and her childlike mind brought her Light's profound wisdom clothed in a garb of simplicity and grace.

The Christ becomes the tutor of earthly knowledge as well. Do you remember the story about Paramahansa Yogananda?

He was enrolled in the University of Calcutta but he'd been spending all his time sitting at the feet of the guru and hadn't studied all year. And he thought he didn't have a chance of passing the exams, which were five days away.

His guru, Sri Yukteswar, reminded him of the verse, "Seek ye first the kingdom of God and his righteousness; and all these things shall be added unto you," and told him to ask a certain boy, Romesh Chandra Dutt, who was at the top of the class, to tutor him.

Yogananda expected that Romesh, who never had any time, would instantly turn him down. But he went back to his boarding house and asked him. Amazingly, he agreed. And miraculously, Romesh knew almost every topic that would be covered on the tests. He coached the "mad monk," as his classmates called him, for the remaining time, never once saying that he was too busy. Yogananda passed all of the exams, to the astonishment of his classmates, family, and the entire university.[8]

This, too, reveals the universal availability of the intelligence of the Christ Mind to those who with childlike simplicity will accept it as the answer to all their needs. Although Yogananda would no doubt not recommend that students follow his truant example, his experience shows the value of throwing oneself upon the Rock of that Christ Mind.

There are many convergent paths of Self-realization through Christ. We don't all have to take it as far as Ramana Maharshi (1879–1950) did back in the 1890s. He was an Indian schoolboy who early realized that his real nature was imperishable and unrelated to his body. So he left his family, went to the holy mountain of Shiva, Arunachala, threw away all his possessions and money, and sat down to meditate. His body began to waste away, his hair and fingernails grew to unmanageable lengths and insects ate away at his legs. He had such a longing for God that nothing else really mattered.

Soon that Christ radiance began to shine through, and he attracted a large following, ultimately becoming one of India's most popular holy men. He was showing one path of God-realization. And beyond the childlike mind, the Mind of God was to be seen clearly reflected in a mature soul who knew one note of cosmic harmony and played it well: communion with the All—one attainment that all can tell: he became the All.

Anandamayi Ma acted in the same way. You know, she used to forget about her body in her devotion to God. Her motto, *"Jo ho jaye"*—"Let come what may"—showed her lack of desire for anything outside of the will of God.

Her disciples had to take care of everything. They said, "We have to mother her; she takes no notice of her body. If no one gave her food, she would not eat or make any inquiries. Even when meals are placed before her, she does not touch them. To prevent her disappearance from this world, we disciples feed her with our own hands.

For days together she often stays in the divine trance, scarcely breathing, her eyes unwinking."[9]

This merging with the universal consciousness of Christ allowed her to be one with the wisdom of the ages with which she astounded people.

You know, people would ask her why she was in the world, and she would say, "I am not anywhere. I am myself reposing within myself."[10]

That is the mystery of oneness with God. And it comes from the childlike mind. It doesn't matter what religion you are, you will find it anywhere. And it can be developed by anyone of any faith.

Look at Brother Lawrence, a humble man too. He was a French footman who lived in Paris in the seventeenth century, a big, clumsy fellow who broke everything. He was converted at the age of eighteen and became a Carmelite monk who worked in the kitchen of the monastery. His writings have inspired people for centuries. He taught that "we ought to give ourselves up to God, with regard both to things temporal and spiritual, and seek our satisfaction only in the fulfilling of His will, whether He lead us by suffering or by consolation, for all would be equal to a soul truly resigned."[11]

It was the same with Anandamayi Ma. When she was first married, and she had to do all the cooking and cleaning at the house of her husband's family, she worked so hard and with such joy that no one noticed that she had scrubbed her hands raw and there were wounds all over them. And she

What and Who Is Real?   197

didn't notice it either! She didn't call any attention to it, because she accepted what came to her and she delighted in serving God in the entire household.[12]

She and Brother Lawrence were certainly on the same wavelength! As the cook at the Carmelite monastery, he had to do all kinds of things that people would not consider spiritual activities. They say, "Well, I can't keep my mind on God while I'm mopping the floor or doing the dishes." But he said, "We ought not to be weary of doing little things for the love of God, who regards not the greatness of the work, but the love with which it is performed."[13] And in the bustle of the kitchen, this possessor of the childlike mind made it his business never to allow anything to come between himself and the Presence of God.

He said, "The time of business does not with me differ from the time of prayer, and in the noise and clatter of my kitchen, while several persons are at the same time calling for different things, I possess God in as great tranquillity as if I were upon my knees at the blessed sacrament."[14] And that Presence which surrounded him is available to everyone, no matter what their religion.

The saints of all ages are above the divisions of race and creed. Sri Ramakrishna, the Hindu saint (1836–1886), said that he could arrive at *samadhi* by any of the various religions he practiced. He not only had visions of the Divine Mother, but also of Allah and Jesus. He said, "I have found that it is the same God toward whom all are directing their steps, though along different paths."[15]

Sri Ramana Maharshi taught oneness with the Presence of God as did Brother Lawrence, but clothed in the Eastern cosmo-conception. After attaining Self-realization, he taught his thousands of followers for many years in a community near Arunachala. His basic principle was that oneness with God, or the Self, is not an "alien or mysterious state, but the natural condition of man."[16] How does one become aware of the Self?

> The Self is ever-present. Each one wants to know the Self. What kind of help does one require to know oneself? People want to see the Self as something new. But it is eternal and remains the same all along. They desire to see it as a blazing light, etc. How can it be so? It is not light, not darkness. It is only as it is. It cannot be defined. The best definition is 'I AM THAT I AM'. The *srutis* [scriptures] speak of the Self as being the size of one's thumb, the tip of the hair, an electric spark, vast, subtler than the subtlest, etc. They have no foundation in fact. It is only Being, but different from the real and the unreal; it is Knowledge, but different from knowledge and ignorance. How can it be defined at all? It is simply Being.[17]

And so, while each religion may define the I AM THAT I AM, that Presence of God, in different ways, they are essentially one. But not everyone has to follow the same path, the same religion; as you go along on the Path, you find that they all become the same.

An Irish journalist asked Anandamayi Ma, "Which is the best path to Self-knowledge?" She said, "All paths are good. It depends on a man's *saṁskāras*, his conditioning, the tendencies he has brought over from previous births. Just as one can travel to the same place by plane, railway, car or cycle, so also different lines of approach suit different types of people. But the best path is the one which the Guru points out."

So then he queried, "When there is only ONE, why are there so many different religions in the world?" And she answered, "Because He is infinite, there is an infinite variety of conceptions of Him and an endless variety of paths to Him."

"What have you to say about those who insist that only one religion is the right one?" the journalist asked.

"All religions are paths to Him."

"I am a Christian..."

"So am I; a Christian, a Muslim, anything you like."[18]

And when a Christian girl asked the Mother to initiate her, she told her to "meditate on the form of Christ surrounded by heavenly radiance, and await His guidance."[19]

We are all manifestations of God, and we all worship the same Spirit.

Longfellow wrote in *The Song of Hiawatha* of "Gitche Manito, the mighty," of the Great Spirit, the Creator, the Master of Life descending, who preached peace to the tribes of men, preached the strength of their union through one brotherhood of nations and one heart of the Prophet whom he would send.[20] This promised deliverer we see as the descending Universal Christ exemplifying the Law of the One as the true self of every *mani*festation of God.

The Great Spirit—it doesn't matter to him what name we call him: Allah, Brahman, Elohim, the Father, the Eternal God, the Prince of Peace—reveals in manifold ways to his people the message of cosmic consciousness and its attendant demand for change in man. It doesn't matter. Call him anything you want to call him—just be sure that you *do* call him.

Because when you call him, he *will* answer.[21] And the answer will not be some stereotyped phraseology, some frozen religious concept. It will be an activating, pulsating flame in your own being. It will quicken you and it will quicken in you that Christ Self-awareness which brings new dimensions of Reality to your being.

Christ the Judge of the Quick and the Dead

There are only two kinds of people on this earth, and men fall either into one category or the other: the quick and the dead.[22] Peter spoke on this subject when he was at Cornelius' house. He

Christ the Judge of the Quick and the Dead 201

proclaimed to all present that Jesus had sent him and the other apostles to testify that their Master was ordained of God to be the Judge of the quick and the dead.

When you stop and think about it, this is an astonishing, in fact, a revolutionary idea! It gets us back to the separation of the sheep and the goats[23] and our discussion of what and who is real defined in terms of who is really alive and what constitutes our 'aliveness'.

It reminds me of what someone once said: "They have never lived. They can wait to die."

And so I think that we are wasting our time whenever we approach the so-called 'dead'. These are the ones who know all the answers, who consider that because the alphabet has twenty-six letters and because the dictionary has a finite number of words, that mere words alone, "the letter," are enough to stipulate doctrine, to open the way to a man's soul to breathe the air of freedom and to contact his God.

They think that words alone can bring salvation—it is not *words*, it is *The Word*, the Logos! And it is not a man-made idea of Logos, it is a God-made idea of Logos by which the heavens were framed.

John saw in the vision that in those days men shall "seek death and shall not find it, and shall desire to die and death shall flee from them."[24] Who are they, then, these dead who dwell in the vanity of the twilight zone between the Real and the Unreal—tethered neither to the Dark nor the Daylight?

Are they the grey ones who so very long ago left off the tending of the divine flame on the altar of Being? The self-extinguished ones, whose devotion having failed them, their oil wasted, have no smoking furnace or burning lamp[25] wherewith to offer sacrifice to the LORD? The very ones who live in darkened houses where no Light (no figure of Christ) may enter?

Even Seneca said of these, "They are unwilling to live, and yet they do not know how to die."[26]

And all the while the heavens are telling of the LORD's endless glory shining in the hearts of the LORD's anointed. Yes, the quick are those in whom the divine spark is yet kindled—whose warmth radiates a golden compassion, a roseate dawn of merciful love and a gracious understanding to all life.

When we look at the great sidereal universe, when we see through the lens or "voice" of a telescope the power of infinity in space, or we look deep within ourselves into our hearts, into the consciousness that is indwelling there, we are aware of a most marvelous system, far exceeding a computer with all of its complex technology. And we glimpse what the heavens and the inner universe of man are telling us through many branches of science.

Last week, as I was passing through the Midwest on the way from Washington, D.C., I picked up the car phone to make a call. And I wanted to get directory assistance. And the operator said, "Where do you want to call?" And I said, so and so. She said, "Alright."

So I heard the clicking of buttons. And the next thing, I heard a voice say: "eight, one, six—three, three, one—zero, eight, nine, six" very mechanically. It sounded like a bunch of metal plates rubbing together!

And I said to the operator, "What in heaven's name is that?"

She said, "Oh, that's the computer talking to you."

I said, "You mean some human being has had his voice recorded, and the recording of his voice is cut up into little digits, and the computer selects these digits?"

She said, "No, not at all. The computer is speaking to you with its own voice."

And so for the first time in my life I can actually say that I have heard the voice of a computer. And it didn't sound a bit like God! No, it sounded like mechanization man speaking out of the mechanistic age in which we live.

While we are approaching the pinnacle of achievement, relatively speaking, insofar as material science goes—the biological and the behavioral sciences, astro- and geophysics, computer and laser technology and all of them put together—as far as our divinity is concerned, man's understanding of himself in relationship to the Deity, we are but infants.

Psychological Problems of the Ego in Rebellion

In my travels around the country and in the contacts I have made with businessmen—in fact, all over the world—I think that probably the greatest impression I have received is how quickly people are fall guys if someone will only give them a little flattery. Everyone wants to be praised. They are all concerned with their own ego.

Great fund-raisers who raise millions of dollars for certain stated purposes know this, and therefore when they build their libraries they always arrange to say, "This will be the Carnegie Library." Or, "This will be the Peabody Museum Library." When they raise funds for colleges and universities or they're looking for endowments, they arrange to call the institution or the center by the name of the donor, as they have done in the case of Temple Buell College in Denver.

People just love to have their names etched on a piece of stone as a monument to themselves for future generations to gaze upon. And this should indicate to you that "as Maine goes, so goes the nation." In this case it's: as the businessmen go, as the egoists go, so goes everybody. And "there, but for the grace of God, go I!" If it weren't for his grace, we would all be in the same boat, because we're all fall guys for this.

Now ask yourself this question: Can you rise higher than the highest in all of us or fall lower than the lowest in all of us?

In his book *The Prophet*, Kahlil Gibran made this point. He said concerning religion, "In revery you cannot rise above your achievements nor fall lower than your failures.... In adoration you cannot fly higher than [men's] hopes nor humble yourself lower than their despair."[27] All the world teachers have shown the great common denominator of our Higher Reality and the oneness of the evolving soul of humanity.

The Master says, "What man has done, man can do." We would add, "What man has done, man can undo." We can call upon the Brotherhood for the universal strength of all saints to aid us in our mutual overcoming of the universal weaknesses to which the race is heir.

And so, the plight and the fancy of the ego— and egoism—shows that people actually feel inadequate. They feel frustrated. They are not expressing the God plan, the Divine Image. They are not understanding life properly. And at some level of their being they know it. So they feel a compulsion to attract attention to themselves in the world of form, whether by infamous deeds or great achievements.

Now, some men who are born losers go out and do things that will attract notoriety to themselves—like this Richard Speck who killed eight student nurses in Chicago (July 14, 1966). You probably recall that. He hit the front page of the paper. That's all he wanted. He even said, "One of these days it'll be the whole front page."

Then Charles Whitman followed suit, killing

14 people, including an unborn baby, and wounding 31 others in a 90-minute shooting spree from the University of Texas tower in Austin (Aug. 1, 1966).

Robert Smith, a high school senior, taking both men as his role models, planned and executed his own mass murder in a Mesa, Arizona, beauty shop where he shot five women and two children after lying them face down like spokes in a wheel (Nov. 12, 1966).

These three cases are examples of mass entities working on the weak-willed, triggering an ancient record of depravity in these killers through the mass consciousness. You are witnessing here the power of suggestion transmitted by demoniac forces which convince their victim (the murderer) through his acute need for ego reinforcement that he is acting according to a higher power, compelling voices, or the superior direction of his own rational mind.

Such cases of egomania are often accompanied by entity and demon possession and all manner of forces from "beneath"[28] in the astral plane. They exist as a product of the mass consciousness of mankind and as a race rebellion against God.

Call to Archangel Michael

So when you know about these things and you are able to sense beyond the world of effects the hidden momentums of the mass mind, you can do as the Ascended Masters' students do in order to forestall multiple events of horror, which is to immediately take up their dynamic decrees to Archangel Michael for the binding of all unseen forces (demons, discarnates, and the false hierarchy on the astral plane) and their unsuspecting tools. This is especially important in cases of terrorism, riot, assassination, kidnapping, mass murder, or genocide. Because, in order to intervene on earth, the heavenly hosts must have your prayers and calls for help right away.

Here's how we do it. Following is a decree dictated to me by Archangel Michael for our use in the exercise of God's power according to the science of the spoken Word. He entrusted it to me for your souls in the hour when you should have need of his strength and faith and protection in facing life's karmic adversities. May you learn to appreciate this "great prince," as the prophet Daniel referred to him,[29] and cherish his divine friendship and intercession.

You will recall that as Joshua was by Jericho, the odds of battle stacked against him, he looked up and saw a "man" standing near with drawn sword. And Joshua approached him and asked him point-blank, "Are you for us or for our enemies?"

And the archangel replied, "Nay, but as Captain of the Host of the LORD am I now come." So powerful was his presence that Joshua fell on his face to the earth and worshipped the LORD.

Then the anointed leader of the children of Israel said to the Captain, "What saith my lord unto his servant?"

His reply reveals the absolute God-awareness on the part of the archangel that the LORD God, the I AM THAT I AM, was where he was. Archangel Michael was and is the immediate expression of the I AM THAT I AM who appeared to Moses. Hence he is called the angel of the LORD's Presence—the extension, if you will, of *your* I AM Presence as well as *my* I AM Presence wherever and whenever we should call him into action. (His name translated from the Hebrew means "who is as God.")

Such God consciousness do these God-free archangelic beings have that without hesitation the Captain gave the LORD's command: "Loose thy shoe from off thy foot; for the place whereon thou standest is holy."

And Joshua did so.

In that day the LORD gave Jericho into the hand of Joshua and his men through the divine intercession of Archangel Michael and his legions of Light.[30]

This decree is one of a number of decrees given to me by Archangel Michael for the children of Light who must accomplish their mission in the Aquarian age. Simply give it aloud with a strong voice—with joy, authority, and reverence.

When you come to the insert, state the personal or planetary circumstance requiring the immediate intercession of Archangel Michael and the heavenly hosts. Then give the body of the decree as many times as you like, as often as you will, with a dynamic voice and spirit until Light's action is accomplished. (Be sure to give the refrain after each verse and seal your session with the concluding acceptance. Students of the Masters enjoy repeating this call 3 times or 9 times, 14, 24, 33 or even 108 times in the ancient tradition of the recitation of the mantra of the WORD.)

The emissaries of God are our unseen helpers without whose assistance we of ourselves are incapable of dealing with the forces bent on world destruction. That's why God created angels! These emissaries of Light who frequent the fire rings of the Central Sun always obey the commands of the sons and daughters of God, subject to God's will and loving design.

Light Will Overcome!

In the name of the beloved mighty victorious Presence of God, I AM in me, Holy Christ Selves of all mankind, beloved Archangel Michael and Faith, the seven beloved archangels and their divine complements, their legions of white-fire and blue-lightning angels, beloved Lanello, the entire Spirit of the Great White Brotherhood and the World Mother, elemental life—fire, air, water, and earth!

I decree for a triple blue-ring protection around all potential tools and victims of nuclear, conventional, and chemical warfare, terrorism, riot, assassination, kidnapping, incarceration, suicide, homicide, genocide or mass murder this day! And I demand the binding and the judgment by Archangel Michael and the hosts of the LORD of all malevolent forces—mass entities, demons, discarnates, laggards, fallen angels and the false hierarchy on the astral plane, their plots and strategies toward anarchy and the shedding of innocent blood and the spewing out of the sewers of Death and Hell upon man and society through horror and tragedy.

In the name of the Father, the Son, the Holy Spirit, and the Mother, I call to the Cosmic Christ and Great Teams of Conquerors from out the Great Central Sun, to the Seraphim and Cherubim and the Elohim of God to take immediate action to restore protection and the divine will and consciousness in the following emergency: _____

Insert optional personal prayer here.
---

    1. Blue lightning is thy Love,
       Flood forth to free all;
       Blue lightning is thy Power,
       In God I see all;
       Blue lightning is thy Mind,
       In pure Truth I find...

Refrain: Light will overcome,
            Light will make us one.
           Light from blue-fire sun,
           Command us now all free!

2. Blue lightning is thy Law,
   Blaze forth as holy awe;
   Blue lightning is thy Name,
   Our heart's altar do enflame;
   Blue lightning maketh free,
   In God I'll ever be...

And in full Faith I consciously accept this manifest, manifest, manifest! (3x) right here and now with full Power, eternally sustained, all-powerfully active, ever expanding, and world enfolding until all are wholly ascended in the Light and free!

Beloved I AM! Beloved I AM! Beloved I AM!

May he who is as God be with you.

The Belief in a Personal Devil

At a recent conference—where one of the principal activities we engaged in was the study and mastery of the science of the spoken Word in the giving of such dynamic decrees as this one—we had in attendance a lady minister of a metaphysical church, and she went over to the Broadmoor Hotel and said to her roommate, who was also attending the conference, "Does he really believe in a personal devil? Horrors!" she said, "I like him but I just can't imagine that he believes in a personal devil."

Well, I'm not even going to explain it to you. I'm going to say, pick up your newspaper, look at the front page, read some of the sensational stories there, and see for yourself if you believe people have acted rationally. And if you don't think they have, then tell me who or what is in them that makes them suddenly take on modes of irrational behavior.

Is it a force of Christ or Antichrist—Good or Evil? You decide for yourself.

Because in this world you will never escape the equation of the Real and the Unreal. And believe me when I tell you that your solving of this problem of Being within your own psyche is one of the principal reasons you came into embodiment.

I remember one time when I was a boy, walking through an insane asylum accompanied by a very good friend of mine who was a local official. We were quite close. And so I turned to him and I said, "Ben, these people are possessed with demons."

And there was a woman sitting there who probably weighed 350 pounds. Her face was as red as a beet. And from morning till night she raised her hands up in the air and slapped her knees, just like a printing press—bing, bing, bing, bing—continuously. That's all she did all day. And she'd say, "Whoomp!" along with it.

Was that just a human action? What kind of a possession was that? Something had ahold of her. She'd lived there for eight or ten years continually raising up her hands and bringing them down with no purpose and no reason.

I saw people with legs and arms not much bigger than a broom. I never knew such people existed in physical form. I saw hydrocephaluses with waterheads about as long as a watermelon. I saw monstrosities of human creation.

Then I said to him, "Don't you think they're possessed, Ben?"

He said, "They're not possessed. They just don't have anything up here."

You see, he thought it was the absence of something "up here" that was acting. Well, how can an absence act? What is an absence? It wasn't an absence. Something had ahold of them. They did all kinds of things. And there were even children in that institution.

Well, I contend that if the living Truth about the Mighty I AM Presence and the forces of Light and Darkness were taught by the churches in our land and in all lands throughout the world, you would not have this eruption of sadistic egoism or the insanity of demon possession—whose open door to the psyche, I might add, is always an ancient and very present (whether conscious or unconscious) rebellion against God.

Instead of that, you would have a proper employment of the opportunities of life by people. And oh, how happy they would be to take advantage of the glorious opportunity of real honest-to-goodness living!

Our Victory over Life's Challenges

Now, consider the billions of unascended lifestreams involved with the evolutions of earth at the present time and that less than 50 percent of the planetary quota are in embodiment*—the remainder waiting in the wings to come in. And the Lords of Karma,[31] who oversee the progressive evolution of the lifewaves of earth (functioning, as it were, as 'lords of emigration'), can't find bodies for them!

And therefore, these souls have to wait offstage, like an understudy, until the transition cycles of births and deaths are accelerated and they can be allowed to come in and play their part. You see, there are quotas and the seven Ascended Masters who serve on the Karmic Board actually determine the destiny of every incoming soul according to the dictates of personal karma (the mandates of free will) and the laws of God.

You must recognize that your life is a precious opportunity. You have been given a tremendous gift with your descent into embodiment. And if you don't discover the meaning of life, if you don't really understand who you are and what you are and what your destiny is, you're sort of a chip on the water—and it's an awfully big ocean!

But when you do discover it, it doesn't matter how big the ocean is because you are just as big as the ocean. And this is no figment of the imagination. It's reality. You're just as big as any problem that you have to handle, and you can cope with it. And as you accept the challenges of life and you

---

*As the Great Cosmic Light and the violet flame intensify, this percentage could increase or decrease depending on the number of ascensions (exits) and upcoming root races taking embodiment (entrances) as well as the relative levels of planetary karmic weight; i.e., the total karmic weight of all people in embodiment plus the untransmuted momentums and records of those not in embodiment but requiring re-entry in order to complete their divine plan.

win, you must realize that it is not just a matter of winning for *yourself*—the little self—but it's a matter of winning for the Big Self, the Great I AM, the Presence of Life.

And the LORD God said, "It is not good for man to be alone. I will make an help meet for him."[32] How many see the difference between the negative and the positive? How many see that God is the great positive pole and that the earth and life here in the womb-manifestation is the negative pole?

Here we see that substance is Matter, or Mater. It's the Mother, you see; and God himself, then, has made the creation—the Matter cosmos—as a help meet for himself, the Great Spirit.

And we are androgynous beings holding within ourselves the masculine power of God as the Spirit of Life, the animating principle, and we are a soul (the feminine side of our aspiring nature) clothed upon with material substance, i.e., Mater energy coalesced in matter-form.

This evolving soul, together with its form (the four lower bodies), needs refining so that our bodies can be changed (accelerated) in a moment, in the twinkling of an eye, when the last trump sounds.[33]

And the last trump is the sounding of the trumpet of victory—our victory, yours and mine, over the challenges that life creates for us and that we create for ourselves through our karma. Life gives us these challenges because only through accepting them can we actually become masters of our worlds and inherit our divine destiny.

What is our destiny? I could tell you one little thing: this universe and the star systems within it are expanding so rapidly that there are any number of vacant planets waiting for a 'God' to rule them. And the Father, you know, is not competitive. There is no competition whatsoever in heaven. Why, he is so anxious to turn over a segment of the universe or all of the universe to this 'womb-man', this bride of Christ that he created, that he can hardly wait!

Because, you see, when God made man, he copied himself. He made man in his own image.

Now, that isn't the physical self, it's the spiritual self. You are a spirit encased in a body temple. And as a spirit in a body temple, you have consciousness. And the consciousness is the consciousness of the spirit—not of the flesh, which is dumb.

But whenever free will is given to anyone— whether it's an angel in heaven (who's supposed to be nobody in particular) or it's someone made "a little lower than the angels" down here on the path of the mastery of the self, hoping to be "crowned with more glory"[34]—God is waiting for a manifestation of himself to appear "on earth, as it is in heaven."

We once saw a billboard warning against fatal traffic accidents which particularly amused us. It said, "An angel in heaven is nobody in particular!" In other words, don't become an angelic statistic— you count more down here—so drive carefully.

Well, once you make the acquaintance of the

archangels and many beautiful angels, you realize they are very different and very unique—each one being somebody very special in particular. And this, of course, is precisely the value of free will in the individualization of the God flame. You can be anybody you want to be, and become well known for the particular talent and profile of God you develop.

Free Will—the Necessary Fly in the Ointment

So what happens? Free will gets perverted.

Whenever God gives free will to any part of Life, he is actually giving that part of himself the freedom to move against himself. On the other hand, the conscious, loving acceptance of the gift of free will—really locking in to its responsibilities—is man's prerequisite to receiving the Godhead.

You see, God couldn't convey the allness of himself to man as he wanted to unless man would first prove to him that he was willing to properly exercise the function of will. And therefore, he *had to* give free will to his children. Given the desired end, God *had to* take the chance!

And they in turn would *have to* accept the gift and freely exercise it. For better or for worse, they, too—given the desired end—would *have to* take the chance. Otherwise, God's children could never freely find out for themselves that they wanted to become what he wanted them to become—without divine coercion or his resorting to some sort of cosmic cookie cutter.

And the chance taken would have far-reaching consequences: for God, exaltation or annihilation on earth; for man, exaltation or annihilation in heaven.

That was the covenant, but that was also the fly in the ointment. It was a necessary fly, though—it had to be there. But now it has to be taken out of the ointment. And only we can do it. We've got to purify the ointment of that fly!

This is the mystery of God's gift. And what we've got to understand is that man's free will and his freedom to exercise it are divine rights. All human rights derive from this cornerstone of the pyramid of Life.

And what I've told you is the heart of the mystery of free will that is no longer a mystery—thanks to beloved Jesus and his cohorts of Light—the Ascended Masters!

God's gift of soul freedom is a hallowed thing. This being so, we must give all due attention to this most sacred lever of our soul's going out and coming in from the heavenly to the earthly realms.

Now, it should be obvious to you from your own experience that God could not, nor would he, compel you to do exactly what he wanted you to do. If he did, you would no longer have free will.

You've often heard people say, and you've probably said it yourself, "I've had to learn everything the hard way. Nobody taught me what I know. I've worked for whatever I've got. I come from the school of hard knocks."

Free Will—the Necessary Fly in the Ointment 219

This ought to be a clear indication to you that your soul knows that God put you on earth to learn life's lessons by trial and error, free will and *your* determination to survive.

Well, the same law of free will holds true of the archangels and the cosmic beings and solar lords God created.

And if some of you think for one minute that there was no such being as Lucifer, disabuse yourself of that idea. There are dark and malevolent spirits in the universe. And they are legion. They are the example of the misappropriation of free will to the death, in effect, of the Deity in their sphere of influence. They are the dead whose end is foreknown as the handwriting on the wall—written by the hand of their ancient and current choices.

Oh, there're not as many of them as there are divinely integrated spirits, not by a long shot—but there're enough of them around to cause plenty of trouble to those of us being tested in the crucible of earthly life!

No less than a third of the angels of a certain heaven-world, a certain octave, were cast out of the etheric plane at the time that Lucifer himself, that "son of the morning" who led the revolt, was cast down to the waste places of the earth, "to the sides of the pit," by none other than, you guessed it, Archangel Michael and his legions of the First Ray.[35]

This was the result of the archangel Lucifer's vow to ascend to heaven and exalt his throne above the Sons of God and the "stars"[36] whom we know as

Elohim. Imagine! He led many fledgling angels—whose wills were not yet firmly set in God's will and who were glamoured by their hierarch—in the expropriation of the divine energy and consciousness. With art and cunning he caused them to reject the path of initiation leading to the bestowal by the Cosmic Christ of the gift of Divine Selfhood.

He exhorted the angels to bow down and worship him as their god—he the one who betrayed his office as the bearer of God's Light (*Lux-fer*, from the Latin, meaning "lightbearing"). Engendering in them the pride of the intellect's scientific superiority which sets itself above the Will and the Wisdom and the Love of the LORD God, he ignited in them the ambition to wage intergalactic wars against all who would challenge his supremacy.

Thus, the mystery of Evil germinated from the seeds of direct defiance on the part of some among the divine retinue, challenging the LORD God himself and his heavenly hierarchy who embody the eternal WORD. To this hour, beloved, the fallen ones make mockery of the devotees of the eternal Light who perpetually intone the I AM THAT I AM, saying,

"Holy, Holy, Holy, LORD God Almighty, which was, and is, and is to come. Blessing, and honour, and glory, and power, be unto him that sitteth upon the throne, and unto the Lamb forever and ever."[37]

Well, as it is chronicled in Revelation 12, these rebels were defeated in an intergalactic war by Archangel Michael and his legions of Light who cast them down into the lower octaves of the physical/astral planes. Their punishment (i.e., karma) was to embody like mortals subject unto the laws of mortality—separate from, and therefore without access to, the Presence of God, the Tree of Life in the midst of Paradise. This karmic condition compounded their mortal desire with its sense of sin and its attendant suffering—disease, disintegration and death.

Nevertheless, once encased in flesh, unrelenting, they chose to continue their warfare against God and his Sons. Only *now* they would go after the most vulnerable part of himself—his precious children and the holy innocents (virgin souls) embodied and evolving on earth. And the warning went forth: "Woe to you inhabiters of the earth and the sea, for the Devil and his seed is come down to you, having great wrath—because he knoweth that he hath but a short time."[38]

In that Wicked One and his ungodly seed, no wonder, mercy and grace were unknown.

Henceforth they would exercise free will to the destruction, they thought, of the offspring of God. But, in effect, to deny the will of the Father is to deny the animating principle of Life within oneself. And so their denial became their conscious freewill choice toward self-disintegration (in effect, a suicide pact). Yes, it happened to the Luciferians, as well as to the seed of Satan, and it's happening every day all around you, right before your eyes.

And we remember David's contemplation of a mortality that, by choice, will never become Immortal: "As for man, his days are as grass: as a flower of the field, so he flourisheth. For the wind passeth over it, and it is gone; and the place thereof shall know it no more."[39]

Serpents Take the Low Road, Lead Mankind Astray

In one sense, the serpent in Eden[40] can be taken allegorically as symbolic of the intellect, the lower questioning mind which says to itself:

"Why did the LORD God say that we shouldn't eat of this fruit of the Tree of the Knowledge of Good and Evil? Why did he say that we should not know Evil as well as Good?

"Why did he say that we should know only Good, the science of Spirit? What is there about Evil, the science of Matter, that we're not supposed to know?

"Why, it just might be, if we understood the relativity of time and space and the lower order of things, that we would be able to control the universe! I'll bet you that the knowledge of Evil is a secret that God has reserved just for himself!"

Aided and abetted by the race of fallen angels known as "serpents," intellect engaged in its own reasoning and it decided to eat of the forbidden fruit. And in so doing, it dropped the immaculate concept of the Deity.

And the fly dropped into the ointment.

And it would remain the fly in the ointment,

necessitated by impure desire, until the soul's demand for purity would restore free will to the Law of the One.

This is precisely when free will became a thing apart from the seraphic oil of gladness and approbation before the Sons of the Most High God.

And twin flames sent forth from the throne of Alpha and Omega began, slowly, almost unnoticed, to imitate the subtle compromises of the fallen angels—each deepening shade from white to grey being a slight step backwards down, down, down the spiral (spinal) staircase from the crown chakra to the base-of-the-spine—from the nonphysical (etheric) planes to the earth earthy where atomic weight, not light, is become the measure of the "things" a man is and is possessed by.

Reminding us of our formerly exalted state in the Shekinah (Mother) glory of the Word, Jesus said to us, illumining the scripture: "A man's life consisteth not in the abundance of the things that he possesseth but of the Light—God-consciousness—which he retaineth in his chakras."[41]

Alas, for the time being the soul had elected by free will to exercise the thinking process through the instrument of the lower mental body (dealing in relatives) and departed, therefore, from the use of the higher mental body (dealing with the Absolute) and its access to the all-knowing Mind of God.

The die was cast.

The consequences of the freewill choice made between the high road and the low road became an endless pursuit of karma, with the serpent of the lower mind swallowing and regurgitating its tale of endless cause/effect, karmic sequences set in motion by the misguided use of free will.

And millions of years of human, instead of divine, evolution ensued—at a snail's pace—and a snarl.

The Conspiracy against the Children of the Light

So, what was the purpose of these fallen angels, the original false Teachers and false Christs gainst whose coming again and again Jesus warned us?

The answer is easy when you possess its logic. These reprobate angels who yet move among mankind, taking full advantage of their credulity, have but a single goal in mind: to cause the children of earth to forget the immaculate concept—and little by little to commit spiritual suicide. And they are always there with haughty stature and magnetic appeal to achieve compromise, the effective betrayal of the Light and the Truth in every field of human endeavor—and in the human soul.

And afterwards an injection of guilt and condemnation so great that the soul believes the absolute lie that it can never rise again. And subservience and slavedom are the outcome: "I am no longer worthy to live and reign with my Father in his kingdom."

The plot against the Children of the Sun was hatched: once having partaken of the chemistry of lower self-knowledge, their loss of the higher sense of Selfhood in God would be a *fait accompli*—without their ever having realized what happened! Like taking an overdose of drugs and waking up out of the body on the astral plane, unable to get back in. You're dead before you know it!

And so the children of earth began to see people as dual in a brand-new understanding of relativity. The philosophy of *relative* good and evil fabricated by the fallen angels was the modality of compromise which they used to water down and obscure the delineations of the real choice between *Absolute Good* and *Absolute Evil*. Which boils down to the choice of Self or anti-Self that every soul returning to the Father's kingdom must make.

Having descended thus far, it took but a single step for them to now look within themselves and see evil—what the Hindus call maya, or illusion, and what the Ascended Masters have termed the *energy veil*. And what they saw was their own misqualified substance, the by-product of the misuse of free will, in place of the pristine purity of the divine union the soul once knew with its twin flame[42] at inner levels.

Alas, once enmeshed in the veil, they couldn't get past it. They couldn't see through it! And the way of human life opposed to the divine became its own counterpoint: a self-fulfilling, self-perpetuating prediction based on the law of the jungle: self-preservation.

Well, what you look at, the things you envision, what you place your attention on, what you behold in consciousness, is soon outpictured as the 'reality' of your world.

Meet a friend. Love him. Feel that he is a wonderful person and he can do no wrong. Then let there be some lurking suspicion in your mind that perhaps his motives are impure. "Perhaps he's 'evil' after all," you say to yourself, "and besides, he's a hypocrite. He's just putting me on!"

Well, the first thing you know, you've re-created in your own consciousness all of the evil that's ever been created from time immemorial. And pretty soon you no longer have a friend. You don't love him anymore because you've become an iconoclast. You have broken down his image *in your own mind*. You have broken down the 'idol' of your friendship because of the lurking suspicion in your own heart.

And this, too, is one of the subtilties of serpent mind's self-preservation.

And I think that there is nothing worse than human beings suspecting their best Friend, the Lord GOD himself, of some form of perfidy! What in heaven's name are they preserving themselves for or against?

Oh, they won't admit it, people won't voice it—but when they see a child fall off a cliff or they hear of some terrible death by drowning or a freak accident, or they examine the records of a hospital and they hear of the gross sufferings of people with leukemia and other forms of cancer, they say to themselves: "This world's a terrible place! God's a terrible God! Why does he do things like this? Why does *he* allow it to happen?"

They do not understand that it is the freewill agency, the all-power of choice—"this" or "that"—which has been misapplied, that has caused men to create and re-create darkness and then to reap the harvest of their sowings.

Jesus himself spoke on this. He said, "If the Light that is in thee be [turned to] Darkness, how great is that Darkness!"[43] This time we capitalize the *L* and the *D* because we're talking about the Absolute of God's Light and its absolute perversion into Darkness and Death by fallen angels who originally had access to the fount of the Holy of Holies.

That Darkness is only great because it is the Light of God turned inside out to no good purpose; nonetheless, the power of the Light imprisoned in a deathlike matrix yet grips the victim with a certain "power." As those who work with insane criminals know, Evil has a power all its own. What they don't know is that that very Evil is the ill-gotten Good of the LORD turned upside down through the fallen angels' manipulation of the purest Light of his children.

Actually, the fallen angels have just about mastered every trick in the book to extract the Light from the chakras of God's children. Just look all around and see how the unsuspecting get sucked into all kinds of things and don't even know they're being had.

But don't you for one moment think we're idly spinning yarns about our pet conspiracy theories, pinning the tale on the Nephilim[44] by way of providing a scapegoat for humanity's milk of human kindness gone sour. Believe me, our fiery spirits are beyond any such chicanery or psychological self-delusions.

We have seen the penalty of the Law for spiritual fraud that is the yoke of the fallen angels in their role as false prophets, false pastors, and false Christs, especially as they sit in their seats in religion, in government, and in the economy. Their end is the self-fulfilling prophecy that Daniel read to Belshazzar, who had desecrated everything holy in the temple of God and man:

"'Mene, Mene, Tekel, Upharsin.' God hath numbered thy kingdom [consciousness, domain] and finished it [put an end to the cycles of thine opportunity to glorify the I AM THAT I AM]. Thou art weighed [thy karma—thy words and thy works are weighed] in the balances [the scales of Cosmic Justice] and art found wanting."

And so it is written: "In that night was Belshazzar the mighty king of the Chaldeans [the Nephilim god] slain."[45]

And so it is written of every fallen angel who does not repent of his wicked deeds, who does continue as the destroyer of the Temple Beautiful, the false priest who steals into the secret chamber of the heart—the slayer of the Christ in his little ones.

The Lost Teachings of Jesus on Planetary History

This which we are telling you *is* the Lost Teaching of Jesus Christ. With Saint Germain, Mother Mary, and Archangel Michael, the Lord has gone to great lengths to explain to us life's mysteries, interpreting for our benefit the complex causes behind the outplaying of events on the world scene, giving us an overview of hundreds of thousands of years of planetary history, including our own past lives.

We have been taken in our finer bodies to the pits of the astral plane, there to observe its denizens. We have spent hundreds of hours in the record room of the Royal Teton Retreat, principal etheric retreat of the Great White Brotherhood on the North American continent, focused in the heart of the Grand Teton in the Teton Range near Jackson Hole, Wyoming.

Here we have studied under the Lord's servant, the Keeper of the Scrolls, the karmic sequences of many civilizations and the roles of Good and Evil which men and women and good and bad angels have played in turning the tide of events toward the upside or the downside of history.

If you think these claims wild and outlandish, then you must likewise doubt that God holds the solution to the world's problems and that in order to effect that solution he works through people as he always has and always will. The fact is that we volunteered for this mission and have been serving in this capacity of messenger and prophet—admonishing the people, enlivening their dulled memories, and warning them of the seed of the wicked—for just about as long as the fallen angels themselves have been around. And many of you whom we know and love have been a part of this mission from the beginning.

For a while all of us experienced setback and we even became enmeshed with the evolution of the fallen ones, incurring karma and having to be extricated by divine intervention. This has happened to quite a number of twin flames who came to earth with Sanat Kumara, great hierarch of Light, known in the East as Kārttikeya and in the West as the Ancient of Days.[46]

So we can say with a certain burden of regret, as well as with the confidence of firsthand knowledge, that what we tell you is the culmination of scores of embodiments on planet earth going back to the early days of Lemuria.[47]

In addition, we have been God-taught by our Saviour Jesus Christ and by the councils of wise ones—the Council of the Royal Teton, and the Darjeeling and (East) Indian Councils of the Great White Brotherhood—where the beloved Son of God often presides. We have also benefited by our personal examination of galactic and intergalactic archives shown to us at inner levels by certain hierarchs concerned with the immediate future of this system of worlds.

Our purpose is one: to chart for you Truth and Error side by side so that you can decipher your destiny and become the master of yourself instead of serving the Egyptian taskmasters. So that you can balance the unresolved situations in life—the karma of ignorance and misplaced desire—and get in the charioteer's seat and drive those four horsemen of your four lower bodies by your Christ-centeredness in the God Flame and the Law!

In other words, we're here to help you get free—by your God-given free will (which you haven't necessarily been exercising to its highest and best use lately)—from the round of rebirth in these dense spheres of enslaving ignorance and desire, so you can get on with the cosmic romance of you and your twin flame!

We're here to help you learn how to scale the heavens of your causal body, chart the stars of your God-attainment in a sea of light, take dominion in all planes of your God-free Being, and use all the divine and developed human resources at your command from the joint causal bodies of your twin flames to help the hosts of Light set every single solitary child of Light on planet earth free!

And then take on the next planet and the next until those rebel angels without a justifiable cosmic cause receive full circle the karma of their deeds and no longer taunt and tempt our little ones!

Yes, if you believe God has a solution to our pitiable human condition and the mess we've allowed the fallen ones to make of our beautiful world, then believe us for a while, at least until you've given yourself and God and us a chance to prove to you that the violet flame works, that the science of the spoken Word works, that the archangels and chohans of the rays work, and that God in you can work hand in hand with cosmic law and cosmic forces to save this world!

If you believe there is a way out of the age-old dilemma of mortality, then come believe with us for a while until you, too, possess the scientific and spiritual proof that what we say is Real is true. Our only motive is your freedom, for we have long ago outgrown any desire we ever might have had for anything more from planet earth or her evolutions except their God Victory in the Light.

We, too, like most of you who read our writings with an inner knowing and response, are sojourners here—not natives but pilgrims still serving in Sanat Kumara's rescue mission, ministering in his name who sent forth the twelve and commanded them, saying:

> Go not into the way of the Gentiles [alien powers] and into any city of the Samaritans enter ye not.
> But go rather to the lost sheep of the house of Israel. And as ye go, preach, saying, The kingdom of heaven is at hand.

> Heal the sick, cleanse the lepers, raise the dead, cast out devils: freely ye have received, freely give.⁴⁸

The lost sheep are those souls of Light who accompanied Sanat Kumara, descended through Abraham, obeyed not the covenant which forbade intermarriage with the seed of the aliens—UFO people, fallen angels and laggard evolutions from other systems⁴⁹—and became enmeshed in their karma, which was the karma of the original Evil One. As a result, their blueprint (genetic code) was marred and they lost the memory of their origin. Now they must be restored to their lawful inheritance through the lawful exercise of God's light, energy, consciousness, and free will.

Initiation at the Twelve Gates of the Holy City

We understand that the offices of the twelve apostles hold the archetypal patterns of the path of our soul's perfectionment leading to the initiations of the twelve gates of the City Foursquare. At these gates (thresholds of initiation) Christ stands with hierarchs representing schools of Light under the twelve solar hierarchies. The greeting of the One "that openeth, and no man shutteth; and shutteth, and no man openeth"⁵⁰ to each soul who would enter there is the same:

> I know thy works: behold, I have set before thee an open door, and no man can shut it: for thou hast a little strength, and hast kept my word, and hast not denied my name.

> Because thou hast kept the word of my patience, I also will keep thee from the hour of temptation, which shall come upon all the world, to try them that dwell upon the earth.
>
> Behold, I come quickly: hold that fast which thou hast, that no man take thy crown [thy Light in the crown chakra].
>
> Him that overcometh will I make a pillar in the temple of my God, and he shall go no more out: and I will write upon him the name of my God, and the name of the city of my God, which is new Jerusalem, which cometh down out of heaven from my God: and I will write upon him my new name.[51]

Thus, the World Teachers Jesus Christ and Saint Francis (the Ascended Master Kuthumi) welcome citizens of the world to the twelve gates of Christic initiation whereby they may study to show themselves approved unto God[52]—and then enter in, received by the Ascended Masters who tend the flame of the Holy City. To that end God has declared his covenant:

> Behold, the days come, saith the Lord, when I will make a new covenant with the house of Israel and with the house of Judah:
>
> Not according to the covenant that I made with their fathers in the day when I took them by the hand to lead them out of the land of Egypt, because they continued

not in my covenant and I regarded them
not, saith the Lord.

For this is the covenant that I will
make with the house of Israel after those
days, saith the Lord. I will put my laws
into their mind and write them in their
hearts, and I will be to them a God and
they shall be to me a people.

And they shall not teach every man
his neighbour, and every man his brother,
saying, Know the Lord: for all shall know
me, from the least to the greatest.

For I will be merciful to their unrighteousness, and their sins and their iniquities will I remember no more.[53]

And to that end—that all who are the Christic, *anointed*, seed of Light understand this covenant, this I AM Presence, this High Priest who is the Holy Christ Self, and this deliverance from the sins of straying from Sanat Kumara's sheepfold through the fiery baptism of the Holy Ghost—we say as One: *"Ich Dien"*—"I Serve."

If you knew the Truth—and you can know it, if you have the patience and the guts to submit to its two-edged Sword that will cleave asunder the Real from the Unreal within you—you could separate the Darkness,* as can the divine swan,

---
*Again, *Darkness* is uppercased because it consists of God's Light misqualified by man's free will. Thus, until man strips this Darkness of the God-Light with which he alone endowed it, it retains the inverted Life force—the Evil force. When stripped of its God-Light by the Judgment Call of the embodied sons and daughters of God, Darkness loses its power and its capital D.

the Paramahansa, from the Light. You could skim it off from yourself. And you would be very careful, after a while, to let only the Light in. And you'd stem the tide of Darkness. You'd say, "I don't want you! Stay out!" And then, you see, you could become the arbiter of your destiny.

This is where your soul's instinct toward *spiritual* self-preservation comes in, prompted by your guardian angels.

By contrast, the subtleties of the world and the machinations of the colorful personalities of the Evil One come into your subconscious through the mass mind as you gorge yourself (or used to before you knew better and decided to do better) on the channels of the mass media. These thoughtforms are taken in by the eye, the ear, and the spiritual orifices known as the chakras. And they gain entry through the similarity in vibration of the records of your own past lives magnetically recorded in the memory body—your Book of Life.

Such negative thoughtforms remain in the subconscious as a deleterious influence until you make up your mind to exercise the power of the spoken Word to strip from those very thoughtforms that misused power which was originally God's and which must be returned to him alone.

And so the only way to get rid of that fly in the ointment is to let your free will merge with the greater will of God until, a day at a time, decision by decision, you make his will your own. Thus consciously, by choice, you can return to the pristine state where there is no longer the warring of the law of God and the law of sin in your members, but only the supreme will of God. And you yourself have become that One—*consciously, by choice*. Our Father would not have us any other way.

We Have Lived Before

For we have lived before. The products of this generation did not attain even the present majority of worldly wisdom and functional abilities to move the frame in a matter of six months or a year.

Yet a child can both walk and talk in just twelve months! A child can come into the world and in 365 days be an animated creature that functions biologically as an adult—eats adult food, walks around and talks and has a great deal of intelligence and environmental cognition.

And some have such amazing talent! We have heard of a boy genius in Korea who began writing at seven months. His parents happen to be university professors, but we don't believe for one moment that the genes were the *sole* cause for this carry-over. By the time he was two and a half he could read, write, and speak Korean, Chinese, German, and English and he even published his own book of poems, essays, and letters.

At two years he composed a letter recommending the unification of Korea and objecting to war upon earth and the depredations of the adult world, which he severely criticized, saying he hoped they would do better. For a photographer from *Look* magazine he wrote this poem: "This camera takes picture of Ung Yong; But this time, please take my spirit; It is a picture-taking, telling and accurate."⁵⁴

Great musicians have been able to play the piano at a very early age. Why? Because they were maestros of music in past lives and possibly took further training under the Masters in temples of music on the etheric plane between embodiments. Our destiny comes to us from the near and distant past. And we have lived before and often.

What difference does it make if you go to sleep in one body at night and wake up in another one in the morning? Oh, you'll forget who you were, you won't know where your home is—you won't remember your mother and father.

But this going to bed in one body and waking up in another is more or less what death really is. But why is it necessary? Why doesn't the body sustain itself?

Alexis Carrel kept tissue from a chicken's heart alive for over thirty years in a test tube in his laboratory. Why don't our body cells renew? Well, as a matter of fact, they do. And the better we take care of the body, the better it takes care of us.

Mankind's Ignorance of the Law of Karma

But what happens to us in this world is that the grease factory takes care of us. French-fried potatoes—hot fat, 350 degrees Fahrenheit—clog the arteries, giving young people at seventeen atherosclerosis. Athletes, boys on the football field drop dead at seventeen and eighteen. Men are dying like flies at forty and forty-five—heart trouble, hardened arteries full of cholesterol, all types of diseases.

Because the furnace inside is all clogged up! There're clinkers in the grates. The great bellows of the lungs can't breathe.

People have no life in them because the system of this free society plays upon the lowest common denominator of that lower mental body—greed— and people put the dollar ahead of everything else. This is ignorance! They put the dollar first. The majority of the restaurant owners don't say, "How much good food can I give for this number of dollars?" but "How much profit can I make?"

I'm not condemning any person or organization, but I am speaking a truth to society. They are self-indicted. I do not have to indict them. I'm a part of them and supposedly, by my presence here, I consent. But I don't. And many of you don't. And many in the world do not consent to it. But many are ignorant of it. They do not understand.

So we have a very peculiar situation. People in the world are fed an abominable diet. Twenty years ago DDT, which had been thought to cause leukemia and other diseases, was finally recognized for the villain it is. Rachel Carson in her book *Silent Spring* warned of it.[55] And then Michigan and other states began to pass laws restricting the use of such lethal chemicals or banning them altogether. But we've still got a long way to go to make the environment safe for our children.

Perhaps someday we will return to organic farming. Perhaps our people will once again return to Eden to eat proper food. And perhaps our universities will be free—and rid of the tribe that seeks to subvert the principles of freedom to a collective society. Either they do not understand the Law of the One or they understand it all too well and are consciously subverting it and the minds of the youth, step by step.

We do not have sickness in the world because God wills it so. We do not have war in the world because God wills it so. We do not have hatred in the world because God wills it so. We have these conditions in the world because of the law of cause and effect. Every evil that men do returns to their own doorstep.

The fallen angels know that, so all they have to do is to set up some ungodly cause and convince people it is in their political or social interest to espouse it, and self-serving men and women will be self-bound by their ignorant misuse of the law of cause and effect. And I tell you, the consequences of ignorance of God, of Self, and of the law of karma are far-reaching!

Believe me, people do reembody—they do come back into embodiment—and they bring with them a certain karmic record. This is their own record, not someone else's. The government of heaven does not mix our records. Thank heaven for that! The Keeper of the Scrolls and the recording

Mankind's Ignorance of the Law of Karma   241

angels and the Lords of Karma—they know you and they know me and they know all people.

And therefore, because of the law of karma you cannot equalize a society and make everybody in a society equal economically or in any other way. You couldn't do it if you wanted to! You couldn't do it because of birth factors alone. People's genes and chromosomes, their inheritance, their karmic circumstances are physically different. Some are born with a father and mother and some are born without a father and mother, in the sense that they lose both father and mother.

Our karma is different—each and every one of us. And we need not despair over it because, as Bernarr Macfadden used to say, and he said it correctly: If you don't like your life, you can always make it over. And this is truth. That's one thing God has done. "We make or unmake our lives every day,"[56] he said. God has given us this opportunity to re-create ourselves daily.

So, we have to come back to the point where we can recognize the realities of ourselves—and then motivate ourselves to separate ourselves out from the unrealities! We have to know who we are and understand that the universe has judged us according to our own record.

In other words, all our endowments come from past effort and achievement. If we want more than we have of any virtue or commodity or talent of heaven or earth, all we have to do is work for it to God's glory, and we'll get it. If we see to it, he'll see to it.

Jesus knew this law and he stated it very clearly and succinctly. You know, the occasion was the anointing of his body by the woman—thought to be Mary of Bethany.[57] She came to him with the precious oil of spikenard, very costly, and she broke the alabaster box and poured the ointment on the Master's head.

But some who were on hand at Simon's house were indignant and they said to themselves, "Why was this waste of the ointment made? It might have been sold for three hundred pence and given to the poor." So they murmured against her—even his disciples.

They were upset because they were socially minded people. They thought in terms of world equality: Everybody should be equal. Everybody should be given the same thing. Well, they are! They're given opportunity. But their opportunity is to some degree overshadowed by, and even severely limited by, their karma.

Jesus defended her on the basis of divine principle and her devotion: "Let her alone. Why trouble ye her? She hath wrought a good work on me. She is come aforehand to anoint my body to the burying." Evidently, Mary perceived the spiritual as well as physical necessity to perform this ritual *before* the crucifixion, rather than afterwards.

And then Christ looked at them and he made

a most significant statement that you want to remember. He said, "The poor you have with you always, and you may do good for them whenever you will, but me you do not have with you always."

Now, the poor are thought to be the lowest dregs of society, while the rich are, supposedly, economically speaking, the higher elements. But Christ spoke not only of the physical poor but of the poor in Spirit whose karma placed them on the low side of the karmic spectrum. He taught that they had needs beyond the immediate—needs which only his resurrection and victory over Death and Hell could provide for.

And so, whether the people who come to us are physically or spiritually poor, we are taught by Christ to help them and to heal them of their impoverished sense.

But when Christ is come, the incarnate Word, we leave off our social do-good programs and even our busyness about our 'religious' rituals and church work. We put all that aside and we rise up and anoint the Lord's body unto the initiation of the Resurrection and the Life.

For only through him are the temple doors opened to us, that we might also attain to the inheritance of his Christhood and thereby have the wherewithal to give something to the "poor" who are beneath us on the initiatic ladder.

Therefore, to underscore his approval of this deference to the Master by the female initiate,

Jesus said, "Wherever this gospel is preached, what she has done shall be spoken of as a memorial unto her for all generations."

Master El Morya says there's always someone above you and someone beneath you on the ladder of life. Serve both and you will be richly blessed.

In the course of our lifetimes, we have all been located on the various degrees of this karmic scale. We have been rich and we have been poor. And sometimes we're poor in one lifetime because we so abused our riches in another. And then again, because we were poor in one lifetime and used what little talents we had so wisely, we are given great riches in another.

Heaven knows what it's doing!

You see, you really can't create social justice in the absolute sense, whether in a free society or in a communist state. It simply won't work. There are too many inequities in any system. And inequities begin with our karmic levels. And these are self-leveling no matter what system we're forced to function under. Water—the water of the human consciousness—will always seek its own level.

That's why most welfare programs don't work. You simply can't artificially elevate people, by money or whatever means, above the level of their own attainment or self-mastery. These states of self-awareness are expressions of their free will, you see. And you can't raise anybody above the level of his own free will or his nonexercise thereof! Now, that doesn't say you can't love him or you can't teach him a course or two in self-improvement. You can give him as much training and apprenticeship as he's willing to apply himself to. But in the end he's got to do it for himself.

Helping people to help themselves and to improve their lot is what the instruction of the Maha Chohan is all about. This great Master, who represents the Holy Spirit and wears the mantle of the office of the Paraclete, trains teachers at his retreat in Ceylon (Sri Lanka) as well as in Darjeeling. Those who really care about souls in need who are reaching out for help should apply to the Maha Chohan to join his classes, out of the body on the etheric plane.

Down here there is only one way of bringing justice to ourselves as individuals and to society. And that is through the God Presence, and the practice of the God Presence by the Golden Rule: "Do unto others as you would have them do unto you." We truly need to give of ourselves to others.

For the salvation of our souls as well as others, Charity must have her place in our lives in a very practical program of self-help for those who are willing to be God-taught to help themselves. Motivation, free will, and individual self-effort is the key here. Without dynamic decrees for the specific binding of the lethargy of the nonwill, no social programs can survive, let alone be successful. We must feed his sheep.

Following in the footsteps of the Masters under the canopy of the I AM THAT I AM will bring us to Love's victory. Overcoming ourselves and the dark side of ourselves (like the dark side of the moon) according to the optimum cycles of opportunity, we can and should chart the ebb and tide of our days on the Cosmic Clock, the new-age psychology/astrology taught to us by Mother Mary. This system makes the returning currents of positive and negative karma *predictable*[58]—and therefore beatable!

When we know what to expect with each new dawn of opportunity (this is the blessing of charting our karmic and initiatic cycles on the Cosmic Clock), we can plan ahead how we are going to stand, face, and conquer life's supposed adversities, sent to test our mettle, and how we are going to ride the crest of past positive momentums into the new wave of the future.

As Brutus said to Cassius, "There is a tide in the affairs of men, which, taken at the flood, leads on to fortune; omitted, all the voyage of their life is bound in shallows and in miseries.... We must take the current when it serves, or lose our ventures."[59] And this is Truth.

Unless we conquer ourselves and our karmic tides, we will be ill-equipped to "love thy neighbor as thyself" or to assist him in his own soul liberation. Let all who would help others help themselves begin at the beginning with Self-help. Help yourself to the divine prerogative of taking dominion over your affairs, your family, your spiritual/mental/physical environment and most of all yourself.

When you do this, you will be the greatest help to others. For the Lord helps those who help themselves in order that they may help others. The Divine Helper, the Holy Spirit in the person of the Maha Chohan, must be acknowledged as the center of every social, educational, medical and family services program. His flame and consciousness must be invoked as the pillar of fire in the midst of community life—his disciplines taught, his Love extended with practicality and spiritual upliftment.

His Teachings must be set forth by example heart to heart—for the sheep who are fed must, above all, find soul nourishment even from secular shepherds who understand that the cause behind boredom, listlessness or violence among the poor is the absence of deep soul satisfaction and contact with Truth.

Thus, touch the needy with Love and Truth and Friendship, and the holy angels will work with you for small victories and great. And your reward and your blessing will be the smile of self-worth, self-appreciation in one who knew not who he was until you loved him.

Truth Vanquishes Doctrinal Delusions

We ourselves should be grateful that we know the Truth and hear the Truth—and know it when we hear it no matter who the speaker or the vocabulary! Because what we may term the Devil's lie is, of course, all of the palliatives in religion and philosophy that seek to justify men's conduct—the idea of someone saying: "Well, God loves me so much that he's going to give me a saviour to save me from my sins." He did! He gave you your Holy Christ Self. Jesus lived and expressed the Holy Christ Self of his being. He was lifted up that he might draw men to God.

But, it is within themselves, within their own beings, that men must come to know God. They cannot know God through the eyes of another, through the words of another, through the spirit of another, but only through the Spirit of the living God—anchored in the spark of Life that we identify as the threefold flame.

If it were not so, Jesus would not have warned his disciples of false Christs and false prophets who would show great signs and wonders, their followers pronouncing with loud fanfare: "Christ has come and he is in the desert!" or "Christ has come and he is in the secret chamber!" Of these flatterers and their vanities, Christ said, "Go ye not after them!"[60]

Don't you remember his instruction to the Pharisees concerning the coming of the kingdom? "The kingdom of God cometh not with observation: Neither shall they say, Lo here! or, lo there! for, behold, the kingdom [consciousness] of God is within you."[61]

Now I ask you, ladies and gentlemen—if the whole wide kingdom of God is inside of *you*, doesn't that include God and his Christ? Doesn't that include the Father and his Son? Aren't *they* a big part of the kingdom? I should say so!

Well, the Chart of Your Real Self illustrates how God's kingdom can be and indeed is in each of you. It's inside all of us. It shows God and his Christ individualized in every one. Drops of the ocean of being are we, each one the point of contact with the Mighty I AM Presence and the Christ Self.

Yes, my beloved, the kingdom of God and his Christ and their triumphal reign *are* within you. And fear not, the Holy Spirit's comforting flame is there, too.

Now, you tell me who are the false pastors of the Word who deny that God's kingdom—the realm of his Universal Mind—and all that's in it is inside of you. Beware of them, for they are the godless in whom the fires of creation were long ago put out by their own denial of God in themselves as well as in you. They are the hirelings that will flee when your need is greatest. Most certainly they will flee when Christ comes to judge them for their infamy—multiple sins of omission of true Charity—against your soul.

But in your extremity, know that God is in you, and your true shepherd, your beloved Christ, will lead you, with good angelic company, into all safety.[62]

The Satanic delusion of only one Son of God, only one manifestation of his Christ, and the rest of us sinners, and of only one embodiment, one chance for salvation and then heaven or hell, has caused so much confusion in the world that as a result of the omission of this Lost Teaching many of the churches have fallen into activities which are severely criticized by their own members.

This delusion has been foisted upon the people through their misunderstanding of the law of karma, the law of rebirth, and their consequent failure to recognize the perfectly natural idea of putting on and taking off the body overcoat.

I often wonder if the undertakers went to work on this doctrine. Sometimes I think it was written by the friendly undertaker! I just don't know.

Reembodiment: The Mercy and Justice of the Law

Take a baby borne in its mother's womb—it springs from the fusion of the sperm and the ovum and in nine months' gestation grows to a mature child with all of its organs in position and functions with divine precision as it comes forth and assumes its place in the world, once the umbilical cord is cut and the breath is come in.

Sooner or later this child comes to the point where he is going to give up his body, when the spirit that animates the form is going to depart. Now, to even suspect that God who was capable of producing the babe in the first place would be incapable of taking that same spirit and putting it into another body is simply preposterous!

What a waste! Why would an intelligent Potter break the mold of the soul every time the body wore out, when there is no end to its usefulness?

My mother did not believe in reembodiment. She was horrified when she found out that

I did. She was a victim of the system that promoted the idea that we live but once. And because of that idea, men are often put in terrible straits. Some of these are very interesting situations.

People say they live only once. Well, then, if that's true, what about the boy who dies at three years of age?

What about the little babe, the little waxen-faced babe that lies dead in its mother's arms at birth, stillborn?

What about the man who lives to be twenty-five and then perishes?

Or those who die on the battlefield for their country?

Or the man who lives to be a hundred and ten and says that he's had five wives and smoked and drank heavily all his life and attributes his long life to all of his excitement and fun?

Doesn't it seem to you as though there would be some equality in the eyes of God, some equality in the longevity of a person's life if we all lived but once? Why shouldn't we all have the same amount of time, then, if such be the case?

Well, you see, heaven is not concerned. Heaven winks at this, because our life is not in the body. Our life is in the soul and the soul can change garments as often as it wishes or as often as life (karma and the divine plan) necessitates it. And actually, this is a great blessing.

I recall having stood at various times and asked the mercy of God to take someone out of a broken body because of the intense pain and suffering that person was experiencing with no hope of recovery. This is particularly true of accident victims when they're in a terrible condition.

If there is no hope, isn't it a wonderful thing that that soul can actually pass through that change? Isn't it wonderful that the consciousness can leave the body and not have to remain there to feel the pang of severed limbs or mutilation beyond repair?

Isn't it a wonderful thing that Life in its great mercy can just gently lift the soul out of the body and then in due course of time put it sweetly into another woman's womb?

My mother was particularly concerned because, as she said, "Well, I don't like the idea of my being someone else." Well, dear hearts, you can never be anyone else but yourself. You couldn't possibly be anyone else but yourself!

If you became a victim of amnesia today (God forbid!) and then you recovered your memory and you found you'd married a woman while you were suffering from amnesia, as has happened—and you had had three or four children and then you met your first wife—well, you see, you'd really have a double life, but you'd still be the same person.

So, it doesn't make any difference, does it? Just think of it in this way—are you a different person each day because you wear a different suit? Don't you think your real friends love you for what you are and not for what you wear? So it goes.

Heart-friends of the ages recognize one another no matter what overcoat they're wearing.

Why, just come to a Summit University conference sometime. It's like old home week. People recognize each other on sight though they've never laid eyes on one another in this life. And quite a number of people have found their soul mate or twin flame sitting next to them at one of our classes!

Don't tell me people don't know who they are or who their friends (or enemies) are just because they've changed garments! It just isn't true. It's a most interesting thing when you stop and consider it. But we have to understand our lifestreams according to their innate purpose—as a continuous stream of consciousness moving in and out of many planes and systems of worlds, always wearing the appropriate garment for the mission.

The Living Christ Is the Universal Saviour

When we understand the Christ in the proper perspective, we have to realize that there was provision made for the salvation of man from the foundation of the world—through the Lamb of God, who was "slain," as Jesus revealed to John the Revelator, "from the foundation of the world."[63]

What this means is that Christ, the Light of every son and daughter of God, has been persecuted unto the death from the foundation of this world as we now know it, subject as it is to the Cain civilization of the fallen angels.

The living Christ—self-realized in men of God such as the great priest/king Melchizedek, who himself came and met Abraham returning from the slaughter of the kings and blessed him, he being without father and without mother, without beginning of days and ending of days[64]—is always the Universal Saviour who makes God and his salvation accessible to his own through his best servants.

So was Jesus the Christ from the beginning. So was he the Logos universal. He was with the Word who went forth from the beginning and created all things. He himself knew that his Reality was a continuum just as your soul knows that her Reality is from the beginning.

Therefore he declared, "Before Abraham was, I AM," in the full awareness that the "I AM" of him had always been the Christ. And he also knew that the permanent part of each one of you was and is that same Christ. Yes, one Universal Christ (*the* Son) but many sons and daughters of God embodying and personifying that One.

But, you see, he equates and he relates with the Holy Christ Self of each of us. This is the "I AM He"[65] consciousness of the perpetual Christ which Jesus maintained. God did not make *one* beloved Son in human form. He made *all* beloved sons in human form and an "only begotten Son"[66] in the spiritual sense that there was only one e-*man*-ation—*emanation*—from the heart of God, which was known as the Logos, or the Word, whose image dwells in every heart.

This personification of the Universal One within you (the Emmanuel) manifests as your Holy Christ Self. Jeremiah called this personal Christ THE LORD OUR RIGHTEOUSNESS.[67] He knew our righteousness (i.e., our standard for right action) must come from the LORD's presence within each one—lest every man should become a law unto his human self.

So you see, without Christ in us, we have no hope of rising beyond the human potential. Therefore Paul said Christ in you is the hope of glory[68] — because he is the only hope and the only means whereby the soul may glorify God in her members.

Now, if you'd learn to read the scriptures properly, you'd see that John brings this out clearly. He says, "In the beginning was the Word, and the Word was with God, and the Word was God...All things were made by him—the Christ—and without him was not any thing made that was made... I and my Father are one...Before Abraham was, I AM."[69]

Well, you see, the Christ, then, far antedated Jesus. And Jesus, the *man*, became the Christ in *mani*festation. That is to say, he personified the Christ by the assimilation (and the assumption) of the Word.

The Romanization of Christ and Christianity

Looking back through the evolution of Christian theology, it should be noted that it was the emperor Constantine who did more than almost anyone else to introduce the subtleties of pernicious precepts into Christianity. "If you can't lick 'em, join 'em," he said. Why, he was Machiavellian before Machiavelli was ever born! Let the ends of world domination justify the means of a quasi religious freedom.

Whereas before him under Diocletian, in the last and most severe period of persecution, the catacombs of Rome were full of Christian renegades, Constantine, seeing that the old gods of Rome were losing their popularity because so many people were turning to become Christians and confronted by the rising tide toward Christianity, decided, "I can't lick 'em so I'll join 'em."

While yet competing for control of the Roman Empire in A.D. 312, Constantine, according to Christian legend, was told by God in a dream to have his soldiers paint the Chi-Rho (a Christian symbol consisting of the first two letters of the Greek word for Christ) on their shields, and as a result won a decisive battle.

He went on to defeat his rival and became the "holy" Roman emperor Constantine, who has been portrayed in all his regal robes celebrating Christian rites and declaring himself a Christian yet still tolerating the pagan cults of the day—using them all as a means to his political ends of unifying the empire. And to this day Constantine is remembered for 'freeing' the Christians and 'Christianizing' the empire. In fact, he and his cohorts 'Romanized' Christ and Christianity.

The degree to which Constantine sought to synthesize Christianity and paganism can be seen in one of the emperor's commemorative medallions that shows him with a Chi-Rho monogram on his helmet and a Sol Invictus (pagan sun god) chariot horse below.[70] In addition, author Ian Wilson tells us, "How far Jesus had become divorced in western Christians' minds from the Jew of history is forcefully illustrated by a portrait of him as a beardless Apollo-like youth in a mosaic that once decorated the floor of the Romano-Christian villa at Hinton St. Mary in Dorset. Only the Chi-Rho monogram identifies it as Jesus."[71]

And what did they teach? They taught what Romans would be expected to teach. They presented Jesus as a god. They led the people astray into a cult of idolatry more Satanic than Christ-like. They taught them to worship Jesus as a flesh-and-blood martyr and messiah.

Just as Constantine, in the tradition of his predecessors, bore for life the title of *pontifex maximus*, chief priest of the pagan cults supported by the State, so he was to bear with singular pomp his position and power in the Christian church. In 325, when the bitter Arian controversy threatened schism in the Church—and with it Constantine's goal of a "universal empire" for which he had worked long and hard—the emperor called the first ecumenical council of over 300 bishops in Nicaea, had the state pay for all their expenses, and lodged them in his palace. Constantine himself presided over the opening session of the council and took part in its debates.

The conflict centered around Arius, a pastor in the Alexandrian Church who taught that Jesus Christ was not equal or eternal with the Creator but, as the Logos, was the first and highest of created beings—"divine only by participation," by God's grace[72]—whereas his opponents said the Son was "of one substance with the Father."

"In the simplest of terms, the point at issue was whether Jesus was a mere being...who had been brought into existence to serve God's purpose—to act as the 'word' of God—at a particular time in the early first century A.D., or whether he had been God for all eternity, 'of one substance with the Father' (as those in the West expressed it)," writes Wilson. "If the latter, then he was effectively a supraterrestrial entity easily compatible with Sol Invictus, but light years removed from the Jesus envisaged by Arius and the Antiochenes"[73]—supporters of Arius who emphasized the human element as distinct from the divine in Jesus.

When all was said and done, the council rejected Arius' position and, urged by Constantine, adopted the Nicene Creed:

> We believe in one God, the Father Almighty, maker of all things visible and invisible; and in one Lord Jesus Christ, the Son of God, the only-begotten of his Father, of the substance of the Father, God of God, Light of Light, very God of very God,

begotten, not made, being of one substance with the Father. By whom all things were made, both which be in heaven and in earth. Who for us men and for our salvation came down [from heaven] and was incarnate and was made man. He suffered and the third day he rose again, and ascended into heaven. And he shall come again to judge both the quick and the dead. And [we believe] in the Holy Ghost. And whosoever shall say that there was a time when the Son of God was not, or that before he was begotten he was not, or that he was made of things that were not, or that he is of a different substance or essence [from the Father] or that he is a creature, or subject to change or conversion—all that so say, the Catholic and Apostolic Church anathematizes them.[74]

The crux of the controversy over the Nicene Creed—which continued on for five decades more until the First Council of Constantinople again condemned all forms of Arianism—was the use of the word *homoousios* ("of one substance") to define the relationship of Jesus Christ to the Father, which is thought to have been put into the creed at the suggestion of Constantine himself.[75]

Athanasius, the patriarch of Alexandria and chief proponent of Nicene orthodoxy, later wrote that the intent of the creed was to show that "the resemblance of the Son to the Father, and his immutability, are different from ours: for in us they are something acquired, and arise from our fulfilling the divine commands."[76]

Only two of the bishops at Nicaea refused to sign the creed. Along with Arius they were anathematized ("cursed") by the council and exiled by edict of Constantine, who also ordered all of Arius' books to be burned upon penalty of death. After returning home a few of the bishops expressed their remorse for assenting to the new formula. "We committed an impious act, O Prince," Eusebius of Nicomedia wrote to Constantine, "by subscribing to a blasphemy from fear of you."[77]

"Although no gospel regarded Jesus as God, and not even Paul had done so, the Jewish teacher had been declared *Very* God through all eternity, and a whole new theology would flow from this," says Wilson, pointing out that even in the Gospel of John, "the one most inclined to make Jesus divine," Jesus is reported as stating: "I go unto the Father: for my Father is greater than I."[78]

Nicaea was indeed a turning point in more ways than one. Constantine's involvement in Church affairs also created a precedent for civil leadership in Church councils. Nicaea "marked the replacement of paganism with Christianity as the religious expression and support of the Roman Empire," observes historian Will Durant. "By his [Constantine's] aid Christianity became a state as well as a church, and the mold, for fourteen centuries, of European life and thought."[79]

And we may ask the question: Who ever gave the Roman emperor the right to decide Christian doctrine? Yet in the centuries following Constantine's reign, this became the tradition, as we can clearly see in the case of the sixth-century emperor Justinian I. Justinian also played a leading role in the continuing controversies over the divine and human aspects of Christ. He issued his own edicts condemning the doctrines of those he branded "heretics" and then summoned Church councils to do the same.

One of those condemned was Origen of Alexandria. Oddly enough, Origen's seemingly paradoxical statements on the nature of Christ were used by both sides in the Arian controversy to support their views. Among the chief accusations against this eminent theologian by which Justinian and the Fifth Ecumenical Council anathematized his teachings three centuries after his death was the charge that, like Arius, Origen had made the Son inferior to the Father.

But his theology was not that simple. As one author summarizes the issue: "Origen taught that Christ was the only-begotten Son of God, and that since God the Father had always existed, He could never have existed, even for a moment, without having generated the Son. The Son, therefore, is coeternal with the Father and existed before all worlds.... Origen seemed also to say that Christ is a creature, and that as the image of the Father he is secondary to the latter and subordinate to Him."[80]

262 CHAPTER 9 • A CONTINUATION OF OPPORTUNITY

Another observer of the controversies surrounding Origen has noted that "the charges against Origen boil down to the accusation that his theology was adulterated by his philosophy.... The distinction between what Origen had actually said and the opinions thought to be implied by what he said began to be lost. And no real attempt was made to distinguish Origen's own thought from what his later followers had made of it."[81]

And so, the religion of Rome that had co-opted Christ as the new head of their pagan cult went marching on. Its exponents bequeathed to all Catholics the Good Friday fix—a fixation on the crucifix. And often a bloody crucifix at that! Why, it was a cult of death robed in the black of perpetual mourning and the *via dolorosa*—the sorrowful way. All the while neglecting to carefully instruct them in the catechism of joyous salvation by Jesus' *joyous* victory over Death and Hell through the living Christ within themselves! They taught men to adore—"*Adoremus!*"—the man Jesus to the utter neglect of the Universal Divinity he portrayed—the universally available Divinity that is everyone's to claim in Jesus' name.

Jesus' clear message is: Because Christ is raised up in me, he shall be raised up in you, whereas in the Roman hierarchy and rituals to God and to Jesus, there was, more often than not, complete disregard of Christ's principles and love. And the history of the Church has shown that orthodoxy for the sake of orthodoxy has been incapable of feeding the sheep the true Bread of Life which came down from heaven in the pure person of the Christ Jesus.

Just look at the historical evidence of this Satanic delusion. Ever since the Christian era, throughout Western civilization we find the pages of the centuries bathed in blood because of religious wars, crusades, persecutions, and inquisitions instigated by the seed of Satan in our midst—whose sole aim was and is to destroy the true doctrine and divinity of Christ as present potential in all God's children just as that divinity was the fully realized Godhead who dwelt bodily in Jesus.

And the Church has survived, in spite of its materialistic hierarchy, solely because of the saints embodying the living Word in the very midst of a corrupt or stupefied clergy!

Enough of that. I think I'll tell you another one of my Pierre stories which brings to mind at least one of the reasons why the doctrines of reembodiment and karma were knocked out.

Well, since the people knew they had lived before and that they would live again another day to obtain salvation, they got a little complacent, a little independent of the religion of fear/sin/punishment and hellfire and brimstone—which is not the religion of Christ but of Satan.

They were saying, "Pierre, are you going to church today?"

"Aha, I'm not going to church today. I'm not going anymore in my whole life!"

"Why not, Pierre?"

"Because I'll go in my next life, that's why."

And so, you see, the wise and crafty priests deemed it expedient, in order to maintain control and a fair livelihood ("the end justifies the means"), to alter Christ's doctrine and the sacred scriptures.

They took out the great truth of the law of reincarnation and karma because, they said, "the ignorant masses are unable to cope with this teaching. The unwashed masses do not understand the Law. We will keep it a mystery. We will give them the bread—only that which they need for their subsistence in this life—and we will keep the wine, the essential Truth, for ourselves (in secret)."

They did not convey the Truth to the common people because it made it much harder to control them. Besides which, it would become obvious to the people, if they were taught the Law, that the clerics themselves did not obey the Law nor did they bow before Christ in their hearts.

They were incapable of conveying the Law because they themselves didn't live it and, what's more, in many cases they didn't know it! They, too, had become the victims of the blind leaders of the blind. For down the centuries ignorance had begot ignorance, and density more of the same. Corruption was in the Church. It was everywhere.

Of no surprise—Jesus warned of the mentalists without heart, the scribes and Pharisees who still proscribe with the authority of Moses yet show not forth the good works of the Anointed One.[82]

Likewise, let us follow the Universal Law and

be unmoved by the barrenness of the false priests. And let us not allow these false preachers to take from us the cup of our Christhood or to turn us off to the Lord's true religion.

We who know the Truth must proclaim it and live by it and set the example of the way of Love—his Love!

For he gave his Word for us: And ye shall know the Truth and the Truth shall make you free![83]

The Age of Apostasy and an Angry God Is Not Over

Today we have a better world than we had back then. And do you know something? Some of us have some serious illusions about history. We think because we love Jesus, because we love God, because we have respect for Truth, that they lived very wonderfully back then.

I tell you, the age of apostasy was really a dark age. And it did invade the Church. And then, you see, it also set forth the picture of an angry God—a God of wrath, of lightning and thunder, who was constantly seeking to throw the souls of men into a hell from whence they could never escape. That was the devil's portrait of our heavenly Father.

Yet you and I know that there are people in the world today, fathers and mothers, who have had a daughter come home to them *enceinte* (with child) without the benefit of a wedding ring. And these parents have accepted their errant daughter back into their home. Some of them have even raised the child and walked proudly down the street with their grandson, who in the eyes of many in the world wasn't so grand at all.

Well, you see, this makes man much better than God. He can forgive, but God is a God of wrath who will cast out people forever—this is *not true!* It never has been true.

The fact that men make their heavens and their hells was written about quite beautifully, I think, by the great writer Omar Khayyam, who said: "I sent my Soul through the Invisible, / Some Letter of that After-life to spell: / And by and by my Soul return'd to me, / And answer'd, 'I Myself am Heav'n and Hell.'"[84] We ourselves occupy the consciousness of that heaven or hell which we have created.

I must say that I could not explain in one night every facet of this Great Law to the satisfaction of all minds. But give me any man or woman on this earth who will listen and who will leave aside their illusions and confusions, and I will show them the Law that God has clearly revealed to me.

Why, he has revealed that this universe as well as your soul is a place of great beauty, intense beauty, and that this world would not be the way it is today at all if the Truth had been exalted.

He has shown me that the Church was invaded centuries ago by the fallen angels who were cast out of heaven into physical embodiment in order that they might work out their karma on earth for their sin against the Sons of God. Instead of taking their just penance as a continuation of Life's opportunity, they penetrated the Holy Church to continue their blasphemy against the Son by betraying his little ones.

Thus the children of his heart who deserved true shepherds and trusted these wolves in sheep's clothing[85] have been led doctrinally astray. And, as a result, many of the ministers today are taught from childhood to believe the lies of Serpent as though they were out of the mouth of Christ himself.

They are taught that we live but once and then we die and that's the end of us—and we are weighed, then, according to that life. And if we are good, we're going to heaven; and if we are bad, we're going to the other place. That's what they're taught.

The false pastors take the scripture which says it is appointed unto men once to die, but after this the judgment,[86] and on this they hang their false doctrine of only one embodiment—although it doesn't even say it is given man once to live!

Now, what it really means is that the ego must die, and it dies but once and after that the soul may obtain the resurrection through the just judgments of God. But until free will says die to the ego, it lives on, incarnation after incarnation. It's plain to see that for many the ego does not die at the death of the body. Thus the soul must be born again in Christ,[87] this time to slay that dweller on the threshold[88]—*once* and for all, thence to attain immortality.

In reality, beloved, because God so loved our souls as his own he has given us many, many opportunities to return to his heart through loving obedience to his Son.

We don't have an angry God. You know who gets the most angry with you when you do wrong? I'm going to tell you who gets the most angry with you when you do wrong. *You* do. You get angry with yourself. You are the most wrathful god in all the universe with yourself. And this, too, is the product of the diabolical doctrine of sin and condemnation.

We say we are a Christian nation and we say that we are a Christian world and we say that this is an era of Christendom—in fact, *anno Domini*, the year of our Lord 1986. And where is our Lord today?

Madalyn Murray O'Hair said in the '60s that we have no right to pray—not in school and not in space.[89] And the voice of one woman swayed the mindless idiots that occupy high positions in our society. Why? Because from their seats of authority they, too, promulgate the devil's doctrine. Whether ignorantly or with malice aforethought, the result is the same: Prayer is banned in the public schools to the hurt of a generation of schoolchildren, and needlessly so.

"In God We Trust" is on our coins. The statue of the Goddess of Liberty holds her torch high in New York harbor. She still cries out, "Give me your tired, your poor, your huddled masses yearning to breathe free..." Yet this modern society compresses people like old cars in stamping presses, packing them down with the vibrations of negativity that are thus compounded in their worlds until they can no longer rise.

If today's Christianity is the religion of Christ, then will somebody please tell us where is the true transmission by its adherents of the all-consuming fire of the Holy Ghost, the promised Comforter which should come for the deliverance of his dear followers?[90]

Christ, the Law, the I AM in Every Man

Be not dismayed—the flame is still exalted! The flame breathes on, even though the votaries are gone. And the flame is the Truth. And that's what we proclaim: The Christ is within every man. He's a spark in some and a burning brand in others. And he can be exalted in you, and he *is* the Saviour of mankind.

The man Jesus, who was and is the Son of God, is your elder brother. And he is not in the least offended by this concept because Truth is what he stands for. Messias, yes, but we are all intended to be a messiah—all of us, the whole world. Each in his own way can become through Messias a deliverer and a leader in the cause of Christ—in the hope that the spark of Life can be reignited in full conflagration in those in whom it flickers near death.

As we mentioned earlier, quoting from the book of Hebrews, God made a new covenant with the seed of Abraham, which is the seed of the

Universal Christ who descended from the Ancient of Days. They are the quick, defined neither by race nor by religion, nor by human ancestry but by the divine spark and the interior Light. We present herewith the Lost Teachings of Jesus in the Lord's interpretation of his promise to the redeemed of the Great God Self:

I will put my Law—which means the Logos, "my Christ"—**in their inward parts** (in their genes) **and write it in their hearts** (I will etch on crystal in letters of living fire in the secret chamber of the heart the image of the Christ, after whose image ye are made) **and will be their God** (I will be to them the ever-present I AM).

The personal God who becomes the ownership of each individual is the Beloved Mighty I AM Presence, which you see depicted in the Chart of Your Real Self. This is your very own God Self, your personal refuge and your strength (energy Source), a "very present help in trouble" as the psalmist said.[91]

And they shall be my people. You are "God's people," his very own pure son (person). You are God's person—his personal self in earth—even as he is your Real Self in heaven.

And they shall teach no more every man his neighbor and every man his brother, saying, Know the LORD. They will no longer teach, every man to his neighbor, who is the LORD; for the LORD, even the Mighty I AM Presence, shall be known by every man and woman as "my Father and your Father, my God and your God."[92]

In this wise did Jesus also explain the Presence to his beloved Mary Magdalena on resurrection morning. Indeed, this Truth is the Resurrection and the Life of every disciple of Christ—i.e., of the I AM WHO I AM.

"For they shall all know me, from the least of them unto the greatest of them," saith the LORD. From the lowest to the highest caste, from the untouchables to the Brahmins—everyone has an I AM Presence and a Christ Self. And everyone shall know Me as the personal God of very gods. And because they shall comprehend Me and My all-comprehensiveness in their life, they shall contain Me and I shall contain them.

In this Light **I will forgive their iniquity, and I will remember their sin no more.**[93] For all is God and in God and of God; and in this knowing, this reality, and this love, all else shall cease to be, save the I and the Beloved.

And every man shall sit under his vine—his Beloved Christ Self—**and under his fig tree,** his own Tree of Life—the Beloved I AM Presence laden with the fruits of his causal body.

For all people will walk, every one in

the name of his god—his individual I AM Presence—and we will walk in the name of the LORD our God forever and ever.⁹⁴

And there shall be one altar, one temple, one world—not according to the United Nations, not according to the Babylonian one-world economy concept of Nimrod,⁹⁵ but according to a union of hearts where all embrace the ideals of their Divine Presence and find union with one another through the Universal Law of the One.

This is the path that leads to the abundant Life for all—free from the deadly controls of international capitalist/communist conspirators who, aided and abetted by the international money changers, are destroying the economic balance of nations and the power base that belongs to the people.

"Behold, What Manner of Love..."

I heard a man say the other night, "I don't care what you were, it's what you are today that I'm concerned with." And this is something we should remind ourselves of often. To see ourselves and one another as we really are in God, like God—as God.

Consider Love's mystery unveiled to John in his perception of the identical nature of God and his offspring.

> Behold what manner of Love the Father hath bestowed upon us that we should be called the sons of God!

"Behold, What Manner of Love..." 273

> Therefore the world knoweth us not because it knew him not.
>
> Beloved, NOW are we the sons of God!
>
> And it doth not yet appear what we shall be.
>
> But we know that when he shall appear we shall be like him.
>
> For we shall see him *as he is.*
>
> And every man that hath this hope in him purifieth himself even as he is pure.[96]

And that's the prerequisite for being like him. You have to see him as he is. You have to see yourself as God sees you. You have to have hope—the hope of *Christ in you*, which is our only hope. For no one can be saved unless Christ live in him truly.

That's why we're telling you these things and that's why it's so important for you to tell the world.

Because Christ is in you—the same yesterday, today, and forever[97]—this change of garments, this different embodiment, is no problem at all. It's no problem to God. No more a problem to put your soul in another body than it was to put you together in the first place! No problem at all. And it's much better than going to Hades.

Don't you see? Your re-incarnation is really an opportunity—a continuation of the opportunity that began when God first conceived you in his Mind. When you were a God-idea gathering more of his Love, being draped with his immaculately moving conception of You.

Getting down to earth, stop and think for a

moment: If you're not ready for heaven when you make the transition—you know, you have a few more worldly attachments to get over—do you think God's hands are tied? that he's not free to give you a few more decades or lifetimes to really overcome the world and its pulls and come to the place where you truly want to be up there with the angels and the saints?

Just 'cause you're not quite a saint yet doesn't make you a hardened sinner and it's no reason for an all-loving and all-wise Father to throw you in the dump to burn forever with the rest of the refuse!

Now, to say that God *has to* send you to hell if you're bad or that he *has to* send you to heaven if you're good is making him the prisoner of a law he never ordained!

Both 'good' and 'bad' people may be ill-suited for either extreme; but a more temperate zone in between may be just the thing they need in order to evolve—one way or the other. And so you see just why God keeps the earth spinning in space. We may be neither "here" nor "there," but we're getting there—wherever "there" may be.

Well, one of the most amazing arguments I've heard for going to heaven as opposed to hell was put forth by a preacher who said to me, "If I'm good and I do all the things the Bible says I should, then God *has to* take me to heaven. By his own law, he *has to* forgive my sins."

Well, dear heart, you see, God doesn't *have to* forgive your sins and take you to heaven anymore than he *has to* send you to hell. He can put you anywhere he wants to. And you may find one day that he just might want to put you back on earth to finish what you started in your last life. And he just may keep on sending you back until you complete the assignment and do it right—like he wants it done.

And he'll do it whether you like it or not or whether you believe in reincarnation or not! Because in the end, it's not what you believe that counts, it's what God believes that will make it all happen.

And you can be sure that whatever the Father does do, he'll do it because he loves you.

> Verily, verily, I say unto thee, When thou wast young, thou girdest thyself, and walkedst whither thou wouldest: but when thou shalt be old, thou shalt stretch forth thy hands, and another shall gird thee, and carry thee whither thou wouldest not.[98]

The Church's Doctrine of Sin Begets More Sin

One of the worst things the Church ever did was to teach the doctrine of sin the way they teach it. Because that's responsible for more sin than anything else!

If you don't believe it, you take a man who's in debt. And he's so badly in debt that he doesn't know what in the world is going to happen to him. He's on the verge of bankruptcy. That man will go out—if he's got a credit card—and buy more stuff on his credit card than anyone else, because he knows he can go into bankruptcy and he can get right out of the whole thing.

"Jesus paid it all. All to him I owe. Sin had left a crimson stain. He washed it white as snow."[99]

But what about where it says in the scriptures that if you sin willfully after you have already received the knowledge of the Truth, there remains no more means of atonement for your sins? And then it says you can only expect a certain fearful looking for of judgment and fiery indignation, which will come upon the ungodly and devour the adversaries of the living Truth.[100]

Go to Saint Peter, he tells it like it is. He talks about the apostate teachers—the fallen angels upon whom Enoch and John the Baptist and Jesus and Jude also raised the right hand of God's judgment, inasmuch as these proud ones had worn out the grace of the merciful Law:

"For if after they have escaped the pollutions of the world through the knowledge of the Lord and Saviour Jesus Christ, they are again entangled therein and overcome, the latter end is worse with them than the beginning. For it had been better for them not to have known the way of righteousness than, after they have known it, to turn from the holy commandment delivered unto them."[101]

I am not belittling the Law, but I think the crime fits the punishment or the punishment fits the crime, whichever way you want to say it. I think that a man has to have some intelligence, some awareness to know that he has erred.

If a man ignorantly errs, I consider that the laws of God will bring to his doorstep recompense, but it will not be the same recompense as for the one who knowingly errs. And I think also that the one who knowingly errs does not really know the Truth either and is still in a certain amount of ignorance. And therefore he, too, is given a certain amount of mercy.

But I do not believe in the law of mercy as some have chosen to interpret it to their own advantage or disadvantage, as the case may be. Although the mercy of God endures forever, as the Bible says, I believe, as it also says, that his Spirit will not always strive with flesh.[102]

I believe that if a person continues in wrongdoing over and over again, he can lose his soul or become a castaway;[103] that he can pass through the change called the second death[104] and cease to be an individual in God (an individed 'id-entity') and not reembody. And this, too, is scriptural.

Yes, I believe that and I know that to be true. For we also know that this occurred with Adolf Hitler. And it has occurred with others—people whose karma was so great that if they went through the whole sosophoric round, they would still be unable to pay it all. So this, too, is an example of the mercy of God that endures forever. For the cancelling out of that soul whose karma decrees he shall live in karmic torment forever is indeed mercy.

God's mercy that endures is bestowed upon his beloved, but the embodied devils and fallen angels who come as betrayers of the Word, molesters of the holy innocents, must one day, after the longsufferingness of the Law is spent, meet with full force the infamy of their words and works against the Person of God in his little ones.

This denouement ought to be considered as the end product of the multiplication of our own sowings and reapings—as the mathematics of Divine Justice mandated by our exercise of free will, rather than as Opportunity's grand finale scripted by an angry, vengeful, whimsical God.

I will say this: that the people who lead a life of happiness and joy and peace, having families with few untimely deaths, few tragedies, are many times people whose good deeds (good karma) have merited them great rewards.

Jesus said: "Verily I say unto you, There is no man that hath left house or brethren or sisters or father or mother or wife or children or lands for my sake and the gospel's, but he shall receive an hundredfold now in this time houses, and brethren and sisters and mothers and children and lands, with persecutions, and in the world to come eternal life."[105]

Well, you figure out how you're going to get that reward unless you have more than one life!

So, you see, when you understand the Bible as God said it—not just as it's been interpreted to you by your parents, not just as some preacher's told it to you, but as it really is (including the most important parts they left out, which we're getting back now directly from the Lord Christ by his Holy Spirit—you see, they couldn't keep it from us forever!)—then you'll have true freedom, the freedom to be and to espouse your Real Self.

And that's why I'm telling you these things—because, you see, *you* have to discover the Path for yourself. I can tell you things that will clue you in, but you have to be able to put them together for yourself.

It's not a matter of accepting me or rejecting me. It's not a matter of accepting or rejecting what I say or of accepting or rejecting what someone else says. It's a matter of understanding what is Truth.

So, here we're not dealing too much with the Masters, we're dealing with you. You and your twin flame and how your spirits came forth from the fiery ovoid in the beginning. But, oh, what a wonderful story the Masters are! What a wonderful story the heavenly hierarchy is! What a wonderful story the divine flames are! What a wonderful story Truth and the history of Truth is!

But it can't all be told in a nutshell. It can't all be told in a few words. We can touch it lightly, as we have done here, and it will inspire us to seek further, to learn more, and to realize the greatest hope of all—that the laws of God are already working within ourselves.

Notes

For an alphabetical listing of many of the philosophical and hierarchical terms used in *The Lost Teachings of Jesus*, see the comprehensive glossary, "The Alchemy of the Word: Stones for the Wise Masterbuilders," in *Saint Germain On Alchemy*.

Chapter Five KAL-DESH: THE INTERMINGLING OF TIME AND SPACE

1. When Mark Prophet delivered this lecture, he used the Hindi pronunciation of the words *kal* and *desh* (from the Sanskrit *kala* and *desha*) in which the final *a* of both words is silent. The alternate spelling without the final *a* as written in the title retains this pronunciation and vibration for the reader of the word.
2. **Rebellion,** which often begins to manifest at the age of puberty, is in reality a rebellion against returning karma. In most cases, the individual's karma descends for the first time at age 12 and he is forced to deal with the effects of causes he has set in motion in past lifetimes. The only reprieve in the face of the relentless law of karma that we face from puberty on is the grace of Christ when we receive him as our personal Saviour and Teacher in place of the impersonal Law. The confirmation of the child in the Law of the One at age 12–14 is for the sealing of the soul against the day of reckoning with his karma, and for the anointing of the child with the responsibilities of

adulthood. This initiation—commemorating Jesus' coming of age, when he discoursed with the doctors in the temple (his final exam), and his going forth to the East in preparation for his mission—is for the confirming of the Law by understanding, by teaching, and by action and the dedication of the child as a defender of the faith. By developing a deep commitment to defend the Law, he is thus better prepared to face the onslaught of his own karma and the temptations that come during adolescence—using the pure energies of life flowing through him in devotion to God.

3. Prov. 3:12; 13:24; Heb. 12:6–8; Rev. 3:19.*
4. **Thoth:** the Egyptian God, also called Tehuti; the god of wisdom, learning and literature; the inventor of all arts and sciences, including writing, arithmetic, algebra, geometry, theology, political economy, medicine, surgery, music and musical instruments. He is usually depicted as counselor and friend of the Egyptian rulers Osiris and Horus, the scribe of the kingdom and amanuensis of the gods. Succeeding Horus to the throne, Thoth is said to have reigned for over three thousand years as a model ruler, then to have taken his place among the gods as guardian of the moon, patron of history, herald, scribe, and keeper of the divine archives. In addition, he is the recorder of the judgment who weighs the hearts of the deceased and reports the verdict before Osiris. Thoth is often portrayed as an ibis (a bird related to a heron with a long downwardly curved bill) or an ibis-headed man; the exact significance of this symbology has never been discovered.

Archaeologist James Churchward traces Thoth back to the days of Atlantis using information he claims to have deciphered from ancient tablets discovered in India and Mexico, confirmed by more than fifty years of his own research: "The first we hear about the religion of Egypt is where an ancient record states that about 16,000 years ago Thoth, the son of an Atlantian Priest, planted the Egyptian colony at the mouth of the Nile, and at Sais on the banks of the Nile built a temple and taught the Osirian

---
*Bible references are to the King James Version unless otherwise noted.

religion.... Egypt was a sub-colony of the Motherland [Lemuria] under direct control of the colonial empire—Atlantis" (*The Sacred Symbols of Mu* [1933; Paperback Library, 1968], pp. 197, 199).

The Greeks identified Thoth with their god Hermes (the messenger of the gods, whom the Romans associated with Mercury) and with Hermes Trismegistus (meaning "the thrice greatest Hermes"), author of sacred writings and alchemical and astrological works. On the famous Rosetta stone, inscribed by priests of Ptolemy V (d. 180 B.C.), Hermes is called "the great-great," or "twice great." Hargrave Jennings wrote in his introduction to one of the extant works of Hermes, *The Divine Pymander:* "Hermes was called by the Egyptians TAT, TAUT, THOTH. It is concluded that, because of his learning and address, and in wonder at his profound skill in the arts and sciences, that the people gave him the name of TRISMEGISTUS, or the 'THRICE GREAT.'... Some have been so fanciful as to make him one with ADAM," as well as Enoch, Canaan, and the patriarch Joseph. "Perhaps—in spite of all the foregoing exaggerations, which are always the lot of very great and highly distinguished men, who became deified in after-times—the most probable judgment to be formed concerning him is, that he was some person of superior genius, who, before the time of Moses, had invented useful arts, and taught the first rudiments of science; and who caused his instructions to be engraved in emblematical figures (hieroglyphics), upon tables or columns of stone (obelisks), which he dispersed over the country, for the purpose of enlightening the people, and of fixing the worship of the gods....

"Another Thoth, or Hermes, is said to have lived at a later period. He was equally celebrated with the former, and to him is particularly appropriated, by some, the name of Trismegistus. According to Manetho [an Egyptian priest and historian c. 300 B.C.], he [this second Thoth] translated from engraved tables of stone, which had been buried in the earth, the sacred characters of the first Hermes, and wrote the explanation of them in books, which were deposited in the Egyptian temples. The same author calls him the son of Agathodaemon; and adds that to him are ascribed the restoration of the wisdom taught by the first Hermes, and the revival of geometry, arithmetic and the arts among the Egyptians, after they had been long lost or neglected.... He is said to have written a very large number of books, as commentaries upon the tables of the first Hermes, which treated of universal principles, of the nature of the universe, and of the soul of man; of the governing of the world by the movements of the stars (otherwise in astrology); of the Divine Light, and of its shadow..." (*The Divine Pymander of Hermes Mercurius Trismegistus*, trans. Dr. Everard [1650; San Diego: Wizards Bookshelf, 1978], pp. iii, iv, v).

Manetho said Hermes wrote 36,525 books and the Neoplatonic philosopher Iamblichus (d. c. 330) sets the number at 20,000. Clement of Alexandria, Greek theologian and a father of the Church (d. c. 215), names 42 "Books of Thoth" dealing with priestly education, temple ritual, geography, astrology, guidance for kings, hymns to the gods, and medicine. These were lost in the burning of Alexandria. Writing of the mystical significance of Thoth, one author states, "In the mystic sense Thoth or the Egyptian Hermes was the symbol of the Divine Mind; he was the incarnated Thought, the living Word—the primitive type of the Logos of Plato and the Word of the Christians" (Artaud, "Hermes Trismegiste," in G. R. S. Mead, *Thrice-Greatest Hermes*, vol. 1 [1906; reprint, London: John M. Watkins, 1949], p. 27).

5. Matt. 27:33, 38; Mark 15:22, 27; Luke 23:32, 33; John 19:17, 18.
6. **Level:** a device for establishing a horizontal line or plane by means of a bubble in a liquid that shows adjustment to the horizontal by movement to the center of a slightly bowed glass tube. *Webster's Ninth New Collegiate Dictionary*, s.v. "level."
7. Kahlil Gibran, *The Prophet* (New York: Alfred A. Knopf, 1969), p. 92.
8. Matt. 5:28.

9. John 13:27.
10. See Kyle Crichton, *Subway to the Met: Risë Stevens' Story* (Garden City, N.Y.: Doubleday & Company, 1959), pp. 237–38.
11. Jer. 31:33.
12. Gen. 1:1–3.
13. Robert Louis Stevenson, "Happy Thought," *A Child's Garden of Verses*.
14. Matt. 7:9–11; Luke 11:11–13.
15. Matt. 24:27, 30; Rev. 1:7.
16. Rev. 1:18.
17. Rev. 14:6.
18. Heb. 13:8.
19. In Babylonian mythology, **Tiamat** is the female principle of chaos (represented as the anarchic, tumultuous sea or the powers of salt water) which takes the form of a dragon. She is depicted as the enemy of the gods of light and law. As the story is told in the Babylonian *Epic of the Creation*, Tiamat and her husband, Aspu (the primeval father, a personification of the ocean, the Deep, the powers of the fresh waters), were in existence along with their son, Mummu, before the heavens and earth were created. After a succession of generations of gods came forth from Aspu and Tiamat, Aspu, angered by these turbulent and boisterous beings who were disturbing his former peace, resolved to be rid of the new gods. One of these, Ea, learned of this and destroyed Aspu before he could implement his plans. The vengeful Tiamat thus became the formidable enemy of the new gods, until she and the forces of chaos (including enormous dragons and serpents which she created as her allies) were at last overcome by Marduk, the great god of Babylon, who then fashioned the heavens and the earth and organized the universe. In another variation of the creation legend, Tiamat represents the subterranean waters of chaos, the elementary principle from which the earth arose in the form of a mountain.

Zecharia Sitchin interprets the creation myth as a tale of the creation of our solar system: In the beginning before the formation of the other planets, there was only Aspu (the Sun), Mummu (Mercury), and Tiamat. Tiamat (the "missing planet") was later split in half when it collided with the satellites of Marduk, a large planet drawn into this solar system by the gravitational pull of Neptune. Tiamat's upper half, along with her chief satellite, became Earth and her moon; her lower half, shattered by Marduk during its second orbit, became the asteroid belt between Mars and Jupiter. Sitchin suggests that in this series of events Marduk transferred the seed of life to Earth, giving her "the biological and complex early forms of life for whose early appearance there is no other explanation." He says that at the time the human species on Earth was just beginning to stir, Marduk had already evolved into a planet with high levels of civilization and technology. According to Sitchin, Marduk is caught in a large elliptical orbit around the Sun and returns to the site of the collision between Jupiter and Mars every 3,600 Earth-years. He calls Marduk "the Twelfth Planet" after the ancient Sumerians' scheme of this solar system, which depicts 12 celestial bodies—the Sun, the moon, and 10 planets. See the following works by Zecharia Sitchin: *The 12th Planet* (New York: Avon Books, 1976), pp. 204, 210–34, 255–56; *The Stairway to Heaven* (New York: St. Martin's Press, 1980), pp. 88–90.

20. John 6:53.

Chapter Six THE CHART OF THE I AM PRESENCE

1. Rev. 17:8, 11.
2. John 9:4.
3. Isa. 61:1, 2; Luke 4:16–30.
4. John 10:22–39.
5. Phil. 2:6.
6. Matt. 5:48.
7. Phil. 2:5.
8. James 3:11, 12.
9. Col. 2:9.
10. John 14:23.
11. "Our Constitution is in actual operation; everything

appears to promise that it will last; but in this world nothing is certain but death and taxes." Benjamin Franklin, Letter to Jean Baptiste LeRoy, 13 November 1789.
12. Matt. 5:18.
13. Rom. 12:19.
14. Eph. 4:26.
15. Matt. 24:23–27; Luke 17:20, 21. **"The kingdom of God is within you"** (KJV) has been translated in modern versions of the Bible as "the kingdom of God is in the midst of you" (RSV) or "among you" (Jerusalem Bible). According to G. W. H. Lampe, "in the midst of you" is "improbable as a translation"; three instances in the Old Testament translated into Greek by Symmachus, a second-century translator of the Bible, "are the only real parallel for this meaning of the Greek phrase," he says (*Peake's Commentary on the Bible*, eds. Matthew Black and H. H. Rowley [Walton-on-Thames: Thomas Nelson and Sons, 1962], p. 837). S. MacLean Gilmour notes that "within" does correspond "to the normal Greek use of the word" (*Interpreter's Bible*, 8:300). But scholars have been unable to make sense out of "within you" in the context of Luke's verse because they contend that Jesus would not have answered the Pharisees—who had asked him when the kingdom of God was to come (Luke 17:20)—that the kingdom of God was *within them*.

However, *The Gospel of Thomas*—a collection of sayings which, according to scholar Helmut Koester, "are present in a more primitive form" than parallel sayings in the synoptic Gospels or "are developments of a more primitive form of such sayings"—gives the phrase "the kingdom of God is inside of you" not in the context of a conversation with the Pharisees, but as one of "the secret sayings which the living Jesus spoke": "Jesus said, 'If those who lead you say to you, "See, the Kingdom is in the sky," then the birds of the sky will precede you. If they say to you, "It is in the sea," then the fish will precede you. Rather, the Kingdom is inside of you, and it is outside of you. When you come to know yourselves, then you will become

known, and you will realize that it is you who are the sons of the living Father. But if you will not know yourselves, you dwell in poverty and it is you who are that poverty.'" *The Nag Hammadi Library in English*, gen. ed. James M. Robinson (New York: Harper & Row, 1977), pp. 117, 118.
16. II Cor. 3:18.
17. I Cor. 15:49.
18. Rev. 10:1.
19. Exod. 3:2–4.
20. Dan. 7:9, 13, 22.
21. Rev. 1:8, 11; 21:6; 22:13.
22. Deut. 6:4.
23. James 4:8.
24. I Sam. 2:27–36.
25. Gen. 3:21.
26. Gen. 3:19.
27. **Kundalini:** lit. "coiled-up serpent"; coiled energy in latency at the base-of-the-spine chakra; the Life-force; the Mother energy. When the Kundalini is awakened (through specific yogic techniques, postures and bija mantras, spiritual disciplines, or intense love of God) it begins to ascend the spinal column through the channels of the *Ida*, *Pingala*, and *Sushumna*, penetrating and activating each of the chakras. The raising of the Kundalini before soul purification and the transmutation of negative momentums of past lives have taken place can result in insanity, demon possession, uncontrolled and inordinate sexual desire or a perversion of the Life-force in all the chakras.

The missing link in the Eastern tradition of raising the Kundalini is the use of the dynamic decree in the science of the spoken Word to draw down the Light of the Father from the I AM THAT I AM and causal body and the realization that the Light of the upper chakras is intended to magnetize the Light from the base of the spine to the heart. The descending Light of the Father uniting in the heart with the Light of the Mother raised up from the base of the spine results in the awareness of the sacred heart and the wholeness of Alpha and Omega.

The Blessed Mother has provided the rosary as a safe method of raising the Mother Light by the fervent heat of love and adoration, without a violent eruption of energy. The cleansing of the aura and chakras with the violet flame also enables the Kundalini to rise gradually without danger. When used in conjunction with the violet flame, the bija mantras to the Divine Mother are safe under the sponsorship of Saint Germain, whose East/West experiment in transmutation, combining dynamic decrees with meditation and the recitation of mantras to the feminine deities, provides a path of acceleration for disciples of both traditions. Saint Germain recommends decrees for the tube of light and protection by Archangel Michael as the foundation for these sessions.

For further teaching from the Ascended Masters and Messengers, see "The Raising-Up of the Energies of the Mother" in Djwal Kul, *Intermediate Studies of the Human Aura*, pp. 78, 95, 108–14; *Pearls of Wisdom*, vol. 26 (1983), no. 38, p. 454 n. 1; Elizabeth Clare Prophet's 1985 European and North American Stump for Saint Germain's Coming Revolution in Higher Consciousness and *Mantras of the Ascended Masters for the Initiation of the Chakras*, 36-page booklet; Mary's Scriptural Rosary for the New Age, in *My Soul Doth Magnify the Lord! New Age Rosary and New Age Teachings of Mother Mary*; *The Fourteenth Rosary: The Mystery of Surrender*, booklet and 2-cassette album; and *A Child's Rosary to Mother Mary*—15-minute scriptural rosaries for children and adults, four 3-cassette albums. See also Chapter 7.

28. **"The form of the fourth is like the Son of God,"** Dan. 3:25: RSV reads, "the appearance of the fourth is like a son of the gods." The Jerusalem Bible reads, "the fourth looks like a son of the gods." Arthur Jeffery explains (*The Interpreter's Bible*, 6:403) that a son of the gods means "an angel, a celestial being, a divinity, such as were commonly called 'sons of the gods.'" Further evidence that Nebuchadnezzar thought the fourth figure was an angel is found later in the chapter when he says, "Blessed be the God of

Shadrach, Meshach, and Abednego, who hath sent his angel, and delivered his servants" (Dan. 3:28).

Whether the fourth appeared as an angelic being or as the Son of God, the lesson is well taken that the Christic Presence reflects through the etheric body the highest patterns of the heavens that are to be outpictured in the lower three. The story illustrates the personification of the Light descending as the intercessor in the plight of the three Hebrew boys, who symbolize the mental, emotional, and physical bodies of man. The updated translation of RSV and Jerusalem Bible neither diminish nor alter our understanding of the passage.

29. **Electronic belt:** The momentums of untransmuted karma in orbit around the 'nucleus' of the synthetic self (or carnal mind) form what looks like an 'electronic belt' of misqualified energy around the lower portion of man's physical body. Diagrammed at the point of the solar plexus, extending from the waist downward in a negative spiral to below the feet, this conglomerate of human creation forms a dense forcefield resembling the shape of a kettledrum. Referred to as the realm of the subconscious or the unconscious, the electronic belt contains the records of unredeemed karma from all embodiments. Each day, according to the law of cycles, a certain portion of this energy returns to the individual for transmutation. See "Our God Is a Consuming Fire," in Mark L. Prophet and Elizabeth Clare Prophet, *Climb the Highest Mountain: The Path of the Higher Self, The Everlasting Gospel,* Book I (Livingston, Mont.: Summit University Press, 1972), chap. 6, and table, "Flame Color-Qualities of the Seven Rays and Their Perversions"; Elizabeth Clare Prophet, "The Psychology of Wholeness: The Karmic Clock" delivered at *Higher Consciousness: A Conference for Spiritual Freedom,* July 2, 1976.

30. **Enoch taken up to ten heavens:** See Elizabeth Clare Prophet, *Forbidden Mysteries of Enoch: The Untold Story of Men and Angels* (Livingston, Mont.: Summit University Press, 1983), pp. 370–84.

31. Mark 16:19; Col. 3:1; Heb. 10:12.
32. I Thess. 4:16, 17. See Jesus Christ, "The Second Advent: 'The Day of Vengeance of Our God,'" in *Pearls of Wisdom*, vol. 26 (1983), no. 43, pp. 511–19.
33. John 14:2, 3.
34. Heb. 9:23, 24.
35. "... Yet in my flesh shall I see God," Job 19:26: Controversy surrounds the translation of this verse. Most scholars agree that the Hebrew text of the first half, which the KJV renders "and though after my skin worms destroy this body" and the RSV as "And after my skin has been thus destroyed," is corrupt—i.e., has been distorted from its original meaning and thus is impossible to translate correctly. They say the second half of the verse is probably better Hebrew, but its meaning remains as elusive as its translation. One source of confusion is the preposition *min*, which can mean "from within" or "from without." Thus the KJV renders the clause "yet *in my flesh* shall I see God" and the RSV "then *without my flesh* I shall see God."

    The Jerusalem Bible says in an explanatory note that the entire verse is corrupt and that the various Bible manuscripts differ widely. The Vulgate, a Latin version of the Bible prepared by St. Jerome in the fourth century, gives the verse as "At the last day I shall rise from the earth and be clothed in my skin again; and in my flesh I shall see my God." Perhaps it was inevitable that the Church Fathers would translate this verse in accordance with Christian doctrine. In light of the discrepancies among the manuscripts, the Jerusalem Bible gives the verse as: "After my awaking, he will set me close to him, and from my flesh I shall look on God." "There is no approach to agreement as to the meaning of this verse," says E. F. Sutcliffe, who suggests rearranging the words to get meaning out of them: "Should my skin be flayed from my flesh, even after this I shall see God" (*A Catholic Commentary on Holy Scripture* [New York: Thomas Nelson and Sons, 1953], pp. 431–32).

    The difficulty in translation lies in the implication

of the phrase "in my flesh." Will Job see God before or after death? If after, in the spirit or in the flesh? Samuel Terrien in *The Interpreter's Bible* (3:1055–56) leans toward translating the crucial phrase as "in my flesh" since "there is no doubt that when used with a verb expressing vision or perception, the same preposition [*min*] refers to the point of vantage, the locale from which or through which the function of sight operates," as in "Yahweh looketh from [*min*] heaven,...from [*min*] the place of his habitation (Ps. 33:13, 14)." Terrien goes on to say that this translation possibly infers that Job believed he would in some way receive new flesh after death "for the specific purpose of the divine-human interview."

This verse is meant to tell of Job's hope of incarnating the Universal Christ image. But scholars have been unable to escape orthodox mind-sets and thus have had an ongoing problem in translation. Perhaps the Hebrew was originally corrupted by a manuscript copyist who determined to change it to what he perceived the meaning to be. From Genesis to Revelation, the Bible shows the path of the gradual process of the incarnation of the Word, or the Christ. It was Job's glimpsing of this path that bound him in the faith that one day, in his very flesh, he would realize the Son of God.

36. Rev. 22:1.
37. See Djwal Kul, *Intermediate Studies of the Human Aura* (Livingston, Mont.: Summit University Press, 1976), pp. 38–47.
38. Luke 1:80; 2:40.
39. Aimee Semple McPherson, "Fling Wide the Pearly Gates."
40. Max Heindel takes up the subject of the loosing of the **silver cord** at death in *The Rosicrucian Cosmo-Conception* (1906; reprint, Pasadena, Calif.: Wood and Jones, 1974), pp. 97–102.
41. Charles A. Lindbergh, *Autobiography of Values* (New York: Harcourt Brace Jovanovich, 1978), pp. 394–95.
42. Gen. 5:3–32.

43. The Great Divine Director, "The Mechanization Concept," in *Pearls of Wisdom*, vol. 8 (1965), no. 14 (Livingston, Mont.: Summit University Press, 1980), pp. 72–73.
44. Matt. 7:7, 11; John 15:7, 16; 16:23, 24; I John 3:22; James 4:3.
45. See *Saint John of the Cross on the Living Flame of Love*, for **the alchemical marriage** on earth as in heaven, taught by Mark L. Prophet and Elizabeth Clare Prophet. This 8-cassette album of indispensable teaching on the soul's mystical experience in Christ offers an in-depth study of *Living Flame of Love*—the literary and religious masterpiece penned by Saint John of the Cross in the sixteenth century—with penetrating insights into how to get beyond the burdens of personal karma and psychology in preparation for the Divine Encounter.
46. Saint Germain, *Pearls of Wisdom*, vol. 10 (1967), no. 7; "A Valentine from Saint Germain," in *Saint Germain On Alchemy: For the Adept in the Aquarian Age* (Livingston, Mont.: Summit University Press, 1985), pp. 350–52.
47. I Pet. 3:4.
48. Rom. 7:22; Eph. 3:16; I Pet. 3:4.
49. Exod. 28:36; 39:30; Zech. 14:20, 21.
50. For Saint Germain's teaching on the scientific and controlled release of energy from Spirit to Matter through the thoughtform of the Maltese cross—"a thought and energy matrix whereby the ill effects of personal and planetary karma can be brought under control"—see "A Trilogy On the Threefold Flame of Life: **The Alchemy of Power, Wisdom and Love**" in *Saint Germain On Alchemy: For the Adept in the Aquarian Age* (Livingston, Mont.: Summit University Press, 1985), pp. 265–345.
51. Hab. 1:13.
52. Jer. 23:6; 33:16.
53. Matt. 25:21, 23; Luke 19:17–19.
54. John 3:13.
55. Col. 3:3.
56. Col. 2:9, 10.
57. Acts 1:9–11.

58. Prov. 4:7.
59. I Cor. 15:41, 42.
60. I Cor. 10:31. The understanding of the principle of dedicating one's life and service "to the glory of God" and acknowledging Him as the source ("I can of mine own self do nothing.... The Father that dwelleth in me, he doeth the works," John 5:30; 14:10) was given to Saint Catherine of Siena (1347–1380) during the heights of her intimate communion with God, which were epitomized in her great mystical treatise, the *Dialogue*. This fundamental truth inspired in Catherine the humility and the conviction that enabled her to confront head-on the forces threatening the Church in the turbulent fourteenth century, when she acted as peacemaker and unofficial diplomat, traveling widely and addressing hundreds of letters to the prelates and sovereigns of the day.

In the *Dialogue*—conversations with God the Father dictated by Catherine to her secretaries during a five-day state of ecstasy—the Father explained to his "dearest daughter," as he often called her, that "the root of discretion is a real knowledge of self and of My goodness, by which the soul immediately, and discreetly, renders to each one his due. Chiefly to Me in rendering praise and glory to My Name, and in referring to Me the graces and the gifts which she sees and knows she has received from Me; and rendering to herself that which she sees herself to have merited, knowing that she does not even exist of herself, and attributing to Me, and not to herself, her being, which she knows she has received by grace from Me, and every other grace which she has received besides....

"The tree of love feeds itself on humility, bringing forth from its side the off-shoot of true discretion, in the way that I have already told thee, from the heart of the tree, that is the affection of love which is in the soul, and the patience, which proves that I am in the soul and the soul in Me. This tree then, so sweetly planted, produces fragrant blossoms of virtue, with many scents of great variety, inasmuch as the soul renders fruit of grace and of utility to her neighbour, according to the zeal of those who come to receive fruit from My servants; and to Me she renders the sweet odour of glory and praise to My Name, and so fulfils the object of her creation" (Algar Thorold trans., *The Dialogue of the Seraphic Virgin Catherine of Siena* [Rockford, Ill.: Tan Books and Publishers, 1974], pp. 51–52, 54).

Biographer Igino Giordani records that "on another occasion while she was praying—as she herself related to several spiritual advisers—Jesus Christ appeared to her and asked: 'Do you know, daughter, who you are and who I am? If you knew these two things, you would be blessed. You are that which is not; I am He who is. If you have this knowledge in your soul, the enemy can never deceive you; you will escape all his snares; you will never consent to anything contrary to my commandments; and without difficulty you will acquire every grace, every truth, every light.'... With that lesson Catherine became fundamentally learned: she was founded upon a rock; there were no more shadows. *I, nothing; God, All. I, nonbeing; God, Being*" (Igino Giordani, *Saint Catherine of Siena—Doctor of the Church*, trans. Thomas J. Tobin [Boston: Daughters of St. Paul, 1980], pp. 35, 36).

61. Matt. 6:20.
62. Portia in Shakespeare, *Merchant of Venice*, act 4, sc. 1, lines 183–86.
63. Luke 8:43–48.
64. Josh. 1:9.
65. Ps. 139:8–10.
66. Zech. 2:8.
67. Exod. 13:21, 22.
68. Exod. 14:19.
69. Zech. 3.
70. Mic. 4:4.
71. Jer. 31:34; Heb. 8:11.
72. Zech. 2:1, 5, 10, 11.

Chapter Seven THE INTEGRATION OF THE CHAKRAS

1. Exod. 3:2.
2. Job 22:25, 27, 28.
3. Exod. 3:14, 15.
4. Matt. 5:37.
5. Matt. 12:36, 37.
6. From *Spring Session M* by Missing Persons. © 1982 Capitol Records, Inc.
7. Ps. 19:14.
8. Matt. 6:22.
9. Matt. 26:11; Mark 14:7; John 12:8.

For further teaching from the Ascended Masters and Messengers on the **chakras,** with color illustrations, visualizations, and meditations, see Djwal Kul, *Intermediate Studies of the Human Aura*; Elizabeth Clare Prophet, *Mother's Chakra Meditations and the Science of the Spoken Word*, 8-cassette album; and Gautama Buddha, "The Prayer Wheel of the Crown Chakra," in *Kuan Yin Opens the Door to the Golden Age: The Path of the Mystics East and West*, Book II, Pearls of Wisdom, vol. 25 (1982), pp. 327–30, also available on *The Seventh Commandment: Thou Shalt Not Commit Adultery*, 2-cassette album.

Chapter Eight THE ETERNAL VERITIES

1. II Chron. 32:7, 8; Jer. 17:5.
2. Luke 10:29–37.
3. Matt. 18:12, 13; Luke 15:4–7.
4. John 10:11–15.
5. Matt. 19:19; Mark 12:31; Luke 10:25–28.
6. I Cor. 11:24.
7. Exod. 3:14.
8. Ps. 103:15, 16.
9. I John 4:18.
10. See Mal. 3.
11. Gen. 3:19; "Life is real! Life is earnest! / And the grave is not its goal; / Dust thou art, to dust returnest, / Was not

spoken of the soul," Henry Wadsworth Longfellow, "A Psalm of Life," stanza 2.
12. Gen. 1:26, 27.
13. John 8:58.
14. John 1:9.
15. Gen. 3:21.
16. I Cor. 13:9, 10, 12.
17. Matt. 10:9, 10; Mark 6:8; Luke 9:3; 10:4.
18. John 10:10–18.
19. II Cor. 3:18.
20. Acts 2:2.
21. John 1:14.
22. Acts 17:28, 29; Rom. 8:16, 17; Gal. 4:7.
23. Mal. 3:1.
24. John 11:27.
25. **Golem:** Hebrew for embryonic or incompletely developed substance, shapeless matter (used in the Bible, Ps. 139:16: "Thine eyes did see my *substance, yet being unperfect*"). In Jewish folklore, a robotlike servant made of clay and brought to life by pronouncing the sacred name of God over its form, writing God's name on a piece of paper and putting it in the golem's mouth, or inscribing the word for truth *(emeth)* on its forehead. If the paper or inscription were removed, the golem would be reduced to a pile of clay. In medieval times, the belief in the creation of golems was common and was attributed to various rabbis throughout Europe. In fact, this belief was so strong that Jewish scholar Rabbi Zvi Ashkenazi seriously debated the question of whether or not a golem could be included as part of a minyan (quorum of 10 adult men required to be present for a religious service). Belief in golems was also widespread among the Jews of Eastern Europe during the nineteenth century.

    The golem of the early legends, though unable to speak, was a perfect servant that fulfilled all his master's orders. Starting in the sixteenth century, he was characterized as the protector of persecuted Jews. It was not until the seventeenth century that the Frankensteinlike golem—who in some versions of the tale grew larger in size each day—was portrayed as a physical threat. In some earlier versions of the legend, the golem is seen as dangerous not because of his potential for violence but because he poses the threat of idolatry. For example, in one thirteenth-century legend the golem supposedly created by Jeremiah and Ben Sira, this time endowed with the faculty of speech, warns the two men that their followers may begin to worship them for their seemingly extraordinary powers in bringing the clay man to life. In one variation of this story, the golem himself removes a letter from the words inscribed on his forehead—*YHWH Elohim Emeth*, or "God is truth"—thereby changing *truth* to the word *dead (meth)*. The resulting blasphemy, "God is dead," is a clear message to the golem's creators. As in most of the legends, man triumphs over golem; Jeremiah heeds the warning and destroys his creation.

The most famous golem legend, which has several different variations and has inspired novelists and playwrights, is that of Rabbi Judah Loew (or Löw) of Prague (c. 1520–1609), a historical figure who was a practitioner of the Kabbalah and a Talmudic scholar. He is said to have created a clay man and endowed him with life in order to defend the Jews of Prague from superstitious Christians who accused them of using the blood of Christian babies to bake their matzohs (unleavened bread). The golem served as the rabbi's agent and successfully apprehended those who were spreading the false rumor. He would perform tasks for Rabbi Loew during the week, and every Friday evening the rabbi would turn him back into a heap of clay by removing the inscription from his forehead, because all creatures are supposed to rest on the Sabbath (or, as another version of the legend goes, because the rabbi feared that the golem would profane the Sabbath).

One Friday, however, the rabbi forgot to do this and the golem turned into a dangerous wildman just before the Sabbath began. Rabbi Loew pursued and finally caught up to his golem run amok, tore from his forehead the sacred name of God, and never brought him back to life again. Rabbi Loew's story was the basis for Gustav Meyrink's famous novel *Der Golem* (1915), a German silent film based on Meyrink's novel (1920) which served as an archetype for later films on the *Frankenstein* theme, and the play by H. Leivick, *The Golem: A Dramatic Poem in Eight Scenes* (1921). See Isaac Bashevis Singer, "The Golem Is a Myth for Our Time," *New York Times*, 12 August 1984; Arnold L. Goldsmith, *The Golem Remembered, 1909–1980: Variations of a Jewish Legend* (Detroit: Wayne State University Press, 1981), pp. 15–20; Gershom Scholem, *On the Kabbalah and Its Symbolism*, trans. Ralph Manheim (New York: Schocken Books, 1969), pp. 180, 199, 202–3; *The Universal Jewish Encyclopedia*, s.v. "Golem."

26. **"Divine Us"** refers to the Elohim (plural of Heb. *'Eloah*, God), one of the Hebrew names of God, or of the gods; used in the Old Testament about 2,500 times, meaning "Mighty One" or "Strong One." *Elohim* is a uniplural noun referring to the twin flames of the Godhead. When speaking specifically of either the masculine or feminine half, the plural form is retained because of the understanding that one half of the Divine Whole contains and is the androgynous Self (the Divine Us). The seven mighty Elohim and their feminine counterparts are the builders of form; hence, Elohim is the name of God used in the first verse of the Bible, "In the beginning God created the heaven and the earth." The Elohim are also "the seven Spirits of God" named in Revelation (1:4; 3:1; 4:5; 5:6), and the "morning stars" which sang together in the beginning, as the LORD revealed to his servant Job (38:7). See *Spoken by Elohim*, Pearls of Wisdom, vol. 21 (Livingston, Mont.: Summit University Press, 1978); *The Seven Elohim in the Power of the Spoken Word*, 4-cassette album, The Summit Lighthouse.
27. I Kings 4:25; Mic. 4:4, 5; Zech. 3:10.
28. Gen. 2:9; 3:22, 24; Rev. 2:7; 22:2, 14.
29. John 15:1, 4, 5.

30. Jer. 23:5; 33:15; Zech. 3:8; 6:12.
31. Rev. 14:6.
32. For further insights into the long-hidden history of these fallen ones, see *The Lost Teachings of Jesus*, Books Three and Four; the Great Divine Director, *The Mechanization Concept: Mysteries of God on the Creation of Mechanized Man*, Pearls of Wisdom, vol. 8 (1965), nos. 3–26 (Livingston, Mont.: Summit University Press, 1980), pp. 9–142; and Elizabeth Clare Prophet, *Forbidden Mysteries of Enoch: The Untold Story of Men and Angels* (Livingston, Mont.: Summit University Press, 1983).
33. **Lemuria:** Mu, the lost continent of the Pacific which, according to the findings of James Churchward, archaeologist and author of *The Lost Continent of Mu*, extended from north of Hawaii three thousand miles south to Easter Island and the Fijis and was made up of three areas of land stretching more than five thousand miles from east to west. He estimates that Mu was destroyed approximately twelve thousand years ago by the collapse of the gas chambers which upheld the continent. See *The Lost Continent of Mu* (1931; reprint, New York: Paperback Library Edition, 1968). **Atlantis:** See *The Lost Teachings of Jesus*, Book One, p. 264 n. 42.
34. Matt. 8:12; 22:13; 25:30.
35. Heb. 10:26, 27.
36. Acts 10:42; II Tim. 4:1; I Pet. 4:5.
37. Rom. 8:25; II Thess. 3:5.
38. II Pet. 2:17; Jude 13.
39. *Encyclopaedia Britannica*, 11th ed.: "**Saint-Germain, Comte de** (*c.* 1710–*c.* 1780) called *der Wundermann*, a celebrated adventurer who by the assertion of his discovery of some extraordinary secrets of nature exercised considerable influence at several European courts. Of his parentage and place of birth nothing is definitely known; the common version is that he was a Portuguese Jew, but various surmises have been made as to his being of royal birth. It was also stated that he obtained his money, of which he had abundance, from acting as spy to one of the

European courts. But this is hard to maintain. He knew nearly all the European languages, and spoke German, English, Italian, French (with a Piedmontese accent), Portuguese and Spanish.

"Grimm affirms him to have been the man of the best parts he had ever known. He was a musical composer and a capable violinist. His knowledge of history was comprehensive, and his accomplishments as a chemist, on which he based his reputation, were in many ways real and considerable. He pretended to have a secret for removing flaws from diamonds, and to be able to transmute metals. The most remarkable of his professed discoveries was of a liquid which could prolong life, and by which he asserted he had himself lived 2000 years.

"After spending some time in Persia, Saint-Germain is mentioned in a letter of Horace Walpole's as being in London about 1743, and as being arrested as a Jacobite spy and released. Walpole says: 'He is called an Italian, a Spaniard, a Pole; a somebody that married a great fortune in Mexico and ran away with her jewels to Constantinople; a priest, a fiddler, a vast nobleman.'

"At the court of Louis XV., where he appeared about 1748, he exercised for a time extraordinary influence and was employed on secret missions by Louis XV.; but, having interfered in the dispute between Austria and France, he was compelled in June 1760, on account of the hostility of the duke of Choiseul, to remove to England.

"He appears to have resided in London for one or two years, but was at St. Petersburg in 1762, and is asserted to have played an important part in connexion with the conspiracy against the Emperor Peter III. in July of that year, a plot which placed Catherine II. on the Russian throne. He then went to Germany, where, according to the *Mémoires authentiques* of Cagliostro, he was the founder of freemasonry, and initiated Cagliostro into that rite.

"He was again in Paris from 1770 to 1774, and after frequenting several of the German courts he took up his residence in Schleswig-Holstein, where he and the Landgrave

Charles of Hesse pursued together the study of the 'secret' sciences. He died at Schleswig in or about 1780–1785, although he is said to have been seen in Paris in 1789.

"Andrew Lang in his *Historical Mysteries* (1904) discusses the career of Saint-Germain, and cites the various authorities for it. Saint-Germain figures prominently in the correspondence of Grimm and of Voltaire. See also Oettinger, *Graf Saint-Germain* (1846); F. Bulaü, *Geheime Geschichten und räthselhafte Menschen*, Band i. (1850–1860); Lascelles Wraxall, *Remarkable Adventures* (1863); and U. Birch in the *Nineteenth Century* (January 1908)."

See Elizabeth Clare Prophet, "The Wonderman of Europe," in *Saint Germain On Alchemy: For the Adept in the Aquarian Age* (Livingston, Mont.: Summit University Press, 1985), pp. vii-xxvii; I. Cooper-Oakley, *The Comte de St. Germain: The Secret of Kings* (London: The Theosophical Publishing House Limited, 1912); Irene Tetzlaff, *Unter den Flügeln des Phönix: Der Graf von Saint Germain* (Marshchalkenzimmern, Schwarzwald: Lichthort-Verlag, n.d.).

40. Job 22:27; Ps. 91:15; Isa. 65:24; Jer. 33:3.
41. Isa. 55:1.

Chapter Nine A CONTINUATION OF OPPORTUNITY

1. Job 38:7.
2. I Kings 19:11, 12.
3. Heb. 9:23.
4. Franz Hartmann, *The Life and Doctrines of Jacob Boehme the God-Taught Philosopher: An Introduction to the Study of His Works* (Boston: Occult Publishing Co., 1891), p. 204.
5. *As the Flower Sheds its Fragrance: Diary Leaves of a Devotee* (Calcutta: Shree Shree Anandamayee Charitable Society, 1983), p. 8.
6. Chandravail, *Matri Darshan: Ein Photo-Album uber Shri Anandamayi Ma* (W. Germany: Mangalam Verlag S. Schang, 1983), [p. 55].
7. *As the Flower*, p. 10.

8. Paramahansa Yogananda, *Autobiography of a Yogi* (1946; reprint, Los Angeles: Self-Realization Fellowship, 1975), pp. 249–54.
9. Ibid., p. 522.
10. *As the Flower*, p. 127.
11. Brother Lawrence, *The Practice of the Presence of God* (Mount Vernon: Peter Pauper Press, 1963), pp. 6–7.
12. Bithika Mukerji, *From the Life of Sri Anandamayi Ma*, 2d ed., vol. 1 (Calcutta: Shree Shree Anandamayee Charitable Society, 1983), p. 5.
13. Lawrence, *Practice of the Presence*, p. 20.
14. Ibid., p. 25.
15. *Encyclopaedia Britannica* (1973), s.v. "Ramakrishna."
16. David Godman, ed., *Be As You Are: The Teachings of Sri Ramana Maharshi* (Boston: Arkana, 1985), back cover.
17. Ibid., p. 12.
18. *As the Flower*, pp. 128–29.
19. Mukerji, *Sri Anandamayi Ma*, p. 85.
20. Henry Wadsworth Longfellow, *The Song of Hiawatha*, "The Peace-Pipe."
21. Pss. 86:7; 91:15; Isa. 30:19; 58:9; 65:24; Jer. 33:3.
22. Acts 10:42; II Tim. 4:1; I Pet. 4:5.
23. Matt. 25:32, 33.
24. Rev. 9:6.
25. Gen. 15:17.
26. Seneca, *Ad Lucilium Epistulae Morales*, trans. Richard M. Gummere (Cambridge, Mass.: Harvard University Press, 1934), p. 17.
27. Kahlil Gibran, *The Prophet* (New York: Alfred A. Knopf, 1969), p. 78.
28. John 8:23.
29. Dan. 12:1.
30. Josh. 5:13–15.
31. **The Lords of Karma:** The seven ascended beings who comprise the Karmic Board, which dispenses justice to this system of worlds, adjudicating karma, mercy, and judgment on behalf of every lifestream. All souls must pass before the Karmic Board before and after each

incarnation on earth, receiving their assignment and karmic allotment for each lifetime beforehand and the review of their performance at its conclusion. Acting in consonance with the individual I AM Presence and Christ Self, the Karmic Board determines when the soul has earned the right to be free from the wheel of karma and the round of rebirth. See the following series by the Lords of Karma in *A Prophecy of Karma to Earth and Her Evolutions: From the Last Days of Atlantis to the Present Era*, Pearls of Wisdom, vol. 23, nos. 6, 8–13 (Livingston, Mont.: Summit University Press, 1980), pp. 25–32, 41–74.

32. Gen. 2:18.
33. I Cor. 15:51, 52.
34. Ps. 8:5; Heb. 2:7.
35. Isa. 14:12–17; Rev. 12:4, 7–9.
36. Job 38:7.
37. Rev. 4:8; 5:13.
38. Rev. 12:12.
39. Ps. 103:15, 16.
40. Gen. 2:15–17; 3.
41. Luke 12:15.
42. **Twin flames:** See *The Lost Teachings of Jesus*, Book One, p. 267 n. 5.
43. Matt. 6:23.
44. **Nephilim** (Hebrew for "those who fell" or "those who were cast down," from the Semitic root *naphal* 'to fall'): A biblical race of giants or demigods, referred to in Genesis 6:4 ("There were *giants* in the earth in those days..."); the fallen angels who were cast out of heaven into the earth (Rev. 12:7–9). Zecharia Sitchin concludes from his study of ancient Sumerian texts that the Nephilim were an extraterrestrial race who "fell" to earth (landed) in spacecraft 450,000 years ago. See Elizabeth Clare Prophet, *Forbidden Mysteries of Enoch: The Untold Story of Men and Angels* (Livingston, Mont.: Summit University Press, 1983), pp. 61–67; The Great Divine Director, "The Mechanization Concept," in *Pearls of*

    Wisdom, vol. 8, no. 15 (Livingston, Mont.: Summit University Press, 1965), p. 80; Zecharia Sitchin, "The Nefilim: People of the Fiery Rockets" in *The 12th Planet* (New York: Avon Books, 1976), pp. 128–72, 410. See also *The Lost Teachings of Jesus*, Book Four, p. 309 n. 60.
45. Dan. 5:25–27, 30.
46. Dan. 7:9, 13, 22.
47. **Lemuria:** See p. 299 n. 33.
48. Matt. 10:5–8.
49. **Laggards:** Those who lag behind the evolutions of their planets; specifically souls assigned to earth who had failed to fulfill their divine plan on schedule on their home star, Maldek, and have continued to lag behind their own God-ordained destiny as well as that of the lifewaves of earth, among whom they continue to reembody. See the Great Divine Director, "The Future of a Planet Read from the Scroll of Cosmic History," in *Pearls of Wisdom*, vol. 17, no. 5 (Livingston, Mont.: Summit University Press, 1974), pp. 19–20; Mark L. Prophet and Elizabeth Clare Prophet, "The Coming of the Laggards," in *Climb the Highest Mountain: The Path of the Higher Self, The Everlasting Gospel*, Book I (Livingston, Mont.: Summit University Press, 1972), Chapter 3.
50. Rev. 3:7.
51. Rev. 3:8, 10–12.
52. II Tim. 2:15.
53. Heb. 8:8–12.
54. Frank Dandridge, "Korea's 2½-year-old Genius," *Look*, 7 February 1967.
55. Rachel Carson, *Silent Spring* (Cambridge, Mass.: The Riverside Press, 1962).
56. Bernarr Macfadden, ed., *The Encylopedia of Health and Physical Culture*, 11th ed., 8 vols. (New York: Macfadden Book Company, 1937), 5:1923.
57. Matt. 26:6–13; Mark 14:3–9; John 12:3–8.
58. **Cosmic clock:** A device used to chart the cycles of the soul's karma and initiations on the twelve lines of the clock

under the twelve hierarchies of the Great Central Sun. See Elizabeth Clare Prophet, "The Cosmic Clock: Psychology for the Aquarian Man and Woman," in *The Great White Brotherhood in the Culture, History and Religion of America* (Livingston, Mont.: Summit University Press, 1976), pp. 173–206; *The ABC's of Your Psychology on the Cosmic Clock: Charting the Cycles of Karma and Initiation*, 8-cassette album, The Summit Lighthouse.

59. Brutus in Shakespeare, *Julius Caesar*, act 4, sc. 3, lines 215–18, 220–21.*
60. Matt. 24:23–26; Mark 13:21, 22; Luke 21:8.
61. Luke 17:20, 21.
62. John 10:1–18.
63. Rev. 13:8.
64. Gen. 14:17–20; Heb. 7:1–3.
65. John 8:24, 28; 13:19.
66. John 1:14, 18; 3:16, 18; I John 4:9.
67. Jer. 23:6; 33:16.
68. Col. 1:27.
69. John 1:1, 3; 10:30; 8:58.
70. Ian Wilson, *Jesus: The Evidence* (New York: Harper & Row, 1984), p. 162.
71. Ibid.
72. Will Durant, *Caesar and Christ*, vol. 3 of *The Story of Civilization* (New York: Simon & Schuster, 1944), p. 660; Bernhard Lohse, *A Short History of Christian Doctrine*, trans. F. Ernest Stoeffler (Philadelphia: Fortress Press, 1978), pp. 48–49.
73. Wilson, *Jesus: The Evidence*, p. 166.
74. P. Schaff and H. Wace, eds., *A Select Library of Nicene and Post-Nicene Fathers of the Christian Church* (Grand Rapids, Mich.: Wm. B. Eerdmans Publishing Co., 1979), 2d ser., 14:3.
75. Lohse, *Christian Doctrine*, p. 52; Kenneth Scott Latourette, *A History of Christianity, Vol. I: to A.D. 1500* (New York: Harper & Row, 1975), p. 155.

---

*All references to Shakespeare's plays are taken from *The Complete Signet Classic Shakespeare* (New York: Harcourt Brace Jovanovich, 1972).

76. Schaff and Wace, *Nicene and Post-Nicene Fathers*, pp. 3–4.
77. Wilson, *Jesus: The Evidence*, p. 168.
78. John 14:28; Wilson, *Jesus: The Evidence*, pp. 168, 176.
79. Durant, *Caesar and Christ*, pp. 661, 664.
80. Latourette, *A History of Christianity*, p. 152.
81. *Origen*, trans. Rowan A. Greer (New York: Paulist Press, 1979), p. 30.
82. Matt. 23.
83. John 8:32.
84. *Rubaiyat of Omar Khayyam*, trans. Edward FitzGerald, 5th ed., quatrain 66.
85. Matt. 7:15.
86. Heb. 9:27.
87. John 3:3–8.
88. **Dweller on the threshold**: A term sometimes used to designate the anti-self, the not-self, the synthetic self, the antithesis of the Real Self; the conglomerate of the self-created ego, ill conceived through the inordinate use of free will, consisting of the carnal mind and a constellation of misqualified energies, forcefields, focuses, and animal magnetism comprising the subconscious mind. The dweller on the threshold is the nucleus of the vortex of energy that forms the 'electronic belt', which contains the cause, effect, record, and memory of human karma in its negative aspect. See p. 303 n. 29, Jesus Christ, "The Awakening of the Dweller on the Threshold," and Elizabeth Clare Prophet, "Christ and the Dweller," in *Pearls of Wisdom*, vol. 26 (1983), nos. 36, 38, pp. 383–91, 429–54.
89. **Prayer in school and in space**: In 1963, the United States Supreme Court outlawed prayer in public schools when it ruled 8-to-1 in *Abington School District v. Schempp* and *Murray v. Curlett* that the reading of verses from the Bible violated "the command of the First Amendment that the government maintain strict neutrality, neither aiding nor opposing religion." The latter case was brought by avowed atheist Madalyn Murray O'Hair, who challenged a school

board rule that required "reading, without comment, a chapter in the Holy Bible and/or use of the Lord's Prayer" each day, even though students could be excused from the exercise. She continued to fight what she called organized religion's "inroads on government policy and practice," and when Apollo 8 astronauts orbiting the earth on Christmas Eve 1968 read the opening verses of Genesis, O'Hair objected on the grounds that the reading linked Christianity to the federal government and was a violation of the constitutional principle of the separation of church and state. After Apollo 11 astronaut Col. Edwin E. Aldrin, Jr. celebrated communion and read some passages from the Bible before stepping onto the moon July 20, 1969, O'Hair asked for an injunction to prohibit American astronauts from praying or reading from the Bible during televised space flights. Her lawsuit was dismissed by the U.S. District Court in Austin, Texas, on December 1, 1969. This decision was affirmed by the U.S. Court of Appeals for the Fifth Circuit on September 22, 1970, and in 1971 the U.S. Supreme Court let stand the lower court's decision by refusing to hear the case.

90. John 14:16, 26; 15:26; 16:7–14.
91. Ps. 46:1.
92. John 20:17.
93. Jer. 31:33, 34.
94. Mic. 4:4, 5.
95. Gen. 10:8–10; 11:1–9.
96. I John 3:1–3.
97. Heb. 13:8.
98. John 21:18.
99. "Jesus Paid It All," refrain. Words by Elvina M. Hall, music by John T. Grape.
100. Heb. 10:26, 27.
101. II Pet. 2:20, 21.
102. Gen. 6:3.
103. I Cor. 9:27.
104. Rev. 2:11; 20:6, 14; 21:8.
105. Mark 10:29, 30.

Index of Scripture

Genesis
- 1:1–3   21–22
- 1:26, 27   95, 173, 216
- 1:26, 28   16, 179
- 2:9   179, 221
- 2:9, 15–17   222–24
- 2:18   215
- 3   143, 222–24
- 3:19   67, 173
- 3:21   67, 175
- 3:22, 24   179, 221
- 5:3–32   78
- 5:25–27   127
- 6:3   277
- 9:28, 29   127
- 10:8–10   272
- 11:1–9   272
- 14:17–20   254
- 15:17   202

Exodus
- 3:2   126
- 3:2–4   60
- 3:2–14   208
- 3:14   166
- 3:14, 15   130
- 13:21, 22   104, 247
- 14:19   105
- 14:24   247
- 28:36   85
- 39:30   85

Leviticus
- 19:18   246

Numbers
- 14:14   247

Deuteronomy
- 4:24   269
- 6:4   62
- 9:3   269

Joshua
- 1:9   103
- 5:13–15   207–8

I Samuel
- 2:27–36   64

I Kings
- 4:25   179
- 19:11, 12   190

I Chronicles
- 16:34, 41   277

Index of Scripture

II Chronicles
5:13	277
7:3, 6	277
20:21	277
32:7, 8	160

Ezra
3:11	277

Nehemiah
9:12, 19	247

Job
19:26	73, 290–91
22:25, 27, 28	130
22:27	186
38:7	189, 219, 298

Psalms
8:5	216
19:14	140
46:1	270
86:7	200
91:15	186, 200
103:15, 16	170, 222
106:1	277
107:1	277
118:1–4, 29	277
136	277
138:8	277
139:8–10	103–4
149:6	235–36

Proverbs
3:12	4
4:7	93
13:24	4

Isaiah
7:14	90
14:12–17	219–21
30:19	200
55:1	186
58:9	200
61:1, 2	45
65:24	186, 200

Jeremiah
17:5	160
23:5	179
23:6	87, 255
31:33	14
31:33, 34	271
31:34	107
33:3	186, 200
33:15	179
33:16	87, 255

Daniel
3:25	68, 288–89
3:28	288–89
5:25–27, 30	228
7:9, 13, 22	60, 230, 270
12:1	207

Micah
4:4	107
4:4, 5	179, 271–72

Habakkuk
1:13	87

Zechariah
2:1, 5, 10, 11	109–10
2:8	104
3	106
3:8	179
3:10	179
6:12	179
14:20, 21	85

Index of Scripture

Malachi
3	171
3:1	177

Matthew
1:23	90, 255
5:3	243
5:18	52
5:28	10
5:37	136
5:48	46
6:10	216
6:20	99
6:22	143
6:23	227
6:33	194
7:7, 11	80
7:9–11	30
7:12	245
7:15	267
7:15–20	224
8:12	182
9:20	48
10:5–8	232–33
10:9, 10	175
12:36, 37	136
13:19, 38	221
14:36	48
15:14	264
16:18	191, 194
18:12, 13	163
19:19	165, 246
22:13	182
22:39	246
23	264
24:23–26	56, 224, 248
24:27, 30	31
24:30	71
25:21, 23	89
25:30	182
25:32, 33	201
26:6–13	242–44
26:11	144–45, 242–44
27:33, 38	7

Mark
6:7–13	232–33
6:8	175
10:29, 30	278
12:31	165
12:31, 33	246
12:38–40	224
13:21, 22	224–25, 248
13:26	71
14:3–9	242–44
14:7	144–45, 243
15:22, 27	7
16:19	70

Luke
1:80	75
2:40	75
4:16–30	45
6:20	243
6:31	245
8:43–48	101
9:1–6	232–33
9:3	175
10:4	175
10:25–28	165
10:27	246
10:29–37	162
11:2	216
11:11–13	30
12:15	223
12:31	194
15:4–7	163
17:20, 21	56, 248–49, 286–87
19:17–19	89
20:46, 47	224
21:8	248
23:32, 33	7

Index of Scripture

John
1:1, 3	255
1:1–3	254
1:9	174
1:14	176, 191
1:14, 18	254–55, 261
3:3–8	267
3:13	90
3:16, 18	254–55, 261
5:30	293–94
6:22–59	263
6:53	37
8:23	179, 206
8:24, 28	254–55
8:32	265
8:58	174, 255
9:4	45
10:1–18	249
10:10–18	175
10:11–15	163
10:12, 13	249
10:22–39	46
10:30	255
11:27	177
12:3–8	242–44
12:8	144–45, 243
12:32	248
13:19	254–55
13:27	10
14:2, 3	70
14:10	293–94
14:16, 26	269
14:23	49
14:26	8–9
14:28	260
15:1, 4, 5	179
15:7, 16	80
15:26	269
16:7–14	269
16:23, 24	80
19:17, 18	7
20:17	271
21:15–17	245
21:18	275

Acts
1:9–11	91
2:2	176
9:1–7	49
10:42	183, 200–201, 219, 270
17:28, 29	176
20:28	245

Romans
7:22	85
7:23	236–37
8:14–17	47
8:16, 17	176
8:25	183
12:19	52
13:9	246

I Corinthians
9:27	277
10:4	191, 194
10:31	98
11:24	166
13:9, 10, 12	175
15:41, 42	96–98
15:47	223
15:49	57
15:51, 52	215

II Corinthians
3:6	201
3:18	57, 175, 176

Galatians
4:7	176
5:14	246

Ephesians
3:16	85
4:26	53

Philippians
2:5	46
2:6	46

Colossians
1:27	255, 273
2:9	48, 90, 91
3:1	70
3:3	91

I Thessalonians
4:16, 17	70

II Thessalonians
2:8	221
3:5	183

II Timothy
2:15	234
4:1	183, 200–201, 219, 270

Hebrews
2:7	216
4:12	235
7:1–3	254
8:8–12	234–35, 269–71
8:11	107
9:23	191
9:23, 24	71
9:27	267
10:12	70
10:26, 27	182, 276
11:5	70
12:6–8	4
12:29	269
13:8	34, 273

James
2:8	246
3:11, 12	46
4:3	80
4:8	64

I Peter
3:4	85
4:5	183, 200–201, 219, 270
5:2	245

II Peter
2:17	184
2:20, 21	276

I John
2:13, 14	221
3:1–3	272–73
3:12	221
3:22	80
4:9	254–55, 261
4:18	170
5:18	221

Jude
13	184

Revelation
1:4	298
1:7	31
1:8, 11	61
1:16	235
1:18	32
2:7	179, 221
2:11	277
3:1	298
3:5	236
3:7	233
3:8, 10–12	233–34
3:19	4
4:5	298

4:8	220	21:6	61
5:6	298	21:8	277–78
5:13	220	21:10, 12, 13, 21, 25	233–34
9:6	201		
10:1	59	21:27	236
12:4, 7–9	181, 219–21	22:1	74
12:12	221	22:2, 14	179, 221
13:8	236, 253	22:13	61
14:6	33, 180		
17:8	236	Enoch*	
17:8, 11	43	47:3	270
20:6, 14	277	48:2	270
20:12, 15	236	70:12	270

*References to the Book of Enoch are from the translation by Richard Laurence. This translation along with all the Enoch texts can be found in *Forbidden Mysteries of Enoch: Fallen Angels and the Origins of Evil* by Elizabeth Clare Prophet (Livingston, Mont.: Summit University Press, 1983).

FOR MORE INFORMATION

For a free catalog of books and tapes on the teachings of the Ascended Masters or for information about Summit University retreats, weekend seminars and quarterly conferences, Mrs. Prophet's cable TV shows, the Keepers of the Flame Fraternity, or the Ascended Masters' library and study center nearest you, write or call: Summit University Press, Box 5000, Livingston, Montana 59047-5000. Telephone: (406) 222-8300.

Reach out for the **LIFELINE TO THE PRESENCE.**
Let us pray with you!
To all who are beset by depression, suicide,
difficulties or insurmountable problems, we say
MAKE THE CALL! (406) 848-7441

Index

Abraham: "Before Abraham was, I AM," 174, 254, 255; seed of, 269–70

Abundant Life, 176

Action(s): the elements that make up our, 15; indelibly stamped on akasha, 11. *See also* Deed(s)

Adultery, 10

Africa, 147–48

America: has enjoyed prosperity, 144; Los Angeles as the soul chakra of, 149; people in, 152

Anandamayi Ma, Sri, 192–93, 195–96, 199

Ancient of Days, 60, 230

Angel(s), 189; "the angel of the LORD," 60, 64, 105; clothed with a cloud and a rainbow on his head, 59; on the head of a pin, 55; of his Presence, 104; the I AM Presence has sealed his promise by his, 109; rebellious, 182; of record, 97; recording, 240–41; reprobate, 181, 224; some spirit guides are really, 78; a third of, 219; those who witnessed, 92; unique, 217; which went before the camp of Israel, 105; who looked like "men in white apparel," 91; who rejected initiation, 220–21; why God created, 209; working with, 38. *See also* Archangels; Fallen angels

Anger, if you go to bed harboring, 53

Animal(s): the human, 27; some walked the earth as, 143

Apathy, 134

Archangels, working with, 38. *See also* Angel(s); Michael, Archangel

Archetypes, 148

Arian controversy, 257–61

Art, today's, 147

Ascended Masters: active and felt today, 181; enlightenment taught by, 184; as graduates cum laude of the Mystery School, 185; helping those earnestly winning our ascension, 186; some spirit guides are really, 78; thread of contact with, 182; willingly tied and obedient to the laws of God, 181. *See also* Great White Brotherhood; Masters

Ascension: goal of, 73; through the violet flame, 51; your, 91

Astrology, 14
Athanasius, 259–60
Atlantean masses, the so-called mindless, 164
Atlantean time warp, 40
Atlantis, Mystery School as in the last days of, 181–82
Atom, the seed, 68
Aura: that belies your size, 102; of a violent orange/black/silver, 152

Baby, at birth, 74–75
Banker, 102
Banks, 145. *See also* Economy
Base-of-the-spine chakra, 68; described and discussed, 152–53. *See also* Chakra(s)
Beatles, 28
Bible: Bible prophecies, 34; as God said it, 278–79. *See also* Paul; Scriptural references; Scriptures
Black magic, 147–48
Blood: cleansing of the, 146–47; venous, 133; violet flame as the, of Christ, 71
Blue: of the causal body, 97, 100–101, 102; a combination of yellow and, 100; and the throat chakra, 135
Blueprint: etheric, 68–69; inner, 78; of life, 122; your molecular and electronic, 24. *See also* Designs; Patterns
Bodies: infested with howling demons, 178; 'plastic' substance of the four, 72; seven, of man, 67, 73; three other, 122; train all four of your, 155. *See also* Body; Four lower bodies
Body: anointing of Jesus', 242; construction of the, 160; physically exhausted, 123; should be kept clean, 24; "Take, eat, this is my Body which is broken for you...," 166; you're not your, 58. *See also* Bodies; Four lower bodies; Physical body; Physical form
Boehme, Jakob, 192
Brain structure, 80
BRANCH, 106–7
Brother Lawrence, 196
Brother's keeper, 88

Caduceus, the winged, 143
California, 149
Capitalism, monopoly, 145
Carrel, Alexis, 238
Carson, Rachel, 239
Causal body: on the Chart, 50; described and discussed, 97–104; the fig tree is the I AM Presence and, 107; records stored in, 69; as an upper body, 67
Cause(s): iron law of, and effect, 144; set in motion, 13, 97; we are obliged to uncreate, 14. *See also* First Cause
Cavemen, mankind descended to, 143
Chakra(s), *illus.* 114–18; activated, 171; if any, is clogged, 125; are the centers for the spiritual fire, 68; attached through the central nervous and endocrine systems, 125; base, 223; the channel connecting the, 153; cleanse, 135; dabbler in this science of the, 155; fallen angels extract the Light from, 227; imbalance within, 136;

Joshua's vision of the, 106–7; light of the, woven into the wedding garment, 77; prana in the seven, 133; Saint Germain has given us a mantra for the cleansing of our, 127–29; solar plexus and the throat are corresponding, 141; on the spinal stalk, 7; states and nations have, 149; taking up of the light from the, 77; thought-forms taken in by, 236; toning of all, 135; whirling with light, 8; you *can* exercise your, 122; within your body, 121–22. *See also* Crown chakra; Seat-of-the-soul chakra; Soul chakra; Third eye; Throat chakra

Change: alchemy of, 24; creative, 130; from day to day, 161; laws of, 25

Chaos, 37

Charity, 163. *See also* Love

Chart, *illus.* 111; clouds of glory depicted in, 71; described, 49–50; given to Joshua, 106–7; of the I AM Presence, 43–45; illustrates that day by day you may put on the Son of God, 90; is a diagram of God's kingdom within you, 49–50, 57; is an illustration of the teaching which Jesus gave to Paul, 47–48; is proof that you *do* have a chance, 47; lower figure in, 66–67; in order to understand the, 95; what the, depicts, 77; if you can understand the, 25–26

Chastening rod, 4

Chatter, idle, 136. *See also* Conversation(s)

Children: experiences of, 29; loved for their intrinsic worth, 62–63; recognize you because you are like them, 60; today, 148

Christ: if, had come a hundred years ago, 33; Christ image, 71–72, 73; Christhood, 88; within every man, 269; and the Father, 258–59, 261; First Coming of, 33; if he was still here ruling everything, 33; "his" Christ as "our" Christ, 71; and his disciples in the Himalayas, 39; human and divine natures in, 261; I AM Presence clothed upon with the personal, 177; image of God is, 173, 174; is ordained to be judge, 183; is our original Self, 57; 'my' Christ is the same as 'his' Christ, 174; Origen's teachings on, 261; original meaning of the word, 90; people don't even think they're good enough to talk to, 168–69; persecuted, 253; as potential, 263; Second Coming of, 31, 32–35; selfsame image of, into which Jesus was changed, 176; Universal, 254–55; was uniquely Jesus, 88; when, is come, 243; "Yea, Lord: I believe that thou art the Christ...," 177; of you, 175, 273; you can have an intimate relationship with him, 48; of your being, 25; your thought/feeling modes born again in the encounter with the Universal, 26. *See also* Cosmic Christ; Emmanuel; Jesus; One Sent; Self; Son; Son(s) of God; Word

Christ Mind, 67–68, 87; plane of the, 70; records stored in your, 69. *See also* Mind

Christ Self, 88–91, 271; behold your beloved, 81; in the Chart, 49–50, 57–58; in clouds of heavenly consciousness, 34; contains the image of your soul and your divine plan, 59; does go before and behind your camp, 105; as the eternal Messiah, 109; etheric body is most like the, 68; as High Priest, 235; is the Mediator, 86–87; Jesus comes to us through the person of our, 71; Jesus was the representative of the, 87; Joshua's vision of the, 106–7; and Paul's teaching to the Romans, 47–48; as saviour, 248; as "Sire," 21; the soul united with the I AM Presence through the, 73; as an upper body, 67; as the Vine, 107, 179; when you are one with your, 102; your Presence answers you through your, 105. *See also* Lord; LORD Our Righteousness; Son; Son(s) of God

Christianity, 255–63

Christs, false, 56

Church(es): Arian controversy in, 257–61; corruption in, 264; history of, 262–63; invaded, 266–67; some people turned off by, 29–30; if this Chart could have been in the Christian, 44; of today, 180; if Truth were taught by, 213. *See also* Preachers; Religion(s)

City Foursquare, 233–34

Co-creator(s): with God, 23, 26; with our Higher Consciousness, 130. *See also* Creator

Coats of skins, 67; reincarnation in new, 72; when we didn't have these, 175

'Cocktail party' mentality, 139

Coequality, of the sons and daughters of God, 62

Color, is especially important, 147

Coming Revolution in Higher Consciousness, 145

Communication, 137, 140; peaceful and loving, 141

'Conscience', the still small voice of, 87

Consciousness: planes of, 69; spectrum of, 79–80; stream of, 20, 46. *See also* Mind

Constantine, and Christianity, 255–61

Conversation(s), 140; "unseemly conversation," 135–36. *See also* Chatter; Gossip; Speech; Talk

Cosmic Christ: in the Great Central Sun, 59; personified in our Christ Self, 48

Cosmic Clock, 246

"Cosmic interval," 83

Creation: a distorted, 149; first fiery breath of, 174

Creator, denial of the, 169. *See also* Co-creator(s)

Criticism, 135; mental, 127; when you're engaged in, 64

Crown chakra, 153; described and discussed, 150–51; is a lotus of violet fire, 129; opened, 7. *See also* Chakra(s)

Crystal: etchings in, 24; and the mist, 9, 10, 14, 17, 25, 28

Crystal cord: continuation of, 59; is today a mere thread, 131; pulsation of, 7; and *silver cord* are synonymous, 74; threefold flame is anchored through, 126; was over nine feet in diameter, 127. *See also* Silver cord

Cursing, 135

Dark ones, 178. *See also* Fallen ones

Darkness: as God's Light misqualified, 235n; "If the Light that is in thee be Darkness...," 227; 'outer darkness', 182

Darwin, Charles, 143

De-signs, are the Deity's signature, 23. *See also* Designs

Dead, and the quick, 168, 183

Death, 153; actual cause of, 77; death wish, 127; what, really is, 238

Decree(s): to Archangel Michael, 207, 208–11; for the binding of lethargy, 245; called "Balance the Threefold Flame in Me," 93–94; the correct use of the throat chakra in, 130; a divine, 21–22; intensify and accelerate energy, 102–3; purification through, 142; scientific use of, 144; "...Thou shalt also decree a thing and it shall be established unto thee...," 130. *See also* Mantra(s)

Deed(s): a good, 97; karma of, 11, 12. *See also* Action(s)

Deity, study what, sires, 23. *See also* God

Demoniac forces, 206

Depression, 134

Desh, 36, 37, 40

Desha, 3

Designs, after the heavenly patterns, 23. *See also* Blueprint; *De-signs*; Patterns

Desire(s), 22, 23; cast aside, 175; esoteric interpretation of the word, 20–21; heat of spiritual, 171; karma of, 15; problem of, 19; purified, 20; that come from "beneath," 179–80; transient, 162

Desire body: as one of the four lower bodies, 67–68; patterns outpictured in the, 69; remade after Christ's image, 71–72. *See also* Emotional bodies; Emotional body; Four lower bodies

Devil, belief in a personal, 211

Dictations, energy flowing through you while listening to, 8. *See also* Teaching(s)

Discipline, self-discipline, 148

Disease, 133, 153

DNA chain, 71

Dominion, 73; take, 16; "Take dominion over the earth," 179; over thy human self, 86

Drug abuse, 151

Drug paraphernalia, 29

Duality, 143

Ecclesiastes, the preacher, 75

Economies, 145

Economy, 144–45; chains of control around our, 151

Ecumenical Council, 257–61; Fifth, 261

Eden: return to, 107; serpent in, 222

Educators, tomorrow's, 149
Egg, manufacture of the, 147
Ego: dies once, 267; the personal, 162; if you do what you do to the glory of your, 98. *See also* Personality; Self
Electronic belt: the lower, 98; what is stored in your, 69
Electronic Presence: of God, 58, 61; of ourselves, 44
Elemental builders of form, 38
Elementals, 86
Elijah, 190
Elohim, 178; working with, 38
Embodiment: before we took, 16; your own comings and goings in and out of, 35. *See also* Lives; Reincarnation
Emmanuel, 90. *See also* Christ
Emotion(s): are intended to amplify the potential of the soul, 142; Christ Mind ought to dominate, 68; ebb and tide of, 161; as *energies in motion*, 142; as energy in motion, 5; expressed through two chakras, 141; a lack of prana can influence the, 134; mastery of, 141–42. *See also* Emotional control; Feeling(s)
Emotional abuse, 12. *See also* Emotional malpractice
Emotional bodies, 72. *See also* Desire body; Emotional body; Four lower bodies
Emotional body, 122, 124. *See also* Desire body; Emotional bodies; Four lower bodies
Emotional control, 124. *See also* Emotion(s)
Emotional malpractice, 127. *See also* Emotional abuse

Endocrine system, chakras attached through, 125
Energy: of the causal body comes down through this silver cord, 102; under control, 81; nervous, 81; we are responsible for, 80; which will ascend to your causal body, 98
Enoch, 69, 70; taken up to the ten heavens, 226
Entities, mass, 206
Etheric body, 122; intricate system of nerve passages in, 133; is the meeting ground of heaven and earth, 70; as one of the four lower bodies, 69. *See also* Etheric sheath; Four lower bodies
Etheric octave, plane, 70; Christ Mind descended to, 87; of the heaven-world, 69–70; where the soul of Light abides, 77
Etheric sheath, 72; the soul 'dressed' in the, 77. *See also* Etheric body
Everlasting Gospel, 33, 34
Evil: and good, 143, 152; relative and Absolute, 225; "Thou art of purer eyes than to behold evil...," 87. *See also* Iniquity; Malice
Evildoers, in whom the divine spark has grown cold, 86. *See also* Fallen ones
Eye: "If thine eye be single...," 143; what the, sees is instantly mirrored in the four lower bodies, 148. *See also* Third eye

Faith, 100, 101
Fall, before the, 127, 143
Fallen angels, 227–29, 277–78;

Cain civilization of, 253; Church invaded by, 266; in embodiment, 180, 182; had worn out grace of the merciful Law, 276; known as "serpents," 222; philosophy fabricated by, 225; purpose of, 224–25; set up some ungodly cause, 240. *See also* Angel(s)

Fallen ones, 181; we became enmeshed with, 230. *See also* Dark ones; Evildoers

False prophets, 56

Fasting, 135, 147

Father: father figure, 148; indwelling with us, 49; "Our Father...," 62; a photograph of our loving, 61. *See also* God

Fear, 126

Feeling(s), 26, 72; true, 142; will lead the head, 5–6; your every, contains your electronic blueprint, 23–24. *See also* Emotion(s)

Fig tree: every man sits under his own, 179; is the I AM Presence and the causal body, 107

Fire body, as one of the four lower bodies, 69. *See also* Etheric body; Four lower bodies

Fire breath, sacred, 174

First Cause, 59

Flame: called "threefold," 126; of God's grace, 171; "put it into the flame," 53; that always was, 173; we must believe in the, 172. *See also* Threefold flame

Fohat, 148

Forgiveness, 74. *See also* Mercy

Four lower bodies: are interrelated, 134; defined and discussed, 66–69; out of alignment, 125; what the eye sees is instantly mirrored in the, 148; when we didn't have these, 175. *See also* Bodies; Body; Emotional body; Etheric body; Mental bodies; Physical body; Physical form

Francis, Saint, 131

Free will, 33

Friendships, 73

Future: can be the way you want it, 18; change the, 25; and past and present, 13, 17; rewrite the past upon the pages of the, 16; we think the, is a great mystery, 17

Gemini mind, 35

Genetic code, 71, 73; chakra which governs, 147

Genetic patterns, transcend, 86

Geometric forms, meditation on perfect, 146

Gestation, during, in the womb, 78

Gibran, Kahlil, 9, 205

Givingness, self-givingness, 167, 168

Glory: "to the glory of God," 98; when we are changed from glory to Glory, 176; why one star differs from another in glory, 98

God: in the absolute sense is not aware of sin, 86–87; Almighty, himself, 104; angry, 265, 278; being a manifestation of, 45; believe that, loves us, 172; can save this world, 232; centers his 'Beingness' in the Great Central Sun, 62;

chance to identify with, 66; covenant with, 218; created man in his own image, 95; the creation that he put here, 27; dead in man, 169; devouring, 37; doesn't intend to roast anybody, 30; "to the glory of God," 98; goes with you, 104; has the power to duplicate his image, 62; "Hear, O Israel: The LORD our God is one LORD!" 62; how you feel about your, 165; human beings suspecting, 226; I AM Presence is the replica of, 96; is aware of us, 164; Jesus taught it was not robbery for the Son of God to make himself equal with, 46; making him prisoner of a law, 274; may assume the form of the man he made, 60; within men, 248; name of, 57; oneness with, 196, 198; ourselves and one another as, 272; "partners with God," 90; paths to, 199; personal, 270, 271; as the positive pole, 215; some challenging, 220; in the still small voice, 190; struggles toward, 29; what name we call him, 200; when you draw nigh to, 64; where is, 56; wrathful, 268; "Yet in my flesh shall I *see* God," 73; in you, 169, 249. *See also* Deity; Father; Godhead; I AM Presence; Son; Trinity

God consciousness, 151

God flame, individualization of the, 36, 88. *See also* Threefold flame

God Presence, is the only part of yourself that is absolutely real, 29. *See also* I AM Presence; Presence

Godhead: dwelling with us bodily, 61; an insult to the, 169; your vibration can be a repellent to the, 64. *See also* God

Golgotha, 15; the place of the skull, 7

Good: "Behold the Good," 146; relative and Absolute, 225; relative perspective of, and evil, 152; seeing the, 144; tree of the knowledge of relative, and evil, 143. *See also* Goodness

Good Samaritan, 162, 164; destined to become the Good Shepherd, 163

Good Shepherd, 163

Goodness, Christ goodness, 171. *See also* Good

Gossip, 135; when you're engaged in, 64

Great Central Sun: explained, 58–59; God centers his 'Be-ingness' in the, 62; silver cord originates in the, 74

Great Divine Director, 78

Great White Brotherhood: active and felt today, 181; Mystery School sponsored by the, 183; one of the purposes of the, 88. *See also* Ascended Masters; Hierarchical orders

Green: of the causal body, 97, 100, 102; of the third eye, 143

Guru/chela relationship, 86

Happiness, experienced by man, 80

Hatred: dangerous, 127; resembles

lead or asphalt, 126; self-hatred, 165, 170
Healing, 100; healing arts, 102
Health, 100, 121, 133; positive ions detrimental to, 134
Heart: a central chamber within the, 83–84; hardness of, 127; heart problems, 133; I AM the Light of the, 85; is a chakra of violet fire, 128; leads the head, 5; light from your I AM Presence must pass through the, 131; a mantra affirming the "I AM" as the Light of your, 86; to think and to feel with our, 6; wisdom which is found within the, 160
Heart chakra: as central and most important chakra, 126–27; exercise of, 144; protection of, 131; visualization of, 129
Heaven: God puts us down here to learn to appreciate, 64–65; heaven-world, 69–70
Heredity, the chakra which governs, 147
Hierarchical orders, 70. *See also* Great White Brotherhood
History: backwards and forwards in, 12; before the dawn of recorded, 178; our own past, 15; a piece of string that represents all known, 9; planetary, 229–30
Hitler, Adolf, 277
Holy Spirit, 50
Hungary, royal house of, 186. *See also* Rakoczy

I AM: means "God in me is," 130, 150; "... THAT I AM," 57. *See also* I AM Presence
I AM Presence, 71, 271–72; Almighty One individualized and personified in your, 25; another name for your God Self, 126; clothed upon with the personal Christ, 177; a description of your, 59; expects us to perform well, 14; explained, 58, 59–60; the fig tree is the, 107; God individualized in your, 104; goes with you everywhere you go, 103; has sealed his promise by his angel, 109; is an individualized expression of our God, 60; is the common denominator, 62; is the omnipresence of the Father where you are, 63; is the replica of God, 96; Joshua's vision of the, 106–7; know who you are in relationship to your, 47; light from your, must pass through the heart, 131; as a limitless Source, 63; looks just like everybody else's, 95; meditation on the, 153; messenger of your, 105; and Paul's teaching to the Romans, 47–48; shall be known by every man, 271; some call the, "Jehovah," 58; the soul united with the, through the Christ Self, 73; that is yours alone, 63; as the Tree of Life, 179; as an upper body, 67; "went before them by day in a pillar of cloud...and by night in a pillar of fire....," 104; will exist forever, 104; and the word *desire*, 20–21; your causal body enfolding the, 96; your Christ Self is begotten of your, 89. *See also* God Presence; I AM; I AM WHO I AM; Presence

"I AM WHO I AM," 166. *See also* I AM Presence

Id-entity, 161

Identity: in God, 166; God-identity, 162; which is indispensable, 164. *See also* Individuality; Selfhood

Image(s), 150; Christ image, 71, 73; of the earthly creature, 27; falling in love with your own, 81; God created man in his own, 95; God has the power to duplicate his, 61; of God individualized, 58; of God is Christ, 173; and likeness of God, 59; *if* man were remade in the, of God, 180; of the Only Begotten of the Father, 85; our true, in Christ, 176; power to re-create yourself in the, of Higher Consciousness, 21; reflected in the soul, 147; of the Son of God, 71; soot that has marred the divine, 175; for the whole of creation, 59; you as a son of God made in the, and likeness of God, 57. *See also* Synthetic image

Individuality, 167. *See also* Identity

Inferiority, intimidation through, 47

Inheritance, divine, 89

Iniquity, the Presence does not behold, 105. *See also* Evil; Sin

Initiation: angels who rejected, 220–21; first step of, 176; path of Christic, 177

Initiator, Christic, 183

Injustice, no, in the universe, 145

Instructors, our most dedicated, 4. *See also* Teacher

Jesus, 56–57; anointing of his body, 242; and the Arian controversy, 257–61; attunement with the message of, 183; believed words were as important as actions, 136; "the Christ," 88; Christ from the beginning, 254; comes to us through the person of our Christ Self, 71; the coming of Christ incarnate in, 107; expressed the Christ Self, 248; as a god, 257; Godhead dwelt bodily in, 263; is here to give you the keys to time and space, 32; is your elder brother, 269; "Jesus paid it all...," 276; and the only begotten Son of the Father, 87–89; personified Christ, 255; portrayed the Divinity, 262; Ramakrishna had visions of, 197; on resurrection morning, 271; said, "I AM the Son of God," 45–46; and Saint Germain are architects of this age, 186; Second Coming of, 33–35, 71; selfsame image of Christ into which, was changed, 176; son of man, 33; "...This same Jesus which is taken up...shall so come in like manner...," 91–92; warned of the mentalists, 264; was uniquely the Christ, 88; was the Word incarnate, 33; and the woman who touched his garment, 101; you can have an intimate relationship with, 48; if you had ascended with Jesus from Bethany's hill, 32; you may not feel the Master Jesus' vibration, 8; you stand

to inherit the same Sonship which, had, 47. *See also* Christ; Son(s) of God; Son of man
Job, 73
John, Gospel of, 260
Joint-heir(s): with Christ, 47, 48; we are, 176
Joshua, 207–8; vision of the Chart given to, 106–7
Judas Iscariot, 10
Judgment, "...a certain fearful looking for of judgment...," 182
Justice, an innate sense of, 160
Justinian I, 261

Kal, 9, 36, 37, 40
Kala, 3
Karma: bondage to the law of, 48; of deeds, 11, 12; is the iron law of cause and effect, 144; karma-making action, 53; law of, 240–41, 250; memorabilia of your human, 98; of neglect, 145; and opportunity, 242; personal, 145; personal and planetary, 214; predictable, 246; reasons why the doctrines of reembodiment and, were knocked out, 263–64; to remove crusty old, 53–54; responsibilities of, 52; those enmeshed in, 233; those unable to pay it all, 277; of thought, 11–12; violet flame for the transmutation of negative, 128; after you get socked by your own, 65; your own race against, 18
Karmic Board, an edict of the, 79. *See also* Lords of Karma
Karmic cycles, 35. *See also* Karma

Karmic involvements, have a magnetism, 14. *See also* Karma
Kārttikeya, 230
Keeper of the Scrolls, 229, 240–41
Kennedy, John, 66
Kindness(es), 165; Christ kindness, 171
Kingdom of God, within you, 26, 56
Knowledge, storehouse of, 99
Kundalini, 68, 153
Kuthumi, 131

L-field, 69
Lamb, which is lost, 163
Law(s): codifications of, 160; dedicated application of the, 155; "One jot or one tittle shall in no wise pass from the law...," 51–52; restraining, of today, 181; you are never above the, 55
Leaders: our past and present, 145; tomorrow's, 149
Lemuria, 182; embodiments back to, 230
Liberty, Goddess of, 268
Life-force: of the base chakra, 153; at the base-of-the-spine chakra, 68; indulgence squanders the, 136
Life span, decrease in the, 79–80. *See also* Longevity
"Lifestream," as a "stream of Life," 46
Light: a blinding, 64; "Let there be Light," 21–22; "If the Light that is in thee be Darkness...," 227; "...Light which lighteth every man that cometh into the world," 174

Lindbergh, Charles, 76
Lives, past, 15, 27. *See also* Embodiment; Reincarnation
Longevity, of antediluvian figures, 127. *See also* Life span
Longfellow, Henry Wadsworth, 200
Lord, 180; encounter with our, 176. *See also* Christ; Christ Self
LORD Our Righteousness, 87, 107. *See also* Christ Self
Lords of Karma, 55; confront you with the record of your energy, 53; know all people, 241; oversee evolutions of earth, 214. *See also* Karmic Board
Los Angeles, 149
Lotus, thousand-petaled, 7, 150
Love, 167; begin with the, of self, 164–65; without expectation, 164; God's quickening, 172; a person of great, 102; pink plume anchors, 83; self-love, 170; steps and stages of, 167; that is yours to give to everybody, 63; and the three-fold flame, 92–93. *See also* Charity
Lucifer, 219–21

Magdalene, Mary, 102, 271
Maha Chohan, 245, 247
Malice, 126. *See also* Evil
Man: the Divine, 95–96; God created, in his own image, 95; hidden, of the heart, 85; his former faculties, 143–44; is estranged, 179; "Man, Know Thyself," 44; who hates himself, 170. *See also* Neighbor; People; Person

Mantra(s): affirming the "I AM" as the Light of your heart, 86; cleanse chakras, 127–29, 135; scientific use of the, 144. *See also* Decree(s)
Martha, 177
Mary, of Bethany, 242
Mary, Mother, 246
Master R., 78n
Masters, 38; once walked amongst us, 8; walked the earth, 178; when in the presence of the, 8. *See also* Ascended Masters
Mastery: maximum, 155; promises of self-mastery, 16; true, 35
Matter, nexus between Spirit and, 59
"Mechanization Concept, The," 78
Mechanization man, 178
Mediator, 87
Mediocrity, 8
Meditation, 135; purification through, 142
Melchizedek, 254
Memory body, 69. *See also* Four lower bodies
Mental bodies: highly developed and manipulative, 152; identity patterns and 'nucleus' of, 72. *See also* Four lower bodies; Mental body; Mind
Mental body, 122; as one of the four lower bodies, 67; patterns outpictured in the, 69. *See also* Four lower bodies; Mental bodies; Mental plane; Mind
Mental plane, 12. *See also* Mental body; Mind
Mercy, 99–100. *See also* Forgiveness

Messenger(s), 34, 181, 230; of your I AM Presence, 105
Methuselah, 80, 127
Michael, Archangel, 206-8; calls to, 101; decree(s) to, 207, 208-11; does go before and behind your camp, 105; those "cast down" by, 220-21. *See also* Archangels
Mind: the Christ Mind ought to dominate, 68; controlling thought of the, 36; corridor of the, of God, 24; of God in man's own mind, 37-38; a lack of prana can influence the, 134; offspring of your, 23; remade after Christ's image, 71; shield of the, 20; that becomes a clear pool, 81; whatever you feed the, 24. *See also* Christ Mind; Consciousness; Mental bodies; Mental body; Mental plane; Subconscious; Superconscious mind; Unconscious
Mist, and the crystal, 9, 10, 14, 17, 25, 28
Moodiness, 134
Moses: and the burning bush, 60; name of God as spoken to, 130
Mother light, 153
Mu. *See* Lemuria
Music: classical, 148; is the barometer of society, 137; perverted, 147. *See also* Rock
Mystery school(s), 180, 181; Ascended Masters as graduates cum laude of the, 185; sponsored by the Great White Brotherhood, 183

Nicaea, ecumenical council in, 257-60
Noah, 127

Omar Khayyam, 266
One Sent, Jesus was the, 87. *See also* Christ
Only Begotten, of the Father, 71, 85, 87, 176. *See also* Son; Son(s) of God
Origen of Alexandria, 261

Parents, 62; tomorrow's, 149
Pastors: false, 185, 228, 249, 267; trying to tell people they're going to Hades, 30. *See also* Church(es); Preachers; Priest
Patterns: heavenly, 23; "...the patterns of things in the heavens...," 71. *See also* Blueprint; Designs
Paul: the Lord converted and personally overshadowed his ministry, 49; teaching which Jesus gave to, 47-48
People: the little, 145, 151; today, 27; two kinds of, 17; who have a certain karma to work out, 149. *See also* Man
Person, as *Pure Son*, 107. *See also* Man
Personality: a developed and powerful, 98; the human, 72. *See also* Ego; Self
Petals: base chakra has four, 153; crown has 972, 150; the heart has twelve, 129; seat of the soul has six, 147; solar plexus has ten, 141; third eye has ninety-six, 143; throat chakra has sixteen, 135
Physical body: cleansing of,

146–47; is only one-quarter of the whole person, 122; is the focus of integration, 68; patterns outpictured in, 69; remade after Christ's image, 71; subject to total dissolution, 72; what causes the threefold flame to "go out" in the, 77. *See also* Body; Four lower bodies; Physical form

Physical form, 102; polarity between the etheric blueprint and, 68–69. *See also* Body; Four lower bodies; Physical body

Pink: of the causal body, 96, 99; in your aura, 102

Pituitary gland, 7

Poor, "with you always...," 243

Power: of God in yourself, 25; to make things happen, 18; and the threefold flame, 92. *See also* Dominion

Prana, defined and discussed, 132–34

Prayer, banned in public schools, 268

Preachers, haven't opened the true meaning of the scriptures, 39. *See also* Church(es); Pastors

Precipitation, the ray for, 100

Preexistence: in heaven, 69; the soul's memory of, 45

Presence, 105; 'in the air' above your physical body, 59; knowledge of the, 44; people have seen this, and thought it was an angel, 59; rays of light from your, 104–5; you have everything you need in the, 74; if you look up at your, 29; above your head varies in its locale, 63–64. *See also* God Presence; I AM Presence

Priest: High, 71; wise and crafty, 264. *See also* Church(es); Pastors

Prophecies, 34

Prophet, The, 9

Prophets, false, 56

Psychology, insight into your personal, 165

Purification: of the mind and the heart, 23; soul-purification, 73

Purity, 97, 153

Purple: of the causal body, 96, 100; and metallic gold, 141

Quick, and the dead, 168, 183

Rakoczy, House of, 78n, 186

Ramakrishna, 197

Rapture, where souls experience the, 71

Records, reproduced lifetime after lifetime, 72

Reincarnation, reembodiment, 250–53, 273–74; to finish what you started, 275; in new coats of skins, 72. *See also* Embodiment; Lives

Resurrection, where souls experience the, 71

Retreat(s): of the Great White Brotherhood, 38; in Transylvania, 78n, 186

Rock, listening to, 39. *See also* Music

Root races, taking embodiment, 214

Royal Teton Council, 230

Royal Teton Retreat, 229

Saint Germain: a great Western adept, 186; has given us a mantra for the cleansing of our chakras, 127–29; taught us about the threefold flame, 83–85; teacher and sponsor of, 78n; "Violet Fire and Tube of Light Decree" dictated by, 108–9

Sarcasm, 135, 139

Satan: religion of, 263; seed of, 221, 263

Scriptural references, 32. *See also* Bible

Scriptures: altered, 264; preachers haven't opened the true meaning of the, 39. *See also* Bible

Seat-of-the-soul chakra, described and discussed, 147–50. *See also* Chakra(s); Soul chakra

Second Coming: of Christ, 31, 32–35; of Jesus, 70–71

Second death, 277

Secret chamber of the heart, threefold flame in the, 68, 74–75

Self: begin with the love of, 164–65; 'black hole' of the not-self, 179–80; Christ is our original, 57; love-exchange from the Real, 167; "Love thy neighbor" as though he were thy, 165; power that derives from the Real, 160; Real and unreal, 170; reflection of your Real, 81; resurrection unto man's highest, 183; in a state of becoming, 161; striving of the self *for* the self, 166; synthetic, made out of the synthetic image, 43; wick of, 170–72; your finite, 66–67; your Higher and lower, 66. *See also* Christ Self; Ego; Personality; Selfhood

Self-denial, 169

Selfhood: impoverished sense of, 185; outside of God, 177. *See also* Identity; Self

Selfishness: the heart is clogged through, 127; that may subsequently become generous, 166

Serpent, in Eden, 222

Sex, idle, 136

Sheep, lost, 232–33

Silver cord: can be expanded, 80; connecting point of the, 84; connecting you to your I AM Presence, 49; energy of the causal body comes down through this, 102; explained and discussed, 73–78; goes with you everywhere you go, 103; love passes through the, 50; virtue descended down the, 101; was as large as the tube of light, 78, 79. *See also* Crystal cord

Sin, 274; doctrine of, 275–76; flame of freedom forgives, 128; God in the absolute sense is not aware of, 86–87. *See also* Iniquity

Sinners, you're not, 185

Solar-plexus chakra, described and discussed, 141–42. *See also* Chakra(s)

Son: and the Father, 258–59, 261; indwelling with us, 49; Jesus and the only begotten, of the Father, 87–89; "only begotten Son," 254; only one, 249. *See also* Christ; Christ

Self; Sonship
Son(s) of God: becoming one with the, 90–91; the Chart illustrates that day by day you may put on the, 90; comes to live in your temple, 33; "the form of the fourth is like the Son of God," 68; greater Glory of the, 176; image of the, 71; Jesus said, "I AM the Son of God," 45; Jesus taught it was not robbery for the, to make himself equal with God, 46; likeness of the, 60, 73; made in the image and likeness of God, 57–58; as sire, 20–21; son of man called himself the, 87–88; "...there's only one Son of God," 173; who came down from heaven, 90. *See also* Christ; Christ Self; Sonship
Son of man: became both the office and the mantle, 88; called himself the Son of God, 87–88; Jesus as the, 33; lesser glory of the, 176; we love so dearly, 73; "except ye eat the flesh of the son of man...," 37. *See also* Jesus
Song of Hiawatha, The, 200
Songs, where life is degraded, 137
Sonship, you stand to inherit the same, which Jesus had, 47. *See also* Son; Son(s) of God
Soul: came forth from the causal body, 99; images seen with the third eye are reflected in the, 147; intrinsic worth of the, 184; solar plexus is linked to the, 142
Soul chakra: is a sphere of violet fire, 129; perversion which causes a distortion of the, 149; third eye is directly correlated to the, 146. *See also* Chakra(s); Seat-of-the-soul chakra
Speech: our, 23; purify, 140. *See also* Conversation(s); Voice
Spinal ladder, the thirty-three steps of the, 6–7
Spirit, and Matter, 59
Star(s), 31; "For one star differeth from another star in glory...," 96; wandering, 184; why one, differs from another, in glory, 98
Stevens, Risë, 12–13
Stevenson, Robert Louis, 26
Subconscious, 122; what is stored in your, 69. *See also* Unconscious
Success, your guarantee of, 66
Summit University, 253
Sun: "Let not the sun go down upon your wrath," 53; behind the sun, 59. *See also* Great Central Sun
Superconscious mind, 122
Synthetic image, 43

Tablets of *Mem,* 69
Tagore, Rabindranath, 35–36
Talk, too much, 136. *See also* Conversation(s)
Teacher: every one of us is a, 3; who taught me the most, 4; your beloved Christ Self is your, 89. *See also* Guru/chela relationship; Instructors
Teaching(s): of the Ascended Masters, 73, 180; of the Great White Brotherhood, 185; of Jesus taught by the Ascended Masters, 18; Lost, brought to

our remembrance, 9; true, of Christ, 100. *See also* Dictations

Technology, the word, 140

Temples, ancient, 178

Third eye, 146–47, 153; clearing of the, 145–47; is a center of violet fire, 128; is directly correlated to the soul chakra, 146; misused, 152. *See also* Chakra(s)

Third-eye chakra, described and discussed, 142–43. *See also* Chakra(s)

Third-eye vision, 146

Thoth, the Atlantean, 4

Thought(s): clean, 24; controlling, of the Mind of God, 36; gigantic, 8; high and kind, 64; impinging negative, 20; karma of, 11; the mist is the state of, 10; pit of wrong, 11; purifying our, 23; and Thoth, 4; thought/feeling impulses, 72; thought/feeling modes, 26; if you can't control your, 37; your every, contains your electronic blueprint, 23–24

Thoughtforms: impure and imperfect, 147; pure, 150

Threefold flame, 248; an average height of one-sixteenth of an inch, 132; balanced, 92–94, 127; described and discussed, 82–86; of the heart, 126; is one-sixteenth of an inch high, 82; with its three plumes, 129; reached a height of five to seven feet, 127; Saint Germain taught us about the, 83–85; in the secret chamber of the heart, 68, 75; three-in-one of the, 38; through the, you know Christ, 90; withdrawal of the, 77; in your heart, 49. *See also* Flame; God flame

Throat chakra: clearing of the, 140; correct use of the, in decrees, 130; described and discussed, 135–36; exercise of the, 144; is a wheel of violet fire, 128; misuse of the, 143; and solar-plexus chakra, 141. *See also* Chakra(s)

Tiamat, 40; the dragon of chaos, 37

Time, 9; annihilation of, 31; Jesus is here to give you the keys to, and space, 32; stream of, 30. *See also* Future

Transmutation, easier on the mental plane than on the physical, 12

Transylvania, 78n, 186

Treasures: of heaven, 50, 97; how you lay up, in heaven, 99

Tree: of the knowledge of relative good and evil, 143; of Life, 179

Trinity: balancing the, 93; replica of the, 85; three God-qualities personified in the, 126. *See also* Father; God; Holy Spirit; Son

Truth: affirmation of, 136; light of, 100

Tube of light: on the Chart, 49; drops like a curtain around you, 105–6; flowing naturally, 78; pillar of cloud by day and the pillar of fire by night, 105; silver cord was as large as the, 78; why we need the, 64

Umbilical cord: cutting of, 75; of the soul, 74
Unconscious: collective, 149; recordings stored in, 14. *See also* Subconscious

Vengeance, 52
Via dolorosa, 262
Vine, Christ Self as the, 107, 179
Violet: of the causal body, 96, 99–100; of the seat of the soul, 147
Violet fire: both to create and to uncreate, 24; I AM a being of, 128; transmute by, the base metals of your human consciousness, 24–25. *See also* Violet flame
Violet flame, 53–54; abusing it, 55; as the blood of Christ, 71; can permanently alter the effect, 69; on the Chart, 50; no person has ever made his ascension who hasn't had the, 51; some people who used the, to pay their anticipated debts, 54; those who invoke the, 55; for the transmutation of negative karma, 128; use of the, 150. *See also* Violet fire
Virtue: human, 171; "...I perceive that virtue is gone out of me," 101
Voice, tone of, 141. *See also* Speech

Water body, as one of the four lower bodies, 67–68. *See also* Desire body; Emotional bodies; Emotional body; Four lower bodies
White, of the base chakra, 153
White sphere, of the causal body, 97
Wholeness, 163
Will: blue plume is the anchor point for the, of God, 83; God's, 140; obedience to the, of God, 101
Wisdom, 83, 93
Witchcraft, 127, 147–48
Word: disciplined use of the spoken, 135; "every idle word that men shall speak...," 136; importance of the, 140; lost, 36; misuse of the, 135; our society has deemphasized the, 137; power of the, 182; practical applications of the science of the spoken, 130; son of man Jesus was the, incarnate, 33; spoken, 21, 86
Words, 136–37; have become empty, 139
World Teachers, 234
Worth, self-worth, 168–69

Yahweh, 60, 109
Yellow, 100; of the causal body, 96, 99, 102; of the crown chakra, 150
Yoga, 133
Yogananda, Paramahansa, 193, 194
Yukteswar, Sri, 194

THE LOST TEACHINGS OF JESUS 1
Missing Texts
Karma and Reincarnation

Unmistakable evidence that many of Jesus' teachings were altered, deleted or never recorded

Mark L. Prophet and Elizabeth Clare Prophet prove that many of Jesus' original teachings are missing. They show that the New Testament records only a fragment of what Jesus taught. And that what was written down was tampered with by numerous editors. Or suppressed by "guardians of the faith."

Now, in their landmark series *The Lost Teachings of Jesus,* the Prophets fill in the gaps with a bold reconstruction of the essence of Jesus' message. They unfold the lost teachings Jesus gave in public to the multitudes and in secret to his closest disciples. And they answer questions that have puzzled readers of the Bible for centuries.

Their fresh approach, combined with penetrating research and anecdotes, makes this book compelling reading.

Topics include:

- Externalizing Your Divine Self
- Religion and Man's Struggle to Reach God
- The Question of Reembodiment
- Christ the Perfect Design
- The Mysteries of God Revealed to the Prophets
- The Brotherhood and the Path of Initiation
- Karma, Past Lives, and Right Choices
- Positive and Negative Momentums

"I thirsted for this truth all my life. I've been to every church I can think of."
—M.B., secretary, Buena Park, Calif.

"One of the best books I've ever read. I know that every minister should have a copy."
—P.F., minister, Rocky Mount, N.C.

THE LOST TEACHINGS OF JESUS 1
Mark L. Prophet and Elizabeth Clare Prophet

Missing Texts • Karma and Reincarnation
384 pp., 2157, $5.99.

THE LOST TEACHINGS OF JESUS 3
Keys to Self-Transcendence
Paths to soul transformation and spiritual mastery

In this remarkable blend of the practical and the mystical, Mark L. Prophet and Elizabeth Clare Prophet challenge the orthodox view of Jesus. Their thesis: The Gospel writers and early Church councils altered and omitted certain facts about Jesus' life and teaching—pivotal truths you need to advance spiritually.

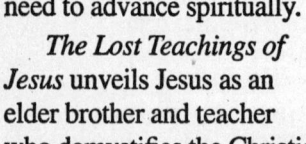

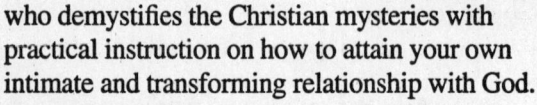

The Lost Teachings of Jesus unveils Jesus as an elder brother and teacher who demystifies the Christian mysteries with practical instruction on how to attain your own intimate and transforming relationship with God.

In Book Three, the Prophets reveal Jesus' lost teaching on how you can move beyond yesterday's awareness and achievements—and take control of the circumstances of your life—by realizing more of your higher self every day.

And they tell the stories of seven saints and mystics who not only reached for but accomplished the goal of self-transcendence. By exploring their unique paths to spiritual mastery, you will find comfort, inspiration and invaluable keys for your own walk with God.

Topics include:

- The Discovery of the Secret Gospel of Mark
- The Laws of Vibration
- Atonement and Self-Transcendence by Rebirth
- Mantra/Meditation: The Soul Omnipresent in God
- Mysteries of the Great Creative Self
- Atlantis Revisited
- Reincarnation: The Prophecy of Elijah Come Again
- Seven Masters Who Tutor Our Souls on the Path of Individual Christhood

"A directory of the way back to God. Will be passed down to my children and theirs."
—A.P., teacher, Tampa, Fla.

"This book has greatly enriched my life and ministry." —R.R., minister, Mountain City, Tenn.

THE LOST TEACHINGS OF JESUS 3
Mark L. Prophet and Elizabeth Clare Prophet
Keys to Self-Transcendence, 337 pp., 2159, $5.99.

THE LOST TEACHINGS OF JESUS 4
Finding the God Within

How to contact your inner source and access your unlimited potential

In this fourth volume of their landmark series, Mark L. Prophet and Elizabeth Clare Prophet show you how to put the teachings of Jesus into action to meet the challenges of life in the '90s and beyond.

This book is full of practical techniques you can use to access the creative love and power of your Real Self.

The Prophets explain why mantras and affirmations work. They show you how to use them with visualizations to help yourself and others.

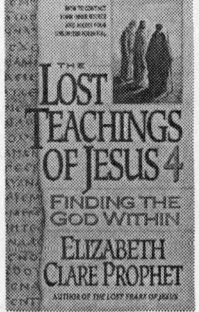

And they give step-by-step instruction on how you can direct the light of God to resolve painful inner conflicts, get rid of bad habits and bring joy to everything you do.

Summit University Press, Box 5000, Livingston, MT 59047
Telephone: 800-245-5445 in the U.S.A. or 406-222-8300

Topics include:

- The Relationship of Man and God
- Christ's Doctrine vs. Church Doctrine
- Seeing God in Yourself
- Jesus' Teaching on Sin, Karma, Reembodiment
- Learning to Command the Powers of the Universe
- The Alchemy of the Violet Flame
- Spiritual Self-Defense
- Structuring Our Lives to Fit Heavenly Patterns
- The Christ Consciousness
- How the Imitation of Christ Can Produce Miracles

"This has been my heart's desire—to have a book that teaches what can't be found in the Bible."
—B.M., student, Chicago, Ill.

"Helps me put His teachings into everyday life."
—M.R., Lancaster, Pa.

THE LOST TEACHINGS OF JESUS 4
Mark L. Prophet and Elizabeth Clare Prophet
Finding the God Within, 349 pp., 2160, $5.99.

Angels
A videotape series by Elizabeth Clare Prophet

Angels can protect and heal. They can bring joy, illumination and comfort. They can help you contact your higher self. And the more you know about what angels can do and how to contact them, the more they can help you. Drawing on her own experiences, Mrs. Prophet explains the unique role of your own personal guardian angel and each of the seven archangels and how you can work with them to create miracles in your life—every day!

Video: 1-hour TV shows: $10.95 each

1.	All about Angels and You	HL93025
2.	Meet Your Angel of Protection	HL93026
3.	How to Meet Your Guardian Angel	HL93043
4.	How to Contact Angels of Love	HL94001
5.	How Angels Help You to Contact Your Higher Self	HL94004
6.	How to Contact Angels of Wisdom	HL94005
7.	How Angels Help You to Effect Personal and Planetary Change	HL94009
8.	How to Call upon Angels to Protect Yourself and Loved Ones	HL94017
9.	True Stories of Archangel Michael's Protection	HL94018
10.	How to Contact Angels: Your Guides, Guardians and Friends	HL94021
11.	How Angels Help You to Recapture the Spirit of Joy	HL94022
12.	How Angels Help You to Create Miracles in Your Life	HL94030
13.	How Angels Help You to Heal Yourself, Your Family and Friends	HL94031
14.	How to Work with Angels for Success	HL94032

THE LOST TEACHINGS OF JESUS
Four-volume pocketbook series with black-and-white pictures.

❏ **BOOK 1:** Missing Texts: Karma and Reincarnation	2157	$ 5.99
❏ **BOOK 2:** Mysteries of the Higher Self	2158	$ 5.99
❏ **BOOK 3:** Keys to Self-Transcendence	2159	$ 5.99
❏ **BOOK 4:** Finding the God Within	2160	$ 5.99

The Lost Teachings of Jesus series is also available in quality paper and hardcover. These editions contain 32 finest-quality Roerich art reproductions and color illustrations of the seven chakras (spiritual centers).

❏ **VOLUME 1** *Quality Paper*	2040	$14.95
❏ **VOLUME 2** *Quality Paper*	2076	$16.95
❏ **VOLUME 1** *Hardcover*	2075	$19.95
❏ **VOLUME 2** *Hardcover*	2077	$21.95

ANGELS – A videotape series by Elizabeth Clare Prophet.
1-hour TV shows, $10.95 each:

❏ 1. HL93025	❏ 6. HL94005	❏ 11. HL94022
❏ 2. HL93026	❏ 7. HL94009	❏ 12. HL94030
❏ 3. HL93043	❏ 8. HL94017	❏ 13. HL94031
❏ 4. HL94001	❏ 9. HL94018	❏ 14. HL94032
❏ 5. HL94004	❏ 10. HL94021	

Books available from your favorite bookseller or use this page to order
Credit card orders call 800-245-5445 *in the U.S.A. or* 406-222-8300

Send checks and money orders to:
Summit University Press, Dept. 764
Box 5000, Livingston, MT 59047-5000

❏ Please send me the items I have listed above. I am enclosing $ _____. (Please add postage and handling charges: for orders up to $19.99 add $2.25; orders from $20 to $39.99 add $3.25; from $40 to $59.99 add $3.75; from $60 to $79.99 add $4.25; from $80 to $99.99 add $4.75 and for orders over $100 add 5% of the total. Prices and postage charges are subject to change.)

Name_____

Address_____

City/State_____ Zip_____

Credit Card No._____

Exp._____ Signature_____

Since 1958 Mark L. Prophet and Elizabeth Clare Prophet have written such classics of spiritual literature as *The Lost Years of Jesus, The Lost Teachings of Jesus, Climb the Highest Mountain, The Human Aura, Saint Germain On Alchemy, The Science of the Spoken Word* and *Forbidden Mysteries of Enoch*. They have also lectured in over 30 countries.

In 1970 the Prophets founded Montessori International and in 1971 Summit University. Mark Prophet passed on in 1973 and Mrs. Prophet has carried on their work. She is based at the Royal Teton Ranch in southwestern Montana, home of a spiritual community.

Here Mrs. Prophet conducts seminars and workshops on the practical applications of the mystical paths of the world's religions. Cable TV shows based on these teachings air weekly across the United States. Mrs. Prophet also appears frequently on national television and has talked about her work on "Donahue," "Larry King Live!" "Nightline," "Sonya Live" and "CNN & Company."